care p series

Sig

A handbook for professional carers

Sarah J Butler

BOOKS

Published by Age Concern England
1268 London Road
London SW16 4ER

First published 2004

Editor Gillian Clarke
Production Vinnette Marshall and Leonie Farmer
Design and typesetting GreenGate Publishing Services
Printed and bound in Great Britain by Bell and Bain Ltd, Glasgow

A catalogue record for this book is available from the British Library
ISBN 0–86242–359–7

Whilst the advice and information contained in *Hearing and Sight Loss* are believed to be true and accurate at the time of going to press, neither Age Concern England, RNIB, RNID nor the author can accept any legal responsibility or liability for any errors or omissions that may be made.

Please note that while the agencies or products mentioned in this book are known to Age Concern England, RNIB and RNID, inclusion here does not constitute a recommendation by Age Concern England, RNIB or RNID for any particular product, agency, service or publication.

Contents

About the author

Sarah J Butler is a researcher and writer who works in a range of fields. She has worked with Age Concern England for many years, contributing to their 'Carer's Handbook' series and to their 'Care Professional Handbooks' series.

Acknowledgements

Many people helped me to write this book, giving their time and sharing their knowledge and experiences. I hope that the result lives up to their hopes and expectations.

Particular thanks go to Beryl Palmer, at Kent County Council Social Services, and to Graham Willetts and Sandra Cronin, both of RNIB, who all gave far more of their time than they could afford. Also to John Crossland, of Croydon Social Services, who helped me to understand the system!

Special thanks go also to the following individuals and organisations:

All of the RNIB staff who helped me -- Jan Henstridge, Gill Levy, Anita Lightstone and her low vision team, Richard Lucas, Julian Rowland and the RNIB library, Graham Smith and Richard Wynn
The people at the RNID – Duleep Allirajah, Brian Grover, Angela King, the media team, Gill Kirby, Gerda Loosemore-Reppen, and the RNID library
Liz Duncan of Sense
Ann Lewis and Chandra Beasley at the Kent Association for the Blind
Barbara Godwin and Jacqui Jackson of Hi Kent
Janine Sykes, Optometrist
Hearing Therapists Alex Willoughby, Val Tait and Bunty Levene
Rehabilitation Workers Marcus Farley and Andy Fisher
Chris Cogdell of Tunbridge Wells Social Services Department, Kent County Council
Nadra Ahmed of the National Care Homes Association
Staff at Headcorn Hall
Staff and users of the Age Concern Day Care Centre in Tunbridge Wells

And thanks most of all to the people who talked about their visual and hearing impairments with such frankness. To maintain their anonymity, their names have been changed in the quotations that appear in the book.

Introduction

Why do we need a book about sensory impairment in older people? One harassed care manager objected, 'If you raise awareness of one disability, what about all the rest?' And in any case, surely it's just part of getting older?

RNIB officer Sandra Cronin visits care homes. If she asks how many have a visual impairment:

> 'The care manager might say no one. But once we've talked about visual impairment ... it turns out that they have six or seven people "who can't see well". The staff's attitude is "well what can you expect?" They don't associate not being able to see very well with visual impairment. They would probably recognise the problem only if someone were registered blind.'

The same goes for hearing loss: it is not uncommon for three-quarters of the residents of a care home to be hard of hearing, though many do not realise it (Willetts 2002).

People with a sensory impairment can easily slip through the net. They may be trying to hide their impairment. They may suspect – or even have been told – that nothing can be done about it. But sensory impairment is as disabling as losing a limb, chronic arthritis or heart disease. And there is plenty that can be done to help.

> Mrs Davidson lived in a care home. She had a visual impairment and dementia. Staff were finding it hard to work with her, and called in a rehabilitation worker specialising in sensory impairment. He watched as the staff fed her, and listened to them talk about how dependent she was. By the time he left, she was able to feed herself again. Magic? Hardly: he had simply put a black place mat under her plate and set up good lighting above her so that she could see what she was eating.

If the staff in that care home had received even basic training in sensory impairment, they would have been able to find a similar solution for themselves. Time and again, care professionals have found that, when they understood more about sensory impairment, they were able not only to provide better care but also to increase the independence of those they worked with. Consequently, they were able both to save precious time and to significantly improve the quality of people's lives.

How many older people have a sensory impairment?

This is not a book full of statistics. It is practical and down to earth. But here are some raw facts that show how widespread sensory impairment is:

> 'One in twelve of us will become blind or partially sighted by the time we are 60. This rises to one in six by the time we reach 75.' *(Vale and Smyth 2003)*
>
> 'Only about 2% of young adults are deaf or hard of hearing. Around the age of 50 the proportion of deaf people begins to increase sharply and 55% of people over 60 are deaf or hard of hearing.' *(RNID 2000)*

There are commonly estimated to be 24,000 deafblind people in the UK, but this figure does not include large numbers of older people who are deafblind or who have some degree of both visual and hearing impairment. So, if you are responsible for the care of any group of older people, it is almost impossible that none of them has a sensory impairment. They may be hiding it but it will be there. Even if you are aware of it, are you providing the best possible support?

This book focuses primarily on the needs of people who lose their sight and/or hearing later in life, because this is when most people develop a sensory impairment. You may, however, be working with someone who has been sensory impaired for many years. Much of what is said in this book is still relevant to them. On the other hand, someone with a long-term sensory impairment will probably already have adapted to it in many ways: for example, someone who is born deaf or becomes deaf young is likely to communicate using British Sign Language (BSL) rather than English as their first language. Someone who was born blind may use Braille to read and write. For them, their deafness or blindness is not a sensory loss but part of the way they are. As with all the people you are working with, you will need to find out from each of them what form of support they want from you.

The need for understanding

Although many people cope well with losing their sight or hearing in old age, others find it harder and may need the support of professionals. This book outlines why people need help, and suggests possible ways for professionals to provide support that makes a real difference to the quality of people's lives.

When the RNIB surveyed blind and partially sighted people in 1995, their response was that 'more understanding about what it is like to be blind' would make most difference to their lives. Deaf people say exactly the same.

Sight and hearing loss can be invisible impairments. Both are often much feared and stigmatised (Ainlay 1989). The result is that many people tend to brush them aside. We refuse to consider what blindness or deafness is actually like. Listen to what people say, and you may be shocked:

> 'Just because we're blind, they think we're stupid.'
>
> 'People often yell at me because they assume blind people are deaf, too.'
>
> 'People don't let me do things – they think I'm incapable, but I'm not. I can do anything.'

Do we talk down to people with a sensory loss without meaning to? Do we expect them not to be able to cope, or step in and do things for them? Do we exclude them from our social activities? All too often, the honest answer would be 'yes'. Sensory loss can threaten independence and dignity. If not taken seriously, it can lead to dependency on others. This is not only counter-productive for staff and service providers; it is also counter to the individual's right to self-determination.

A little understanding can make all the difference.

1 Talking about sensory impairment

This chapter talks briefly about what sensory impairment is and how it is often misunderstood. In particular, we look at:

- Terminology
- Misconceptions about sensory impairment

Terminology

People in the know talk about 'sensory impairment'. But how do older sensory-impaired people themselves describe what they experience? Most of those who acquire a sight or hearing impairment later in life say that they are 'hard of hearing' or 'I'm having problems with my eyes'. They seem often to play down the severity of their impairment, avoiding terms such as 'blind' or 'deaf' as being too stark and absolute. People who have had a sight or hearing impairment since childhood, however, are often proud of being blind or deaf.

Sensory impairment in older age often creeps up on someone, so that they only gradually realise that something is wrong. They see some things and not others; they hear their husband but not their granddaughter. This is not 'blind' or 'deaf', surely? They may fear the darkness and silence associated with such terms, and may not want to be labelled in this way. They may feel, however, a great sense of loss.

Loss, too, is a difficult word. For some in the sensory-impaired world, 'loss' is a taboo word: someone who was born blind does not have a sense of having 'lost' their sight. So, many people do not talk about sensory *loss*.

However, it is clear that most people who have spent their lives as hearing and seeing people, but who become sensory impaired in older age, do experience this impairment as a loss.

This book, therefore, talks both about sensory impairment and sensory loss. When talking to someone about their impairment, however, it is probable that they will be comfortable with neither term: the best advice is to be sensitive to the other person and always to use the terms that they have chosen themselves.

Misconceptions about sensory impairment

Someone who has been able to see and hear all their lives will probably have had very little contact with sensory-impaired people. Their images will be drawn from the heartstring-tugging advertisements of charities, and from literature and film – menacing Blind Pew tapping down the street in *Treasure Island*, tragic Beethoven unable to hear his own genius – not ordinary people like themselves. It is of little use telling them that they will be able to live a full and happy life despite their sight or hearing loss – they have had seventy years or more of being told how terrible it is be blind or deaf. Now that they are impaired themselves, they know from first-hand experience just how hard it can be.

Sensory-impaired older people often treasure the invisibility of their impairment because they know the stigma attached to it. They may find it difficult to tell their friends that they can no longer hear their voices clearly, or see their expressions, suspecting (perhaps rightly) that some might avoid them through embarrassment or because of the difficulty of communicating. Consequently, misunderstandings may arise when they avoid social gatherings or ignore people in the street. They may lose friends who would have shown understanding had they been told about the impairment.

Another effect of this desire to appear like everyone else is that older people with vision or hearing difficulties may feel that they are alone in being impaired – because everyone around them is also hiding their sensory impairment. This, in turn, may delay or prevent them from gaining access to services – because they need to recognise the problem first.

One reason why people fear sensory impairment is that they misunderstand it. At a recent Kent Association for the Blind (KAB) day of awareness training, one participant admitted:

> 'I always thought that blind means no vision at all, but it doesn't.'

In fact, only 4% of the people seen by the KAB have no vision at all. Other common preconceptions about visual impairment are that visually impaired people cannot read print, and that they develop a sixth sense to help them move around. Neither is remotely true and yet they seem to be widely believed.

Ask hearing people what they think being deaf is like and they often describe total silence – although in reality total deafness is extremely rare. Also,

> 'The biggest misconception about deafness is "deaf means you sign".' *Barbara Godwin, Chief Executive, Hi Kent*

Deafness is heavily stigmatised: it is seen as a terrible affliction and is also connected in many people's minds with confusion and ageing.

Richard Binns had to go into hospital for surgery to his heart:

> 'I explained to the theatre nurse that if he would speak directly to me I would be able to answer him. Now this guy would look anywhere but at me and my wife kept saying, "If you look at him he will be able to answer for himself" but it was like talking to the dead. We ascertained that I would be able to keep my aids with me in theatre, and as we prepared to leave, he said to my wife "Does he suffer from dementia?" It took my wife and another member of staff all their efforts to stop me hitting him. When I had calmed down, the ward manager came and apologised and made the weak excuse that the nurse in question had not had deaf awareness training.'

All too often, a person who develops a sensory impairment has to deal not only with the practical effects of the impairment on their life but also with the emotional and social repercussions that result from the impairment.

2 A holistic approach

Sensory impairment affects a person's whole life: its impact is physical, social, emotional and financial. All too often, our response to an impairment is simply to provide practical support, ignoring its non-physical effects. This chapter explores why people need many kinds of support and what that support can achieve. We look at the following areas:

- What do sensory-impaired people need?
- Care planning
- A bit of theory: impairment and the social model of disability

What do sensory-impaired people need?

What do you think someone with poor sight needs? New glasses, perhaps a white cane? And what about someone with hearing problems? A hearing aid, and perhaps a louder telephone bell? This tends to be the limit of what older people receive. But is it enough? And who decides what help they need? If consulted, what would they identify as their most pressing problems?

> Mrs Johnson was in her 60s, and had lost both her sight and her hearing. As a result of diabetes, she lost part of her leg, and her husband confined her to bed, effectively keeping her prisoner – very much against her will.

What would you do if you were called in to help?

> An RNIB dual-loss worker visited Mrs Johnson and asked what she would like to do: she asked to go to the park and feed the ducks. Despite the husband's protests that it would not be safe, they did so straight away and, twice weekly, support was put in

place to do just this. After a while, the support worker suggested a pub lunch after the park, and eventually they graduated to going shopping. When the husband could see that his wife was safe participating in these activities he became involved, and now the couple do everything for themselves again. They have mended their relationship, too.

This case illustrates how important it is to listen to the person with the impairment and to find out exactly what it is that they want to do.

> 'I very quickly learnt how important it is to ask what they want.'
> *Caseworker*

Care planning

Everyone involved in providing care for other people needs to plan their care to some extent, however informally. The care assistant serving meals needs to know who can see their food and who cannot:

> 'When I serve the tea, one of our ladies always gets very impatient but I know it's because she can't see that I'm still serving the others.'
> *Emma, Care Assistant*

On a more formal level, the care manager in a care home assesses the residents individually in order to produce a written care plan. This plan includes information about any sensory impairment.

In fact, good care planning starts even before someone first arrives at a care home. The social services care manager assesses the individual and draws up a care plan – which may recommend residential care. As part of the assessment the care manager finds out about any sensory impairment and includes it in the care plan.

Holistic care goes beyond this, however, and managers of care homes and day-care centres need to consider what it is like for someone with a sensory impairment to come to a day-care centre or to move into a care home: if they have a visual impairment, how will they find their room, the bathroom, the dining room? What will they feel like when faced with a room full of strangers, whose faces they cannot see? If they have a hearing impairment, are they worried that people will think them rude if they do not join in conversation at the dinner table? How will they stay in touch with their family if they cannot hear the phone?

Care planning continues as the new resident settles into life in the home: their vision or hearing may change or perhaps they will develop a new impairment, or an existing one will worsen. Staff here are at the front line – they are the most likely to pick up any problem, however informally:

> **'The first sign might be that they're oblivious to what you're saying, or they rub their ears, or if another resident calls out to them and they don't respond.'** *Gill, Senior Carer, Care Home*

Sensory impairment does not always show itself in such an obvious way, however, and this is where appropriate training is so valuable. Trained staff will be able to recognise the signs of an impairment and give appropriate help:

> Mr Sawyer had poor vision, and staff reported that he had difficulty in washing. He waited each morning for a care assistant to come to help him. They usually took over and washed him themselves. The care manager needed to establish what the problem was. She discovered that the washbasin plug in his room was not on a chain, so Mr Sawyer could not find it to fill the basin and wash. She noted this in the care plan and provided a plug on a chain: with the plug, Mr Sawyer was able to retain his independence and wash himself.
>
> The care manager also arranged for Mr Sawyer to visit his eye specialist again, in case his condition had changed, and asked the rehabilitation worker to come and assess how to help Mr Sawyer to use his remaining vision better.

In whatever context we provide care – in day care, in the home, in a care home or in hospital – that care should foster independence. By helping someone to carry out tasks such as reading, crossing the road, cooking a meal or buying food, we help them to retain their dignity, choice, self-esteem and control.

> 'Homes should be guided by the assumption that an individual has the greatest experience of his or her own needs and disabilities, and may be the best person to give advice about the kind of help he or she needs. The practical implication of this is that staff need to take time and display patience in listening to residents, calmly, attentively and in ways that indicate a clear intention to take action on what they hear.' *(Counsel and Care 1993)*

Staff may therefore have to rethink the way they work with residents and allow them to make their own choices and decisions. This may be difficult for untrained staff, whose instinct is to jump in and help whenever someone is finding something hard. Permitting residents to choose their own clothes or meals can take longer than if a staff member were to intervene – but, ultimately, if the resident maintains their independence, both they and the staff benefit.

This independence also means being allowed to take risks – to go for a walk in the garden, perhaps, despite limited mobility. Staff may want to protect residents from the risk of falling and also may not feel they have time to help that person. Autonomy – or independence – also means being allowed to make your own decisions. For example, someone with a visual impairment might choose to use rehabilitation, and to learn to use a low-vision aid; or they might use Direct Payments to pay someone to read to them for a few hours a week. (Direct Payments enable people to buy their own community care services rather than having them arranged or provided by social services; see page 236.)

A bit of theory: impairment and the social model of disability

Specialists make an important distinction between the terms 'impairment' and 'disabled': *impairment* describes the fact that a limb or organ is missing or does not work effectively, whereas *disabled* describes the fact that society places barriers in the way of someone with an impairment. So, someone with a visual impairment might find it hard to catch a bus: they are disabled by the fact that our bus system depends on travellers reading the bus number and being able to climb the steps of the bus safely. In a society where buses had speaking numbers and no steps, that person would not be disabled.

This is part of the *social model of disability*. It matters because it informs the work of the large sensory campaigning organisations and government policy. It lies behind the Disability Discrimination Act 1995 (DDA) and community care. These are based on the fundamental principle that everyone in society has the same rights – to health, freedom of choice, dignity, and so on. They are not removed when someone becomes impaired. So impaired people must be able to choose to lead full lives as part of society, and to make their own decisions about what they do and how. This model underpins all good practice in care provision – it means giving the people you work with the ability to take control of their lives, to decide what care they want and how they want it.

The social model of disability may seem very abstract for anyone working daily with people who have a sensory impairment, but it is worth considering. Ask yourself these questions:

- What do I think about people with a sensory impairment?
- Do I see them as needing my help?
- Is our relationship one between equals, or am I in a position of power, controlling what they can and cannot do?
- How do I decide what provision to make for someone who is sensory impaired?
- Do I talk first to them, to find out what their priorities are and how they would like to achieve them?

(adapted from *French, Gillman and Swain 1997*)

A care manager described her frustration with one of her staff, who visited newly diagnosed deafblind people, giving each a package of equipment. She particularly favoured liquid level indicators – no matter what the person requested. Usually this was a complete waste of her time. Her clients gained almost nothing from her visits – she never took the time to listen to them and discover their real needs.

As professional carers, it is all too easy to fall into a position of an all-powerful decision maker and help provider. But this is an unhealthy relationship from both sides: a relationship of equals brings great benefits to both professionals and service users.

3 Dual sensory impairment

A dual sensory impairment means more than just sight and hearing loss side by side. This chapter explores why, and what dual impairment is like, under the following headings:

- Why a special mention?
- A definition of dual sensory loss
- Who is affected?
- Causes of dual sensory loss
- What dual sensory loss means in effect
- What support is needed?
- Guide communicators
- Approaching someone with dual loss
- Ensuring that people with dual sensory loss remain integrated
- Mobility
- Dual sensory loss – help from the experts
- Families
- Dual loss and dementia

Why a special mention?

When someone loses both their sight and their hearing, they experience a degree of impairment far greater than the sum of the two individual impairments. The combined effect of losing both sight and hearing fundamentally affects the way the person lives.

This is because someone with a hearing loss may be able to compensate for it to some extent by using their sight – for example, by learning to lipread. But when they lose their sight as well, they lose that resource and can no longer communicate with the people around them using the spoken word. Similarly, someone who has turned to the radio when they could no longer read the paper or see the television loses that contact with the world when their hearing fails.

Dual sensory loss needs, therefore, to be taken very seriously. If it is not, those who experience it become completely isolated. It is our duty to ensure that they maintain the best quality of life possible by keeping the communication channels open.

> 'Being unable to see or hear ... can bring a loneliness beyond compare, because blindness can cut you off from objects and deafness cuts you off from people ... I now live in a dark silent world of my own.' *(Joyce Costie 2001)*

A definition of dual sensory loss

Very few people are completely deaf and completely blind. There are, however, many people whose lives are significantly affected by their dual sight and hearing loss. Where their sensory impairment is severe, they may be called deafblind. Below is a widely accepted definition of deafblindness:

> 'Persons are regarded as deafblind if their combined sight and hearing impairment cause difficulties with communicating, access to information and mobility.' *(Department of Health 1995)*

It has been estimated that, in western Europe, at least 40 people in 100,000 are deafblind. However, these figures include so few older people that they probably significantly understate the true numbers.

There are very many people whose impairment is not so serious as to label them as deafblind but who, none the less, have some degree of both visual and hearing impairment. The National Service Framework for Older People (2001) estimated in 1991 that 22% of people over 60 in the UK have both a visual and a hearing impairment. Therefore, if you work with older people, you will almost certainly be working with dual sensory loss, and will need to take this into account when planning your care.

Who is affected?

It is important to recognise that, whilst most people will acquire both their sight and their hearing impairments in older age, this is not always the case. They may, for example, be blind from birth and acquire a hearing impairment with age.

Although each deafblind person is an individual, it can be useful to recognise four main groups of deafblind people:

- People who are deaf and blind from birth or early childhood.
- People who are blind from birth or early childhood and subsequently experience a significant hearing loss.
- People who are deaf from birth or early childhood and subsequently experience significant sight loss.
- People who acquire a significant visual and hearing loss in later life.

In addition, people from any of these groups may also experience other physical or learning difficulties.

These distinct groups are significant because the age at which a sensory loss occurs may well affect the way that dual loss is experienced. For example, someone who was born deaf or who was deafened early in life may be a British Sign Language (BSL) user or a lipreader, in which case losing their sight will seriously affect their ability to communicate.

A typical feature among older people who develop a dual sensory loss is an inability to recognise this condition in themselves. Those around them often share this.

> 'One person I was working with had very poor hearing, and her vision was not yet seriously affected, but this was the opposite of the way she saw herself.' *(Martha Bagley 1998)*

Rose Arthur has poor vision and hearing, and decided to apply for a hearing dog. But when she rang, and mentioned that she was also blind, the woman refused to help and said she should have a guide dog for the blind. 'It's funny how people get stuck like that – if you're blind you can't be deaf, and if you're deaf you can't be blind.'

Causes of dual sensory loss

In older people, dual sensory loss is most commonly caused by a combination of eye disease and hearing loss. (The main causes of these are described in Chapters 4 and 5.)

People who experience dual sensory loss younger in life or are born deafblind will have a different range of causes, including accident, rubella and Usher syndrome. The effect of their dual sensory loss will depend, at least partly, on its severity and on the age at which it was experienced. For example, a child with Usher syndrome might have been born deaf and grown up in the Deaf community. So they may identify themselves as deaf, first and foremost, and use BSL as their first language. But Usher syndrome causes sight loss in late childhood or early adulthood, which can mean loss of language to a BSL user and a resulting isolation from the Deaf community.

What dual sensory loss means in effect

> 'The biggest barrier to adequately serving the older adult population is a lack of understanding of how vision and hearing loss disrupt communication.' *(Martha Bagley 1998)*

Our ability to communicate underlies everything we do. We communicate to keep ourselves safe, warm and dry, and to eat. Could you buy a week's shopping or choose a meal from a menu or pay the gas bill without sight or hearing?

Imagine the isolation of not being able to hear or see people talking around you: not only would you be unable to hear their words, you would not see their expressions either. You would also realise that, because communicating with you takes so long and demands such patience, people give up and gradually stop making the effort. You are still the same person inside but you know that no one else recognises this.

This is the effect of dual sensory loss: isolation.

Peter Bradbury was profoundly deaf and a good lipreader until he became blind, leaving him with a small amount of residual vision. This meant that lipreading became virtually impossible, although he could sometimes understand his wife. People talked to Peter by writing in large print on a pad, and he painstakingly read this with a magnifying glass. Not surprisingly, conversations lost their spontaneity:

> 'You just feel lost. I can't converse with them so my wife tells me and then I can join in a bit, but it's very brief ... they just talk amongst themselves. So if we're out and we meet friends, well, I don't know what they're saying. My wife tells me afterwards when we come home. I can't converse with them, not now. I could before, because I could see them.'
>
> 'You more or less don't say much. You withdraw inside.' *John Taylor*

John was isolated from other residents in his home and preferred to talk in his own room where it was quiet:

> 'The nearer I am to anybody speaking, the better. ... In a room full of voices where there's a lot of people, the hearing aid is hopeless.'

Esther MacInnes is now 75. She suddenly became deaf at 67 and, since then, her sight has gradually disintegrated. She had been living at home but now lives in a care home. She talks, but receives information through deafblind manual – a means of communication using the hands to form letters (see page 123). She says of the other residents:

> 'They don't have anything much to do with me. They're frightened I'm going to make them talk to me on their hands. ... They seem to pull away from me. I don't bother them now.'

Because Esther did not make relationships with other residents, staff had compensated. They gave her news by finger spelling or by printing capitals on her hand. They had a diary system where they noted information and news they had given Esther, so others could keep her up to date. But, owing to the lack of time, this system had lapsed.

What support is needed?

If you cannot see or hear what is going on around you, your environment is likely to seem threatening and confusing. It can be tiring and frightening to go out. People with severe dual sensory loss therefore often become housebound, and so become even further isolated. Even if someone takes them to the shops or day centre, they will probably go out only rarely. In between, they may feel extremely bored and lonely.

They will also have an emotional reaction to their hearing and sight impairment. The way that they used to experience the world and the people around them has been cut off: no longer can they see facial expressions or a smile, hear gossip, laughter and jokes. Although these may seem trivial, losing them can lead to feelings of grief, loss, frustration and anger, which may be accentuated when in the company of other people.

A person with dual sensory loss is likely to need help in the following areas:

- communication
- information
- emotional support
- counselling
- mobility
- equipment
- independence
- social contact.

You will need to build staff awareness of these needs and provide the social support necessary for working with someone with sensory loss, which can be very demanding. This will involve training, mentoring and, perhaps, counselling. (See also Chapters 6 and 10.)

Guide communicators

One possible answer to the isolation and dependency so often experienced by people with dual sensory loss is the provision of guide communicators – professionals who are trained to support deafblind people. They can help to:

- relieve extreme isolation;
- retain independence, possibly preventing unnecessary entry into a care home;
- provide access to community services;
- enable dual-sensory-disabled people to express their needs;
- give respite to families and carers.

Specifically, a guide communicator may:

- accompany someone to the GP/hospital/dentist;
- go out with the person so that they can visit friends or day care or take part in community activities;
- help someone to go shopping;
- help someone to communicate in groups and one-to-one;
- support the person, using aids such as loop systems, flashing alarms and good lighting;
- make telephone calls;
- pay bills;
- read and write correspondence;
- check labels on medication;
- check food storage for hygiene;
- keep the person up-to-date with news and information;
- help the person to take exercise and participate in other leisure pursuits.

To find a guide communicator, contact your local social services department. Under new guidance about section 7 of the Local Authority Social Services Act 1970 (see page 251) social services must provide specific support for deafblind people, and this includes helping them to make use of guide communicators.

Approaching someone with dual loss

Put yourself in the shoes of someone who has lost their sight and hearing. You are sitting in your usual chair wondering when lunch will be served when someone grabs hold of your hand and shakes it, then starts shouting in your ear. You have no idea who has arrived but they seem angry and aggressive: how would you react?

When approaching someone with dual sensory loss, take care to remember what their disability actually means. Do not be put off making contact, but do take care to be sensitive. Each person is different but the following tips may be a useful starting point:

- Approach from the front or side so that, if the person has any vision, they can see that someone is coming.
- Try using clear speech first.
- If there is no response, try a light touch on the upper arm – leave it there so that they can feel your hand if they want to.
- If they shy away, you may have the beginnings of a problem, but this is rare in older people.
- If clear speech does not work, you can try block – using your finger to 'write' letters on the person's hand (see pages 124–125); they will soon tell you if they want to use deafblind manual.
- If they whip their hand away, this probably means they do not want to use either deafblind manual or block – you could try writing in large print.
- If they choose a method with which you are not comfortable, tell them.
- Remember that they must have some way of communicating, and will probably tell you what it is.

(Communication methods such as block and deafblind manual are described in Chapter 10.)

Approaching someone for whom touch is culturally inappropriate (eg some Muslim women) may be best done by asking a member of their family to tell them that you are there. Some social services have recruited people from within the ethnic community to work with those who are deafblind, but social services and voluntary agencies often rely on family members. Working with the family has the advantage of overcoming some people's reluctance to communicate with non-family members. The family may, in addition, be able to provide language support if the person with dual loss does not use English easily. However, under the Disability Discrimination Act, there is a duty to use professional interpreters. This not only ensures that the interpreting is accurate but also maintains the service user's confidentiality.

Ensuring that people with dual sensory loss remain integrated

Isolation can be a problem for anyone with a sensory loss, and is almost certainly going to be difficult for someone with dual sensory loss. If you are involved in organising social or group activities for older people, you need to ensure that everyone who would like to take part is able to, whatever the degree of their sensory loss. (See Chapter 10 for information on communicating in a group.)

You should also ensure that everyone who will be working with you is aware of the need for clear speech and will use it at all times. This will be more difficult if many of your staff do not have English as their first language, but it is worth persevering and emphasising the need to make themselves understood by enunciating all words clearly.

If you are working with someone who uses deafblind manual or finger-spelling, make sure your staff are aware of this. It is easy to learn, and having a network of people to communicate with will transform the life of the user as well as sharing the responsibility of care among staff. In a care home where one of the residents uses deafblind manual and finger-spelling as their main means of communicating, other residents could also learn this.. Other residents are potentially one of the greatest sources of support, and some will welcome being given a way of helping.

Mobility

Mobility becomes a particular challenge when someone loses both sight and hearing, because they lose access to all the clues they might previously have used. For example, if a blind person used to find their way to the front gate by listening for the sound of cars in the road in front of them, they will need to find a new way of orientating themselves when they lose their hearing. They will need to learn techniques such as using orientation clues – for example, lining themselves up with other landmarks, such as the doorway and fence, to enable them to reach the gate. They will have to be shown these clues first, and will need time to learn them. In addition, they will need to learn safe routes – for example, paths where cyclists will not go, because they will be unable to hear them coming on shared-use paths. (See also Chapter 11.)

Dual sensory loss – help from the experts

People who become dual impaired late in life rarely have links with services that can help them. Although they may well be in contact with social services, their dual impairment and its effects can go unrecognised. Often, too, sensory-impairment services are split into visual impairment and hearing impairment, with very little communication between them and little understanding in either camp of the effects of dual sensory loss.

> 'The term deafblind brings, for most professionals, a vision of Helen Keller. Unfortunately, most older adults who are deafblind are not like Helen Keller.' *(Martha Bagley 1998)*

The result of this lack of understanding when providing support can lead to further isolation. For example, if we offer someone home-delivered meals because they find it hard to communicate, rather than transporting them to the day centre, we will only reinforce their isolation.

Many people do not recognise that they have a dual loss – seeing themselves rather as visually impaired with a bit of a hearing problem or deaf with poor sight – and therefore do not seek out the support specifically designed for them. If recognising that their first sensory loss was traumatic, an older person may find it hard to confront a second sensory loss. The assessment process may not help:

'People can be overwhelmed by the need to go through two assessments, one for vision and one for hearing.' ***Jacqui Jackson, Hi Kent***

Neither will individual assessments for visual impairment and hearing impairment address dual sensory impairment. Sensory specialists' understanding of dual impairment may improve, however, as a result of the new Section 7 Guidance (relating to section 7 of the Local Authority Social Services Act 1970). This places the onus on social services departments to provide specifically for dual-impaired people. (See Chapter 18.)

Dual loss and dementia

It is not uncommon for people to wrongly assume that someone with a dual sensory loss has dementia. This applies to families, to carers and to medical staff. It is an understandable mistake but one that should not be made. The confusion that results from isolation and the inability to experience the world physically is not comparable to that which results from brain damage. If effective means of communication are put in place, it should be entirely possible to reduce the person's distress and confusion so that they may once again lead a full life.

4 Causes and symptoms of visual impairment

This chapter describes the most common causes and symptoms of sight loss in older people. We look at:

- An official definition of visual impairment
- Sight and ageing
- What is visual impairment?
- Signs that someone has visual impairment
- Causes of visual impairment in older people:
  - macular degeneration
  - cataract
  - glaucoma
  - diabetic retinopathy
- Other eye conditions
- Multiple conditions
- African-Caribbean and Asian communities
- Where next?

An official definition of visual impairment

Because there is such a variety of eye conditions, it is only of limited use to label people as 'blind' or 'partially sighted' – this tells us nothing about their particular sight condition. However, as these terms are commonly used, here are two accepted definitions, from the World Health Organization:

- **blindness** is being unable to distinguish fingers at a distance of 10 feet (3 metres) or less;
- **partial sight** is being unable to distinguish fingers at a distance of 20 feet (6 metres).

These definitions are based on the results of a sight test for distance vision for someone wearing correct glasses. They do not reflect problems with field of vision or someone's functional vision (in other words, what *useful* vision they have).

Sight and ageing

Most older people lose their sight because of an eye condition or disease. No one loses their sight purely because they are getting older, although our eyes do change and often function less well as we age.

These age-related changes include the cornea becoming more opaque, which means it needs more light to function properly. The lens becomes thicker, stiffer and denser and moves forward, which is what makes so many people long-sighted in their 50s and 60s, and also affects colour perception, making everything look slightly yellow. These changes are all natural and, whilst they do mean that as we age we need much more light to see, they do not in themselves lead to serious sight impairment. Therefore, anyone with a serious sight loss is suffering from an eye disease or injury – they do not just have 'tired eyes' or 'old eyes'. Because most eye diseases are progressive, it is crucially important to find out what is causing the sight loss and manage it appropriately.

When working with visually impaired people who lost their sight a long time ago, or who were born visually impaired, they should be consulted on the effects of their impairment and how they would like their needs to be met. The RNIB has information on a wide range of eye conditions that can occur at any age. In this chapter, however, we look at conditions that commonly arise later in life.

What is visual impairment?

Visual impairment is caused by a range of diseases and conditions. Each brings different symptoms. So, while someone with a cataract may find their vision blurry and scratched-looking all over, another with glaucoma may have trouble only with seeing at the edges. These symptoms, in turn, bring different care needs.

> 'Don't assume you know how someone else sees – find out what helps and then put it into practice.' *Ann Lewis, Rehabilitation Services Manager at Kent Association for the Blind (KAB)*

The result of this is that, although a group of people may all be visually impaired, they will have different experiences of impairment. While one may see well in daylight, another may favour dim light. One may read small print but be unable to recognise a friend across the road. They may be able to read an eye chart but will fall up the step into the consulting room because of their tunnel vision. There may be variations in colour perception and their vision may fluctuate from day to day, or from hour to hour.

> 'You can't say, "This is visual impairment – this is what to do".' *Ann Lewis*

In addition, we must bear in mind that someone's vision may deteriorate over time, which may mean that they need more or different support. We must therefore understand each individual's eye condition, and listen to what they tell us about what they can and cannot see.

Although we can list symptoms and describe the likely effects of a particular eye condition, we cannot ever understand how much an individual sees. This depends not only on their particular eye condition but also on the intellectual activity of the brain and how it interprets images: some people learn to interpret that information better over time.

> 'Sight is a very individual thing.' *Janine Sykes, Optometrist*

Some eye conditions can be treated and cured, some can be controlled and prevented from deteriorating, and others cannot be treated at all. What all people with an eye condition have in common, however, is the need for proper diagnosis.

Signs that someone has visual impairment

Below are listed signs of an eye condition that needs proper diagnosis. If someone you are working with displays any of these signs, ask them how well they are seeing at the moment. If they are having any problems, arrange for them to see an optometrist.

Common signs include:

- finding it hard to identify faces or objects;
- finding it hard to identify colours or choosing unusual colour combinations;
- finding it hard to cope with glare;
- walking slowly or with less confidence;
- brushing or bumping into things;
- spilling food and drink;
- leaving mail unopened or unanswered;
- needing more light for reading and other activities;
- giving up reading, watching television or other activities;
- becoming isolated;
- moving their head to focus;
- making little or no eye contact (usually only when impairment is severe).

This is not an exclusive list – there are other signs that you may observe – and some people may exhibit none of them at all. None the less, the list gives an idea of the signs that may indicate a sight problem.

Causes of visual impairment in older people

Four conditions account for most sight loss in older people. They are: macular degeneration, cataract, glaucoma and diabetic retinopathy. Each is described below.

A diagram of the eye (Figure 4.1) is included for clarification. It may also help you to explain an eye condition to the person you are caring for – it is most likely that they will want to know why they have an eye condition and what its effects are.

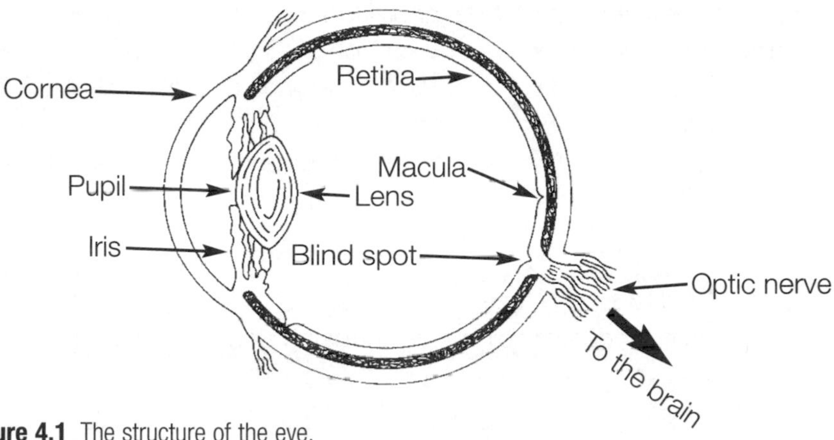

Figure 4.1 The structure of the eye.

Probably the most important fact that you can convey to someone with any of these conditions is that none alone causes total blindness. Some vision will remain, although it may become increasingly difficult to use. Someone with more than one eye condition may, however, face complete blindness due to the combined effects of the conditions. The descriptions of the conditions, below, include a simulation of what each eye condition may be like but it is very important to realise that the same eye condition has a quite different effect on each individual. You cannot know exactly what it is that they are seeing.

Macular degeneration

This is the most common eye condition in the West. In the UK it accounts for one-third of all visual impairment and most of the serious sight loss. It is most often found in people over 60. We do not yet know why people develop macular degeneration.

Macular degeneration causes the person gradually to lose their central vision. Their side, or peripheral, vision remains normal. This means that, although they may see you approach out of the corner of their eye, they may be unable to recognise you when you stand in front of them. It is caused by damage to the macula, which is the part of the retina used for fine-detailed central vision. Most people develop macular degeneration in both eyes, although not necessarily at the same time or rate.

If someone develops macular degeneration, one of the first signs may be that straight lines in the centre of vision of one eye become kinked (eg a shelf or picture rail will look bent). Print on a page or the details on a face will then become blurred and hard to distinguish. Objects may look an unusual size or shape. The person may become very sensitive to light, or see lights that are not there.

> Rose no longer goes out at night because the darkness makes it virtually impossible for her to see, and the street lights produce a terrible glare effect. Luckily, she still manages to maintain some of her social life because a friend takes her out once a week.

Eventually, there may be a blank central area, or a dark central spot, but good side vision means that the person will still be able to move about and continue daily life. Macular degeneration is not painful.

It is very common for the people closest to someone with macular degeneration to wrongly claim that they are being selective in what they see, which is enormously frustrating. Some people with macular degeneration experience visual illusions – a kind of hallucination – which can be doubly distressing if others consequently believe that they have become confused.

Most older people develop 'dry' macular degeneration, for which there is no treatment at the moment. It is, however, possible to treat some 'wet' types of macular degeneration – these types have a sudden onset, so the person will complain of problems very suddenly, and it is crucial that they be referred to hospital immediately.

Some minerals and vitamins, particularly those in green leafy vegetables, may help prevent macular degeneration – although this is not proven. It is a good idea to give up smoking.

TIPS FOR HELPING SOMEONE TO COPE WITH MACULAR DEGENERATION

- Make sure there is good lighting, including an adjustable lamp for close work.
- Use strong colour and contrast.
- Help them to try magnifiers.

Figure 4.2 A simulation of vision for someone with macular degeneration. (Reproduced by permission of the RNIB)

- Help them to practise looking at things from the sides of their eye, not looking directly at them.
- Encourage them to sit close to the television.

Cataract

When a person has a cataract, the lens of their eye becomes clouded. (Cataracts are not caused by a skin growing over the eye.) As a result, what they can see becomes blurred and dim (see Figure 4.3). Most cataracts develop in old age, but they do so gradually and there are wide variances in their severity. Over half of all people over 65 have some cataract development but most are relatively unaffected by it.

If someone you are working with has cataracts, they may describe the following symptoms:

- Things look misty.
- Their colour vision changes: cataracts tinge everything yellow.
- They find it difficult to see in bright light.
- They may see double if the cloudiness in their vision is in more than one place.
- If they wear glasses, they may constantly feel that the lenses are scratched or need cleaning.

If you feel that the person can no longer cope with daily life because of their cataract, you should encourage them to see their consultant, who will

Figure 4.3 A simulation of vision for someone with cataracts. (Reproduced by permission of the RNIB)

probably arrange for the cataract to be removed. This generally involves day surgery … and a waiting list. Waiting lists are very variable, although there has recently been a Government programme (Action on Cataracts) to reduce them.

The surgeon will remove the damaged lens and insert a plastic one in its place. This is not painful, and is usually carried out under local anaesthetic. The stitches will be invisible. You may need to reassure the person you work with that at no stage will the eyeball be removed from its socket.

About six weeks after surgery, the person will probably need to change their glasses. The lenses will only be thick if the surgeon was unable to replace the lens of the eye with a plastic implant. Usually, cataract surgery is successful. However, vision may still be blurred after the operation if another eye condition also exists.

Neither diet nor drugs can improve cataracts.

TIPS FOR HELPING SOMEONE WITH CATARACTS

- Avoid glare – direct or reflected light shining straight into the eyes.
- Too little light may mean they cannot see – but too much may dazzle them.
- Try an adjustable lamp for reading and close work.
- A hat with a brim, a visor or sunglasses may help on sunny days.

Glaucoma

'Glaucoma' describes a range of eye conditions that are very common: in Britain about one in 100 people over 40 years of age have the most common form.

There are two ways in which glaucoma affects sight: either the extreme edge of the field of vision may start to fade, which causes vision to narrow; or blank areas may develop closer to the centre of vision. The effect can be described as *tunnel vision*. Figure 4.4 gives you an idea of the effect of glaucoma on a person's vision.

Figure 4.4 Simulated vision for someone with glaucoma. (Reproduced by permission of the RNIB)

You may realise that someone you are working with has tunnel vision if they seem clumsy, bumping into things that are outside their field of vision, even though they are still able to read a book.

Glaucoma is caused by pressure rising within the eye and damaging the optic nerve. This increase in pressure is caused by the channels that allow the eye's watery fluid to drain becoming blocked. It is nothing to do with blood pressure. Because the pressure usually increases very slowly, someone with glaucoma may not notice the loss of vision for months, or even years. They may still be able to read, because it is their side vision that is affected. They are most likely to find out that they have glaucoma when their eyes are tested: it is therefore extremely important not only that everyone you work with has regular eye tests but also that those eye tests include a test for glaucoma. Glaucoma often runs in families: testing for glaucoma is free to anyone over 40 with a blood relative who has the condition.

It is very important to diagnose glaucoma as early as possible, because prompt treatment can prevent it from getting worse. This treatment involves reducing the eye pressure either by helping the fluid to drain or by reducing the amount of fluid produced. It may be carried out using pills, eye drops or a small operation. It is very important that someone taking medication for glaucoma remembers to take it every day – its effect lasts only 24 hours, after which there is again the danger that pressure in the eye will rise.

TIPS FOR HELPING SOMEONE WITH GLAUCOMA

- They need strong but not glaring light.
- A hat with a brim, a visor or sunglasses may help on sunny days.
- A short white cane (a 'symbol cane') – may help in dim light.
- Colour contrast may help.
- Help them to try using magnifiers.
- Help them to try using a typoscope (a card with a wide slot through which users can read or write) when reading, to cut down glare and help keep the line.

Diabetic retinopathy

Some people who have diabetes may experience changes in their retina over time. These changes are called *diabetic retinopathy*. Although someone may have been diagnosed as diabetic, they may not know that they are more likely to develop a visual impairment because of their diabetes.

Not every diabetic person will develop retinopathy, and it is important to recognise that developing retinopathy is not a consequence of the individual's failure to manage their diabetes. The most common form of diabetes in older people is type 2 and it is often diagnosed only through an eye test. If retinopathy is diagnosed early, it may be possible to keep problems to a minimum.

When someone has diabetic retinopathy, their vision may be patchy and blurred (see Figure 4.5). It may change from day to day or even from hour to hour.

> 'Where sight loss isn't static – say, with diabetic retinopathy – it's harder to deal with.' *Jan Henstridge, Head of Care, Wavertree House, RNIB Care Home*

Figure 4.5 Simulated vision for someone with diabetic retinopathy. (Reproduced by permission of the RNIB)

Diabetic retinopathy is caused when the tiny blood vessels that feed the retina become fragile and start to break, leaking blood. Someone with this condition may see floating spots or areas of blurring, which might clear up without treatment. However, the blood vessels supplying the retina may eventually stop working altogether, and so the cells in the retina die. If new blood vessels grow, they will not be able to nourish the retina and may grow into the inner part of the eye, causing further sight loss.

It is possible to treat diabetic retinopathy with laser equipment. The laser seals the haemorrhages on the retina to stop further deterioration. Eye drops are also sometimes prescribed – it is very important that they be taken correctly and regularly.

TIPS FOR HELPING SOMEONE WITH DIABETIC RETINOPATHY

- They should avoid glare – direct or reflected light shining straight into their eyes.
- A hat with a brim, a visor or sunglasses may help on sunny days.
- Help them to try an adjustable lamp for reading and close work.

Other eye conditions

There are other eye conditions that may cause deterioration in the vision of someone you work with. These are less common and are described briefly below:

Detached retina

It is relatively rare for someone to experience a detached retina, but if they do it is crucial that they receive immediate medical help if their sight is not to be permanently damaged. Most at risk are older people with short sight, although a detached retina may also result from a blow to the head.

If someone's retina is becoming detached, they will probably see a shadow spreading across their eye. They may also see bright flashes and an unusual level of 'floaters'. They will not feel any pain.

Resulting from stroke

If someone you are working with has a stroke, it is important to look out for signs of any resulting sight loss: they are easily missed or misidentified. If someone keeps knocking their teacup over, is it because they are clumsy as a result of the stroke or because they cannot see the teacup?

There are several types of visual loss (called *hemianopia*) that a person may experience after stroke. They may lose all vision in part of their visual field or they may lose the ability to distinguish form and colour but not light. Their visual fields may be affected identically in each eye, but not necessarily. They are most likely to experience visual loss in the nasal half of one eye and the outer half of the other.

There is no specific treatment for the defect to the field of vision after stroke, although it may improve with time. It is important for this to be diagnosed correctly, however, so that you can work with the person to find ways of minimising its effects. Once the person with stroke begins to recover, ensure that they have their eyes tested.

Retinitis pigmentosa

Someone with retinitis pigmentosa will progressively lose their side (peripheral) vision until only a central area of vision is left, which is called *tunnel vision*. They will also experience night blindness, difficulty in seeing in dim light or bright light, and difficulty in adjusting to changes in light levels.

Retinitis pigmentosa is an inherited condition, and is currently untreatable. It is none the less important that it be correctly diagnosed so that appropriate help can be given and other eye conditions eliminated.

Caused by injury or surgery

Some people lose vision as a result of an injury or surgery. This visual loss will clearly depend on the nature of the injury or surgery, but a common factor is that the loss is likely to be sudden. It may also be unexpected. The resulting emotional trauma can therefore be particularly severe.

If someone is to undergo surgery that is likely to result in sight loss, it is crucial that they be well informed, and that you plan together for the immediate aftermath of the operation and for longer-term care.

Multiple conditions

Unfortunately, it is not uncommon for an older person to develop more than one eye condition.

This has implications not only for their vision but also for their treatment. If someone you are working with is diagnosed as having cataracts, they may be extremely disappointed to be told that they cannot be operated on because they also have macular degeneration: the operation might well cure the cataracts but would make the macular degeneration worse.

> 'If someone has cataracts and has heard how much treatment can help, it's hard for them to be told that their sight won't improve because they have other eye conditions as well as the cataracts.' *Jan Henstridge, Head of Care, Wavertree House, RNIB Care Home*

African-Caribbean and Asian communities

People in the African-Caribbean and Asian communities are more likely to develop diabetes and its associated conditions such as diabetes retinosa. They are also more likely to develop glaucoma. They may develop these conditions at a younger age than other ethnic groups – sometimes as young as 30.

If you are working with people from these communities, you should check that they are tested regularly for the eye diseases to which they are particularly prone.

Where next?

Once the person you work with has a diagnosis of their eye condition, you will need to support them and work with them to establish the best way to help them manage their sight. This is covered in Chapters 6–12.

5 Causes and symptoms of hearing loss

This chapter describes the most common causes and symptoms of hearing loss in older people. In particular, we look at:

- Will making things louder help?
- Age-related hearing loss
- Symptoms of age-related hearing loss
- Causes of hearing impairment
- Other ear problems
- The importance of correct diagnosis of hearing loss
- Cochlear implants
- Where next?

Figure 5.1 shows the structure of the ear. When we hear a sound, it has travelled through the auditory canal to the eardrum and made it vibrate. The eardrum is attached to a chain of three tiny bones – the ossicles – that lie across the middle ear, which is a cavity filled with air. These bones carry the vibrations from the eardrum through the middle ear to the inner ear. Inside the inner ear, these vibrations move through a fluid-filled chamber (the cochlea), agitating tiny hair cells. Each hair cell is connected to the auditory nerve, which links the cochlea to the brain. The final stage in hearing a sound is when the brain picks up and recognises the sound.

Most deaf and hard-of-hearing people in the UK begin to lose their hearing as they grow older. Although only 2% of young adults are deaf or hard of hearing, this rises to over 55% of people over 60.

Deafness and hearing loss may result from a wide range of causes. Some cause permanent loss; other types can be treated or may clear up on their

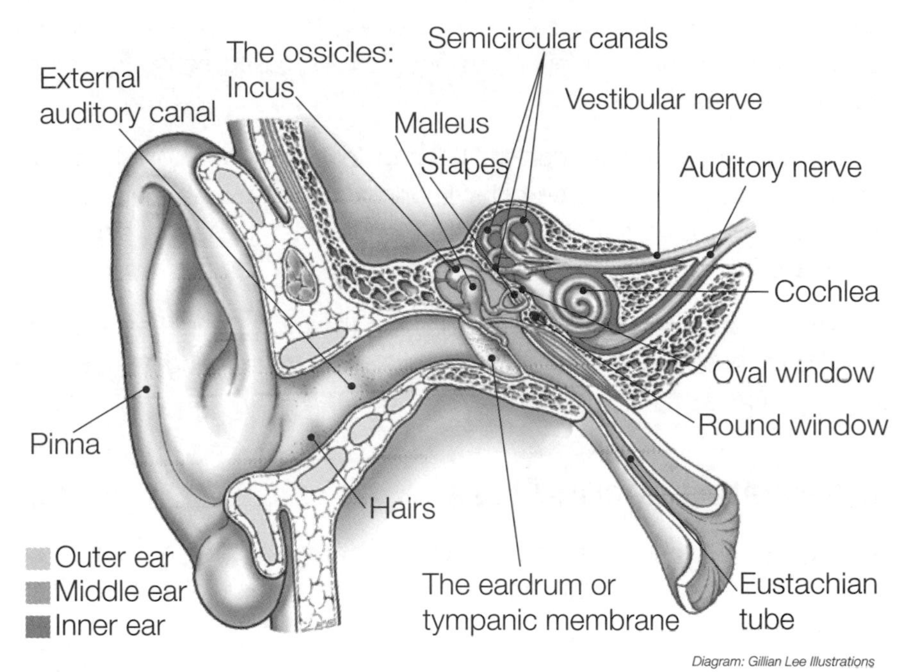

Figure 5.1 The structure of the ear.

own. The various different types are described below, age-related hearing loss being the most common cause of deafness in older people.

Will making things louder help?

For some people, making things louder enables them to hear well; for others it does not help as much – it depends on their type of hearing loss. This is why, although the individuals themselves rarely label their hearing impairment as anything other than 'hearing loss' or 'getting a bit hard of hearing', it is important for those responsible for the care of older people to know exactly what is causing the loss. This will enable you to understand the effect of that particular hearing loss, how it may be treated, and what aids and support might be useful.

Doctors label hearing loss according to the part of the ear that is affected. If sound cannot get through the outer or middle ear, it is called *conductive* hearing loss. Where the cause of the deafness is in the inner ear – in the cochlea or the hearing (auditory) nerve – this is called *sensorineural* or *cochlear* deafness.

People with any form of cochlear hearing loss, including presbyacusis (age-related hearing loss; see below), will experience very similar symptoms. They find it hard to discriminate the sounds of speech, especially against background noise, even when amplified.

Someone with a conductive hearing loss, on the other hand, has a loss of sensitivity – if the sound is made louder, they can hear it and it should be perfectly clear.

Age-related hearing loss

Hearing loss is common in people over 60 because it is a natural effect of the ageing process. This age-related type of hearing loss is called *presbyacusis*.

Inside the ear is the cochlea, which is the part of the ear that processes sounds for the brain to interpret. It has tiny hair cells, which begin to die as we age. The effect of this is that sounds are not as clear as they used to be.

Generally, people who are losing their hearing find the high-frequency sounds (eg the high notes in a tune) hardest to hear at first. Speech contains high-frequency sounds, so it may become harder for someone to understand it. The speech sounds with the highest frequencies are the consonants – sounds such as **s**, **sh**, **t**, **k**, **p** and **f**; for example, 'Did you take them?' might end up sounding like 'Did you shake them?' – very confusing!

Symptoms of age-related hearing loss

If someone in your care has presbyacusis, they may describe the following symptoms:

- Other people seem to mumble.
- They have to ask people to repeat things several times.

- It is hard to understand what is being said in noisy places such as a communal dining room or living room, while others are managing to have conversations.
- They find it hard to keep up with the conversation when talking in a group.
- They get tired listening to conversations because they need to concentrate so hard.
- Other people think that they have their television or music on too loud – but they cannot hear it if it is turned down.
- They find it hard to hear on the telephone.

Alternatively, the person who is losing their hearing may not complain at all: they may not want to admit to themselves or anyone else that they are finding it hard to hear. You may only realise that they are having problems by observing a change in their behaviour. Signs to look out for include not wanting to take part in activities, becoming isolated, seeming to ignore people and turning up the volume on the television.

Someone with presbyacusis may find that their hearing impairment:

- makes it hard for them to hear the high frequencies that are a feature of speech;
- makes them extremely sensitive to changes in the intensity of sound (loudness), so slamming a door may be quite distressing;
- distorts sounds at some frequencies – this will affect their ability to hear speech or enjoy music;
- means that sounds overlap – a ringing phone may blot out the speech that follows;
- means they cannot distinguish between background and close-up sounds.

Causes of hearing impairment

The various other types of hearing loss that might affect the people you are working with are described below, starting with those affecting the outer ear, then those affecting the middle ear, and finally those affecting the inner ear.

Conductive hearing loss

WAX

If the outer ear is blocked by wax, this may affect hearing. The wax usually clears itself, but sometimes it does not and a doctor needs to remove it. It is important not to try to remove it yourself, whether with cotton buds or a finger: this might push any wax on to the eardrum, which can cause pain, infection and deafness.

INFLAMED SKIN

Sometimes the skin of the ear canal becomes inflamed. This may be caused by scratching the ear or because of eczema. It can be painful and there may be a watery discharge. There is not usually any hearing loss. It is important for the individual not to scratch the ear and to keep it dry. The doctor will prescribe ear drops to cure the inflammation.

GLUE EAR (OTITIS MEDIA WITH EFFUSION)

This is most common in children but does occur in adults, too. It happens when the Eustachian (or pharyngo-tympanic) tube gets blocked and air cannot get into the middle ear. The middle ear fills with fluid that becomes gluey, so the eardrum cannot move and hearing is reduced. It usually returns to normal on its own but, if it does not, a tiny ventilation tube (a grommet) can be inserted.

CHRONIC MIDDLE EAR INFECTION

Antibiotics now make this a rare condition but some people have an abnormal eardrum, as a result of chronic infection, behind which dead skin collects. This dead skin may, in turn, become infected and damage hearing. The Ear, Nose and Throat (ENT) specialist may suggest a mastoid operation to remove the dead skin and any infected bone.

OTOSCLEROSIS

This is caused by a bony overgrowth of the stapes, one of the chain of bones (the ossicles) that stretches across the middle ear. The link in this chain becomes rigid and so vibration cannot pass through it, making the individual increasingly deaf. Symptoms include tinnitus (see later) and hearing loss, often at lower frequencies (deeper sounds) to begin with. The person affected may also find it easier to hear in noisy surroundings. People with otosclerosis tend to speak quietly.

Hearing aids are very useful with this condition. If it is severe, people may be offered an operation (a stapedectomy or stapedotomy) that replaces the stapes with a tiny piston, which allows sound to travel to the inner ear again. These operations are usually very successful.

Otosclerosis affects more women than men, and often starts around the age of 30. It can run in families, and is relatively common – affecting about two people in 100.

DAMAGED OSSICLES

The ossicles are the three tiny bones in the middle ear that conduct sound from the eardrum to the inner ear. If they are damaged, it may be possible to replace or repair them in an operation called an ossiculoplasty.

PERFORATED EARDRUMS

A perforated eardrum may have been caused by infection or injury. It will normally heal itself. If it does not, the specialist may recommend an operation to make the ear watertight again, and to prevent discharge. The operation, called a myringoplasty, uses a tissue graft to seal the hole. It is usually successful but may not fully restore hearing if some damage to the eardrum remains.

SENSORINEURAL/COCHLEAR DEAFNESS

This is most often caused by damage to the hair cells in the cochlea. These hair cells cannot be replaced. The most likely causes in an older person are:

- The natural ageing process (as described above).
- A side effect of certain drugs – in particular, aspirin in large doses or the antibiotics streptomycin and gentamicin.
- Exposure to loud noise for a long time.
- A serious head injury with a skull fracture.

People from the same family often experience a similar pattern of hearing loss as they get older.

Hearing aids are usually very helpful for people with sensorineural deafness but will not necessarily make everything perfectly clear.

Other ear problems

Vertigo

Dizziness and balance problems may be caused by damage to the semicircular canals or by a problem with the balance centres at the base of the brain. The cause of this damage can be hard to identify but it may be the result of a virus or poor blood supply. Usually the individual regains their balance, given time, without treatment, but they may need to take a short course of anti-sickness drugs to help with any nausea and a drug known as a vestibular sedative to damp down the dizziness. These drugs should be used for only a few days. Physiotherapy may also be useful to learn some balancing exercises. Some audiology departments run special balance clinics.

Anyone with either vertigo or balance problems should see their doctor.

Tinnitus

People experience tinnitus as noises in their ears or in their head. It is very common – about one in seven people experience it at some time. The noises may be quiet or loud, and can be hissing, 'rushing' or other noises. It can be extremely disruptive and can prevent the person affected from relaxing or being able to sleep. Tinnitus is probably caused by part of the brain making noises louder.

This may happen as a result of exposure to loud noise, hearing loss, injuries to the ear or head, some diseases of the ear or emotional stress – though many people with tinnitus have never experienced any of these.

Anyone with tinnitus should visit their GP to have their ears checked. Some GPs are well informed about tinnitus, and will be helpful and supportive. If not, it is worth asking for a referral to the local ENT department, and perhaps to a tinnitus clinic. The RNID also provides information about tinnitus, and runs a Tinnitus Helpline (see page 290).

If someone's tinnitus is caused by an infection or by medication that they are taking, their tinnitus will stop when the infection is cured or when they stop taking the medication. Other people's tinnitus cannot be cured, so they need to learn techniques to help them to live with it, primarily by reducing their brain's response to the tinnitus sounds so that they intrude less. Together, these techniques are called habituation therapy, and may include:

- learning about tinnitus and what makes it worse or better;
- sound therapy;
- relaxation techniques.

These therapies may be offered by a hearing therapist or by a local self-help group.

Most people find that they notice their tinnitus more in a quiet environment. Sound therapy uses soothing sounds to fill the silence so that the tinnitus is less noticeable. Also possible are:

- counselling;
- treatment for stress, anxiety and depression;
- hearing aids.

Hearing aids may help someone who has both tinnitus and a hearing loss, because they amplify non-tinnitus sounds and so make it easier to ignore the tinnitus sounds.

Menière's disease

Menière's disease is caused by changes in the pressure of fluid in the inner ear, which lead to sudden attacks of severe dizziness. Attacks last between 30 minutes and several hours, and may be accompanied by nausea and vomiting as well as hearing loss and tinnitus.

The attacks of vertigo caused by Menière's disease may be weeks or years apart. The level of the individual's deafness and tinnitus may go up and down. Their hearing may return to normal on its own for a time. It is a progressive disease.

Menière's disease first appears in people around the age of 30: if someone has their first attack of vertigo in their 70s, it is unlikely to be caused by Menière's disease, although some people do develop it later in life.

There is no complete cure for Menière's disease but most people can find ways to relieve and manage their symptoms. These can include managing the tinnitus, changing their diet, complementary therapies, drug treatments to control the vertigo attacks and the sickness that goes with them, diuretics to reduce fluid levels in the inner ear and salt levels in the body, and – usually as a last resort – surgical treatment.

If you think that someone you work with has Menière's disease, you should make sure that they see their GP and are referred to see an ENT consultant.

Deafness as a result of surgery

A very few people lose their hearing because they have to have surgery to remove a tumour on the auditory nerve. Because the surgery severs the auditory nerve, the person enters complete silence. As an American self-help website explains, although people know in advance that they will be deaf when they come round from the operation, 'forewarned does not necessarily mean forearmed … either in the case of the patient or the hospital' (Association for Late-Deafened Adults/ALDA): this is a deeply traumatic experience.

Deafness as a result of injury

Injury may cause temporary or permanent deafness. The sudden and unexpected nature of hearing loss after injury often makes it particularly difficult to cope with, and many people find it hard to accept that their impairment is permanent. People who are deafened through trauma may be beset by feelings of guilt and regret (Woodcock 2001). They are particularly likely to need professional counselling and support to come to terms with their deafness.

The importance of correct diagnosis of hearing loss

Although there is a strong likelihood that an older person with hearing problems has presbyacusis, it is none the less important that the cause of their hearing problems be properly diagnosed by a doctor. First and foremost, the doctor must check for any underlying medical condition that needs treating. They will also establish whether the impairment is a result of presbyacusis or some other ear condition.

If there is any doubt about someone's hearing, it should be checked. All too often, the assumption is made – perhaps even by the person with the hearing problem – that they have dementia, when in fact they are struggling with a hearing impairment.

Of course, it is also important not to jump to conclusions:

> **'If someone doesn't seem to hear, find out why – maybe they just don't want to talk to someone!'** *Gill, Senior Carer*

It is important not only to obtain a proper diagnosis but also for the person to understand what this means. For example, if they have high-frequency loss but can hear low frequencies well, these low-frequency sounds (most background noise) will mask the high-frequency sounds. They may complain 'I hear but I don't understand' and may fear that the resulting communication difficulties come from failing mental faculties.

Some people may find it hard to adapt to amplification and may blame themselves for not trying hard enough or for being inadequate. They may need reassurance that the difficulty results from the limitations of their particular hearing loss.

It is also important to know if someone has an impairment on one side only. They may already realise the importance of listening on their good side but perhaps not that one-sided loss makes it hard to determine the direction of incoming sound. In addition, a hearing loss in one ear makes it difficult to distinguish the sound of a voice against background noise, for which we need good hearing in both ears.

If someone has a sudden loss of hearing in one or both ears, they should see a doctor. If possible, the cause of the loss should be diagnosed to help reassure the person that the loss in one ear will not necessarily happen in the other ear. They could be living in fear of losing all their hearing.

Cochlear implants

You may read about cochlear implants offering a surgical solution to hearing impairment. However, cochlear implants are designed for the small percentage of people who are so profoundly deaf that they cannot benefit at all from a hearing aid. Most older people who are losing their ability to hear in fact retain a significant amount of useful hearing and can be helped by hearing aids – so cochlear implants are not suitable for them.

Where next?

Once the person you work with has a diagnosis of their hearing problem, you will need to support them and work with them to establish the best way to help them manage what hearing they possess. This is covered in Chapters 6–12.

6 Emotional responses to sensory impairment

People react emotionally to sensory impairment in many different ways, and some more strongly than others. This chapter looks at the most common emotional responses, what helps people to cope and how we can help. We look at:

- Sensory loss and old age
- Understanding people's feelings
- The bereavement model and identity
- Making sense of sensory impairment
- Reactions to sensory loss
- Isolation and loneliness
- Passivity
- Responding to a diagnosis of sensory impairment
- How people cope
- Support from family and friends
- When family and friends are not enough
- People who resist help

Sensory loss and old age

Many of the experiences of sensory impairment are shared by people of all ages – everybody is frustrated by broken induction loops in banks, lack of large-print information, others' misunderstandings about their impairment. But developing sensory impairment in old age is different: someone who loses their sight or hearing in old age has lived a whole life as a seeing and hearing person, and seeing and hearing are part of their normal way of life and their identity. As they lose their sight or hearing, they may begin to wonder if they are still the same person.

In addition, an older person may lose their sight or hearing at a time of radical change in their life. As many people age, they may become ill or frail. Their spouse or partner may die. They will no longer work. They will have less money. They may have to leave their home and go into a care home. Their friends may become ill, move away or die. And the world around them will show remarkably little sympathy for the fact that they are dealing with so many major changes in their lives. Add to this a sensory impairment – widely regarded as one of the first signs of frailty in old age – and it is clear that the significance of that impairment for people's emotional and mental health must be taken very seriously.

Many people adapt well – their life experience, personality and support from people around them help them to absorb these changes as a natural part of their lives. But others struggle with the changes of old age, and may need our help. In order to provide this, we need to understand how an older person might feel about the changes associated with old age and, in particular, how losing their sight or hearing will affect their ability to cope with these changes.

Understanding people's feelings

So often, sensory-impaired people say that what they want most of all from other people is understanding. If we do not understand how they feel and how hard it may be for them to express those feelings, we risk, at least, failing to recognise distress and, at worst, missing signs of acute mental illness.

> 'Deafness is invisible, it can so easily be mistaken for something else; for lack of cooperation, stupidity, stubbornness, being unsociable, even for being mentally confused. It may not be recognised by the sufferer himself.' *(McCall 1982)*

Take the case of a new resident in a home, who barely interacts with other residents and who resists offers of help from staff by snapping angrily at them. She is quickly labelled as moody and difficult. Staff and residents rarely approach her, telling themselves that she is not worth spending time or energy on. Everyone becomes set in their ways – she is permanently labelled as 'difficult'.

No one had asked her why she was behaving like this. If they had, they might have discovered that she was struggling to come to terms with the loss of her husband, whose death had precipitated her arrival in the care home. He had been not only her husband but also her carer as she lost her sight and found daily life more difficult.

A listening ear and some understanding about the communication problems faced by someone with a visual impairment could have helped this new resident, not only to settle into her new home but also to cope with her emotional response to such upheavals in her life.

So how can we usefully discuss or predict an individual's emotional response to old age and sensory loss?

The bereavement model and identity

Some people have applied a bereavement model to sensory impairment. According to this, people encounter stages of denial, grief, anger, bargaining, sadness and acceptance as they move through the experience of losing their sight or hearing.

But this can be an over-simplification: if people's feelings are categorised and labelled so neatly, there may be a danger of expecting reactions that are not there or of misunderstanding the way someone feels about their impairment. Such a model also takes little account of the individual's personality, beliefs, past life experiences, support networks and current situation – all of which are important factors in determining how they will respond to sensory impairment.

> 'Each person is an individual and will respond to their sight loss in a personal way. One person might experience deep despair but another

with a similar level of vision may be positive and able to cope with their new situation.' *Chandra Beasley, KAB*

The bereavement model can be useful in helping us to recognise common reactions to sensory impairment. But it should be treated with caution because, as in bereavement, few people progress neatly through the stages in order. Many stick at one stage, or go backwards and forwards through the stages. Almost always, at any one time, their reactions are too complex to be neatly labelled.

Making sense of sensory impairment

Stephen Ainlay (1989) researched the link between sensory impairment and identity. He observed that people often try to make sense of their impairment by finding a reason for it – too much close work or a smoky atmosphere in the office, for example. They feel that their lives must be more than a random series of events. They may feel that their sensory loss is a tragic bolt from the blue, from which they will never recover.

People with a sensory impairment may also wonder if they will be the same person that they always have been, without their sight or hearing.

'I think my personality has changed – it's so hard not being able to see or hear, having to spend so much time thinking.' *Jean Shorten*

Unless they can come to accept that their sensory loss is part of the pattern of their whole life – and not the end of it – they will be devastated by it, and unlikely to be able to cope and retain their sense of identity. They may achieve this acceptance through faith – 'it is part of God's plan for me'. They may come to understand it as just one more challenge, to be faced as they have faced other challenges in life. Or they may be helped by learning that many others have followed a similar path, overcome their difficulties and faced their future, still whole and still themselves, their identity intact. There are many paths to acceptance of sensory impairment. Each, however, depends on the individual's sense of identity and understanding of the world being maintained.

Reactions to sensory loss

As we have seen, it is impossible to predict how any one individual will react to sensory impairment. There are, however, some reactions that commonly occur.

Disbelief or denial

A feeling of disbelief seems almost universal at first. Most people try to put off the realisation of their impairment for a while, attributing any sight or hearing problems to tired eyes, needing new lenses, high blood pressure or to people mumbling. Eventually, they go for a test, still hoping that their vision or hearing problem can be corrected.

> **'People find it hard to accept their vision changing. They expect their eyes to see as well as they have always done. They find it very hard to accept that they can't correct their sight with stronger lenses.'**
> *Janine Sykes, Optometrist*

Maria Conyers interviewed people about their sight loss (Conyers 1986). Until then, many had suppressed their feelings about their impairment, and often the interview was the first time they had reflected on it. Many became distressed; many, too, stated that 'they had, or were able to allow, no feelings whatever about the loss'.

> **'Before I lost my sight, I was a very proud man; this is the worst catastrophe, the worst tragedy that could have happened. I have no future.'**

But, although some were still angry and desperate, others had moved on:

> **'At last I am beginning to live with it instead of fighting it all the time.'**

It may be hard to accept the label of 'blind', 'deaf' or 'partially sighted', but someone who rejects being so labelled risks being misunderstood as senile, incompetent or attention seeking (Cullinan 1986) as they trip on kerbs, mis-hear friends' conversations and peer at the bus timetable. Accepting the label also carries a cost, however, because it may imply to the individual a damaged self-image, which is no less hard to bear late in life. It can be a bitter choice, and it is therefore not surprising that many older people are reluctant to admit to sight or hearing problems.

Hope

In dealing with impairment, hope can be a double-edged sword. For someone with a treatable condition, hope that there may be a cure for failing sight or hearing can carry them through the long periods of waiting for diagnosis and treatment. But if nothing can be done, hope must eventually give way to realisation of the permanent nature of their condition. This can be terribly hard. It sometimes gives way to panic – to maintain the illusion of hope, some people visit a whole series of doctors or therapists to find one who will say that something can be done.

In the long term, however, hope can also be a sign that someone has accepted their impairment, has absorbed it as part of their identity, and is looking ahead to their life in the future with optimism.

Anxiety and fear

Janine Sykes, an optometrist, sees many older people with age-related vision loss. She describes a patient who had the first signs of macular degeneration, which was not severe and was progressing slowly – in fact, he could still drive. But he was terrified – his fear of the future overwhelmed him, apparently quite out of proportion to his actual vision loss.

Maria Conyers' interviewees had almost all felt anxiety or fear at some point. These emotions underpinned an enormous range of other behaviours, touched almost all aspects of people's lives, and might be about something specific or something in the future:

- What effect would their impairment have on relationships?
- Would they be able to maintain their existing roles – as head of the family, as the strong one in a group of friends, as chair of the Women's Institute, and so on?
- Would people assume they could no longer cope with living independently because they made mlstakes such as dropping cups, or giving a strange answer because they had misheard?

- How would their lifestyle be affected?
- Would they be able to carry on living in their home?
- Would they have enough money?

These anxieties about their sense of self and identity were then manifested in feelings of anger, depression, regret, denial, low self-esteem, embarrassment or shame about their impairment, and fear of rejection. They were anxious, too, about their ability to cope with the impairment:

- Would they be able to look after themselves from day to day?
- Would they still be able to get about?
- Would it affect their health?
- Were they getting old?
- Would they be able to learn new skills?

> 'One of our residents had an infection in his ear. He became frightened because he was afraid of what might happen if he couldn't hear in his sleep. We made him feel secure – talked to him, made him feel he was being looked after. The doctor prescribed him antibiotics and he was fine.' *Gill, Senior Carer, Care Home*

Anger

Many people feel anger at their own new ineptness when they develop a sensory loss. They often direct their anger at themselves for being useless, although some direct their anger towards other people.

Anger seems to be experienced by most people in the initial stages of sensory impairment. Sometimes it continues over the years – and may resurface when the impairment becomes more severe.

Avoidance

Some people try to escape coming to terms with their impairment by avoiding tasks that have become difficult. This is not the same as denial – they know they have an impairment but they do not want to address it at that particular moment – although someone in denial may also try to avoid difficult tasks.

Inadequacy and loss of self-esteem

> 'The hearing-impaired person often feels that he or she should be able to cope with the hearing loss more effectively and that difficulties in coping indicate weakness.' *(Kaplan 1992)*

'Confidence can go way down when you start to lose your hearing.'
Barbara Godwin, Hi Kent

Someone's feelings of inadequacy may manifest themselves in frustration at, say, taking an hour to get ready because they cannot find their gloves or in being unable to speak at a community meeting because they cannot hear the speakers. They may also feel inadequate because they equate hearing impairment with other disabilities such as those affecting learning or memory.

Kaplan (1992) describes a deaf man who went on a visit to another part of the country where people had a different accent, making it hard for him to understand what they were saying. When asked to describe his trip, he talked about how ashamed he was not to be able to understand – he saw his communication difficulties as his fault rather than a problem shared by himself and the speaker.

Common responses to the threat to self-esteem presented by sensory loss are denial, hostility and suspicion. For example, someone may blame their friends (perhaps rightly) for mumbling or deliberately excluding them from the group conversation. This suspicion may grow to such an extent that, if they cannot hear well, they may suspect others of saying unpleasant things about them, or mistake their laughter for ridicule.

These feelings of hostility or suspicion are often turned against those closest to the person, or against professionals trying to help them. It is easy for non-impaired people on the receiving end of this behaviour to feel angry and resentful. But we need to try to understand the fear behind the behaviour so that we can remain objective and help the sensory-impaired person to accept their impairment and to be assertive in expressing their needs without being aggressive.

Isolation and loneliness

One woman with a visual impairment told me that the hardest thing for her was that she could no longer recognise people:

> **'It's isolating. But I don't tell people because I think it's off-putting.'**
> *Rose Arthur*

The inability to recognise people, to see their expressions, to tell when they are addressing you, are all significant barriers to communication. Rose continued by describing how she used to ask 'how's the family?' and work out who someone was according to the answer, but as her friends grow older she no longer feels able to ask this because their families might no longer be alive. She tries to avoid this difficulty by training people she knows well to tell her who they are. Before, they used to complain that she ignored them when they greeted her from across the road. Otherwise, she is forced to use people's voices and the subject of their conversation as clues to recognition.

The fundamental effect of hearing impairment on someone's ability to communicate is widely recognised. Unless effective communication strategies are learned and put in place, this leads directly to isolation.

Older people with a sight or hearing impairment very commonly withdraw. This is not only as a result of their communication difficulties but also because of their own and others' increasing perception of them as frail, fallible and no longer at the centre of things. It may also be because of the person's feeling that they are no longer the person they were.

Sensory-impaired people may feel that they have changed, because others treat them differently as a result of the impairment. The older sensory-impaired person is all too aware of the stigma of impairment because, almost certainly before they lost their sight or hearing, they also shared those perceptions. They may have regarded sensory-impaired people as needy, as objects of pity, as no longer fully capable, as being hard to communicate with, and possibly as mentally impaired.

They know full well, therefore, how they themselves are stigmatised now that they are impaired – a situation in which it is hard to maintain a sense of self and dignity. So whilst isolation can result from difficulty in communicating, it can also be a defence mechanism against negative judgements and rejection.

Passivity

Many people become more passive as they age, allowing others to make decisions for them, even when they are fully able to act for themselves. This may result in part from an increasing feeling of vulnerability or frailness, or possibly out of fear of creating anger in others. If they misunderstand, or refuse to do what staff or family ask, they may cause staff to be angry, or their family to stop visiting them or arrange for them to be put into a home. As a result, many older people choose to stay out of sight and out of mind, for safety's sake.

One woman in a care home had seen a member of staff raise her voice impatiently to another resident with poor hearing, and had been so distressed and frightened by this that she said she might pretend to hear when that member of staff spoke to her, even when she couldn't.

This is good for no one – it is not only cruel, it also increases the older person's dependency on others, hastening further frailty and dependence. It reduces their self-esteem and their motivation for living. It is therefore important to encourage people to become more assertive – to ask someone to speak up, or to move the light if they need it – and not to pretend that a problem does not exist because of their fear of becoming an inconvenience.

This is not easy, however. Try saying 'what did you say?' repeatedly during a conversation. How did that make you feel? How did the other person react? Next time you talk to someone who mumbles, consider whether you really would ask them to speak more clearly. Or would you blame yourself for finding them hard to understand? How passive are you?

Responding to a diagnosis of sensory impairment

Quite often, because the person has no reason to suspect that they have a visual or hearing disorder, they blame something else – high blood pressure, tiredness, other people mumbling – for their symptoms. This makes their problems seem routine, and not permanent. So the shock when they receive the official diagnosis may be great.

> 'For many, the initial visit to the eye clinic will be a traumatic time at which they have to confront the prospect of permanent sight loss for the first time.' *(Browne 2002)*

The way that a diagnosis is delivered can make a big difference. Although optometrist Janine Sykes rates the local ophthalmic team very highly, she also feels that they could be more sensitive. She has sent people to hospital for tests, knowing that they have slight macular degeneration, only to discover that they were sent home, worried and distressed, having been told by the consultant that their condition would lead to blindness. It is then up to Janine to explain fully the diagnosis and condition and to reassure them.

She is not alone in feeling that people's psychological needs are not as well catered for as their medical needs.

> 'Attendance at an eye clinic can often be a stressful experience, especially for patients attending the clinic alone. Many feel totally confused, even upset, by the information given to them during the consultation. Clinic staff are frequently pushed for time, and often patients do not know, or are not at a stage to think about, the questions they need to ask. As a result, patients are often left feeling totally bewildered, with little opportunity to absorb upsetting news and discuss any concerns.' *(Browne 2002)*

Indeed, patient support is often provided by voluntary sector agencies using unpaid staff – it is a marginalised service in many hospitals, in both ophthalmic and audiology departments.

Jan Henstridge, Head of Care at one of the RNIB's care homes comments:

> 'It's very hard when the hospital says "there's nothing more we can do for you" and discharges them.'

Jan helps people to cope with a new diagnosis by making sure that the resident knows she is there to support them, both by listening and talking and by making sure their practical needs are still being supported.

> 'I would ask "How did you get on?" and take it from there – I'd see what they wanted. Some might not want to talk straight away. That's where their key worker can be invaluable – they know the resident better than anybody.'

Many individuals face the challenge of adapting to one cause of sensory impairment, only for another to begin or be discovered. Ainlay (1989) interviewed one woman who had glaucoma, which was controlled by eye drops, but was then also diagnosed with macular degeneration:

> 'It is too bad that I had to come down with this other thing. It really is a worse bother. They tell me that I won't go totally blind but with the two problems, you know, it worries me.'

How people cope

> 'I don't think you can predict who's going to be fine. Although the people who cope better tend to be those who think "OK I've got this disability, I'm going to take control of this". Those who accept things as a bad deal – "I can't do this because of my disability" – will find it very hard. They persist in identifying themselves as their disability.'
> *Chris Cogdell, Social Services District Manager*

Optometrist Janine Sykes comments that attitude and personality are very important in relation to sight loss:

'One person with very little remaining vision will cope very well and live life to the full, while another will worry, even though it's only their spectacles that need changing.'

'Often when I ask how they're coping, they may say "Oh, fine," but later, when we're talking, it becomes clear that they're not really coping.' *Jacqui Jackson, Assessment Officer with deaf people*

So what can help someone to cope with sensory impairment?

- Understanding the impairment.
- The people around them understanding the impairment.
- Their personality.
- The ability to maintain their self-image intact, assimilating the impairment into it.
- Support from family and friends.
- The knowledge that they overcame difficulty in the past, will do so now and will continue to do so in the future.
- Security – in relationships, social status, accommodation, finance.
- Faith or belief in some higher order.
- Support from others with a similar impairment.
- And, from professionals:
  - rehabilitation;
  - accessible services;
  - counselling.

Support from family and friends

Support from other people can make an enormous difference to the way in which someone copes with sensory impairment. Friends and family who learn about the impairment and how they can help provide not only practical support but also reassurance that their relationship is still as important as ever, and that they will maintain it, whatever comes along.

Unfortunately, friends and family may find it hard to provide this kind of support. They may be sympathetic but frustrated or angry because of the effect of the impairment on their own lives. They may also fear that the stigma of impairment will cause them, too, to become socially isolated. Some may be unsympathetic, perhaps thinking that their friend or relative is a fraud because their ability to see or hear seems to be so variable.

It is also very common for older sensory-impaired people to be over-protected by their families and by professional carers, who may be worried about whether the impaired person can still look after themselves. This has the effect of isolating the impaired person from daily life, and relegating them to the role of observer, where perhaps before they were always at the centre of things – making decisions, being consulted, participating fully in the lives of the people around them. (See also Chapter 7.)

When family and friends are not enough

In times of trouble, most people turn to their family and friends for help, and older people going through sensory loss are no different. But, because they are older, they may receive less help from these traditional sources, for a variety of reasons:

- The network of people close to them may be relatively small, as people die or move away.
- If they depend on one person for communication – perhaps because they have developed a personal sign language together – the loss of that person will cause isolation.
- Friends and family may be so frustrated that they give up trying to communicate – the impaired person becomes isolated and loses confidence in their ability to communicate.

They need, therefore, to be offered support from other sources. These may be voluntary or statutory, formal or informal.

Staff in health and social care

All care home managers, district nurses and social services care workers need to be aware of the support that older people with sensory impairment need and how they can help. This is where training is so important.

Someone who has recently become sensory-impaired needs, above all, to experience from professionals an understanding of their impairment.

Even seemingly small acts, such as staff identifying themselves before speaking to a visually impaired person, make a big difference. It can be the first time the individual has received reassurance and understanding about their impairment.

> 'If you go into residential care, your ongoing support and friendship counselling is down to the home. The days of care managers regularly visiting the clients on their list are long gone.' *Chris Cogdell, Social Services District Manager*

However, while staff can provide emotional support by listening, understanding and showing sympathy for someone in distress, there may come a time when someone you are working with needs more specialist support.

Counselling and mental health support cannot be provided by untrained staff – they require complex skills and training, and if delivered by untrained staff can do more harm than good. Although most people do eventually find some way of coming to terms with their sensory impairment, a significant number experience depression. Professionals working with older people with sensory impairment therefore need to be aware of the implications for depression and mental health.

If you feel out of your depth, seek expert help. This may include the person's GP – who can provide access to psychiatric services and counselling – and local and national voluntary organisations that provide advocates or befrienders. (See also Chapter 16.)

Advocacy

Even homes that specialise in caring for people with sensory loss cannot offer comprehensive support. For example, a resident of one RNIB home had a severe dual sensory impairment and needed additional support. This came from the local group of DeafBlind UK, which provided a volunteer to befriend the resident, and also offered a monthly lunch service for people with a dual loss.

One resident of a home was referred to the mental health charity Mind because she thought that her family was trying to take control of her finances and have her evicted from the home. Mind has an advocacy service for people with mental health problems, and their advocate was able to resolve the situation and reassure the resident.

Rehabilitation workers

Rehabilitation workers, including specialist therapists in areas such as hearing, can also help:

> 'I have the time to sit down with them. They can talk about all that they are experiencing. They often say, "You're the first person who's listened to me." I have a cupboard full of tissues. But it's OK for people to cry in here – a lot of things have been bubbling for them.'
> *Alex Willoughby, Hearing Therapist*

See Chapter 8 for more on rehabilitation.

Peer support groups

Peer support groups such as Hard of Hearing Clubs offer friendship and understanding about what an impaired person is experiencing, as well as information about their condition and advice about local services. These groups may be run under the wing of local branches of national organisations, such as the RNIB, or by local societies of the blind or deaf, or be set up by rehabilitation workers or hearing therapists. They are often run locally by and for the people who attend them.

Attendance at these groups, however, presupposes that the impaired person knows about them, is able to get to them and is not so isolated that they feel such a group would be irrelevant to them. Whilst they offer enormous support to many people, they cannot take the place of trained, professional care when someone is in real distress. This must be the responsibility of professional health and social care staff. (See also Chapter 7.)

People who resist help

People who do not accept their sight or hearing impairment and seem to resist all offers of help are unlikely to benefit fully from any social or technical assistance they may be offered. This can be extremely frustrating for staff.

'Dependency comes hard to some people.' *Chris Cogdell, Social Services District Manager*

They may be very proud, or unused to accepting help. It can be difficult to know how to provide support in these circumstances.

'Sometimes you can't. It's a really valuable lesson to learn. It's difficult for the practitioner but you have to accept that it is the decision the person has made.' *Alex Willoughby, Hearing Therapist*

There will always be individuals whom it is extremely difficult to help. The best we can do for these people is to make sure they know that we are available.

7 Families, friends and support groups

When someone develops a sensory impairment, relationships with those closest to them are likely to be affected. This chapter examines these changing relationships, and how family and friends are touched by the impairment. In particular, it includes:

- The emotional effect of sensory impairment on families
- People in context
- The effect of sensory loss on relationships
- The role of the professional
- Establishing new relationships

Sensory impairment affects everyone in contact with it: not just the person who is impaired but also their family and friends. If someone loses the ability to communicate effectively, the people with whom they used to communicate also lose the benefit of that communication.

In addition, because hearing and sight loss are stigmatised, the people close to a sensory-impaired person will also be touched by that stigma. They may try to deny the existence of the impairment, or find that others avoid them in the same way as they avoid the impaired person.

> 'Someone came here at Christmas and he had a letter for us. You see it was for my husband as well, and I said "Come in, oh, come on in a minute". He said "I was just writing a letter, it's no use coming in because he can't hear me, can he?" You see, that is the attitude of people.' *Margery, Peter Bradbury's wife*

The emotional effect of sensory impairment on families

In Chapter 6 we looked at sensory-impaired people's emotional responses to their impairment. They are not alone in this response: the people close to them are equally likely to experience an emotional reaction to the impairment, often feeling a similar range of emotions.

> '[They] have a sort of surrogate experience of the resulting frustrations, fears, disbelief and anger.' *(Ainlay 1989)*

The impairment can affect their lives just as seriously as it does the life of the impaired person, and sometimes it seems to affect them more.

Family members may find it hard to believe in the sensory loss – which is both hurtful and frustrating for the impaired person. Usually this is just an initial disbelief, which parallels that experienced by a newly impaired individual. But some family members persist in maintaining their disbelief, and may even set little tests or traps to try to catch the person out, to prove that they are not really impaired. Sometimes family members can be angry, or embarrassed. Often they avoid talking about the impairment, even after a visit to see a specialist. They may also find themselves avoiding the person with the impairment. This avoidance is very common, and seems to be the result of anxiety about how to interact with the impaired person.

People in context

When someone develops a sensory impairment, they reassess how they relate to the people around them. As we saw in Chapter 6, there are many ways for people to respond emotionally to their loss, and this is also true with regard to relationships: they may decide to withdraw from the world; they may decide to connect with other people who have a similar impairment; they may decide to accept or to ignore their impairment and carry on regardless. They may choose more than one of these options.

In order to provide holistic care, we must consider each impaired person's entire world, their complete network of relationships. Older people are likely to have established a number of lifelong relationships – with a spouse, relations and friends – as well as developing more recent friendships, and maintaining these lifelong relationships is likely to be enormously important to them. If these relationships founder because of the impairment, it can be extremely damaging.

Someone who is still living at home in the community should, in theory, find it easier to maintain established relationships. But if they have problems with mobility or communication, their social circle often diminishes significantly as they find it harder to go out and to participate.

> 'I miss a lot. I feel left out. It's like when I went to my niece's wedding. I just sat down and let them get on with it. It's too much of a strain, put it that way.' *Catherine Jameson*

Misunderstandings may also occur, for example, when a family member thinks that the impaired person does not want to talk to them, when they were in fact simply unaware that someone else was there. Many visually impaired people report that when they do not recognise or greet friends in the street, those people feel snubbed.

When someone moves into a care home, their contact with both friends and family will almost certainly be much reduced. This need not be the case – in one care home I visited, one woman's daughter came every week and cooked Sunday lunch for her mother (who lived in a studio flat within the home); another daughter washed her mother's hair once a week. This home has made relatives welcome, so they have no fear of disrupting its normal routines and habits.

On the other hand, family and friends can show a complete lack of sympathy for someone with a sensory impairment.

> 'All too many of these people are described by their family or others with whom they associate as confused, disorientated, non-communicating, uncooperative, an "angry old ...", withdrawn and, most unfair of all, senile.' *(Hull 1992)*

Where conflict already exists in a family, sensory loss can compound it. In some cases, family members may even actively disrupt the impaired person's attempts to adapt – for example, by making so much noise that they cannot use their hearing aid.

The effect of sensory loss on relationships

Reactions to sensory impairment are both complex and unpredictable, so it is not surprising that the arena of personal relationships is a complicated one.

Role reversal

It is not uncommon for roles to be reversed when someone becomes impaired, so that a previously dominant or caring person becomes passive and cared for. In some families, the sensory-impaired person is discouraged from continuing to look after themselves and other family members take control.

> 'Whether someone takes over depends on their personality – whether they have a desperate need to be a carer or not.' *Beryl Palmer, Manager, Sensory Disabilities Services*

This role reversal may or may not be welcome to the individuals concerned. It can be hard for some people to accept the passive role that has been imposed upon them by an over-protective family. On the other hand, some impaired people can be extremely demanding, putting a heavy burden on their family without being aware of the extent of their demands. Social services workers sometimes find that impaired people turn down Direct Payments to enable them to buy in care, saying that they don't need them because their spouse or partner does everything for them.

Some families put a great deal of pressure on the impaired person, perhaps to see a specialist or to give up certain activities. This can be counter-productive:

> 'Sometimes families ... go on about getting a hearing test. It can be very wearing to be nagged by your family.' *Alex Willoughby, Hearing Therapist*

It can have more serious consequences, too:

> 'People may be seen as at risk by an anxious family, demanding a residential placement, rather than looking to support someone at home.' *Gill Levy, RNIB*

Outside the family too, it is common for others to over-compensate, to try to protect the person at all costs from encountering dangers. This is usually because of ignorance, but sometimes these people are professionals who should know better:

> 'I know rehab workers who have recommended the removal of cookers!' *Gill Levy, RNIB*

Stress

Much of the literature about families and carers focuses on the ways that they provide personal care. There is very little mention of the different demands created by looking after a sensory-impaired person, who may need very little help with personal care but has significant problems with communication. The carer may become the only source of information about the world and the only means of communicating with it. There is little recognition of the psychological stress involved in caring in this way, because the focus is always on the physical stress of caring.

The stress caused by dependence on another for communication is also hard for the impaired person and this, in turn, often puts a great strain on a relationship.

Exclusion

Many older people may conceal their impairment because they know that sighted and hearing people are uncomfortable around them and will exclude them if they know about the impairment.

It is common for hearing and sighted people to assume that a sensory-impaired person is impaired in all of their senses: they shout at a visually impaired person, or treat a deaf person as though they are stupid; they assume that the impaired person cannot participate in a conversation or activity and so exclude and isolate them. In a social setting, this means that an impaired person may effectively become a 'non-person' and be treated as though they are not there because of the powerful stigma attached to sensory impairment. This may sound extreme but is in fact very common: in a group of people, anyone with a sight or hearing impairment is likely to be left out of the conversation, often quite blatantly.

Thus at a time when the person most needs to talk about themselves and their changing sense of identity, they may feel inhibited from doing so. They may also feel less and less a part of the world of sighted and hearing people around them.

The role of the professional

The amount of involvement we have with the family and friends of a sensory-impaired person depends largely on the caring context in which we work. However, whether we work in domiciliary care, in a clinic or in a care home, we cannot afford to ignore the family and friends of the people we work with: they are a crucial element in that person's ability to cope with their impairment. We therefore need to find ways of helping people to maintain healthy relationships, by encouraging family and friends to participate and by establishing an environment where they feel welcome.

We need to educate family and friends about the impairment and its effects, and to include them as an integral part of the care that we provide. If they understand the impairment, they may find it easier to understand what is happening to them and to the person they are close to. If they do not, they can make it extremely hard for that person to live with their impairment:

> 'Often the family don't understand that even someone with a serious hearing loss can hear well in good conditions. Hearing loss can cause relationship problems, family problems. It can lead to arguments if the partner's hearing is OK – they may say "You never hear what I say to you" or argue about the volume of the television. This still happens even when they know the other person has a hearing loss.' *Alex Willoughby, Hearing Therapist*

Our involvement could take the form of informal chats or it could mean encouraging the family to attend an awareness training session. If we work in a day or residential care context, we need to include the other service users or residents in this education: they are the people with whom the sensory-impaired individual interacts the most.

If we are involved in providing any kind of rehabilitation, it is useful for a spouse or partner, close family member or friend to join in. In this way, they become more involved, more informed, and are more likely to be able to continue the rehabilitation back at home. There they can provide moral support if, for example, the hard-of-hearing person asks the rest of the family to speak more clearly, or to change restaurants for a quieter one.

This involvement can be extremely important: it is not unusual for a rehabilitation specialist to teach someone new skills and see them carry out tasks successfully but then to find that the same tasks are not performed at home. This is often because another family member assumes control through ignorance of the impaired person's capabilities. Or it may be that the impaired person's new skills, confidence and independence could threaten the dynamics of relationships at home – the family may reject the new skills and confidence, thereby effectively undermining rehabilitation because they have not been part of it.

A family that is involved in rehabilitation is more aware of the challenge that faces a newly sensory-impaired person, and better able to understand how difficult they may be finding that rehabilitation:

> 'The effort required to learn these new skills often induces frustration and anxiety, which can be compounded by a lack of understanding by family and friends.' *(Williams 1994)*

Establishing new relationships

One way in which people cope with sensory loss, and the resulting loss of their old social network, is to establish a new one. They may do this on an informal basis – perhaps forming a friendship with another resident, who may have a similar impairment. This can be difficult to achieve without help because their impairment may, by its nature, restrict their ability to make contact with people. They may need the help of staff to make initial contact.

Another way of making new relationships – which is available to people living in the community or in residential care – is to join a peer support group.

Initially an impaired person may resist going, not wishing to be associated with a stigmatised group – but if they do go, they generally find an enormous source of support. This is not only because of the rehabilitation courses, mobility training, lipreading skills and social activities that such groups offer but also because of the positive effect on self-esteem of membership of a group where impairment is normal.

Meeting people with a similar impairment can help the person to understand that they are not alone in being impaired, and that others have found positive ways of living with their impairment. They can often also find comfort in the fact that there are others whose condition is worse: they no longer see themselves as uniquely singled out for tragedy.

Members of such groups offer a significant amount of support, discussion and preparation for what lies ahead. This cannot help the person to avoid the experiences of impairment, or their emotional reactions to them, but it can help them to learn what to expect, and to know that others have been there before them, and will be there after them. From others in the group they can learn:

- coping strategies;
- assertiveness;
- practical tips.

Sensory-impaired people can also find that the stress of social interaction is removed by choosing a social network among people with the same impairment:

> 'The pressure to perform is relieved in a group of people who share similar loss of vision, know the problems it can create and who take little if any notice when the person falters.' *(Ainlay 1989)*

8 Rehabilitation: making the most of sight and hearing

This chapter describes how, alongside rehabilitation workers, we can work to help sensory-impaired people to maintain a good quality of life. It includes:

- What is rehabilitation?
- Who carries out rehabilitation?
- Working with individuals
- Specialist rehabilitation workers – what they offer
- How specialist rehabilitation can help: a case study
- Learning new skills
- The rehabilitation relationship
- Where to find rehabilitation workers
- How to get the best out of your local rehabilitation service

What is rehabilitation?

When someone leaves the consultation room with a diagnosis of sight or hearing impairment they may feel that nothing can be done to help and that they now must simply put up with poor sight or hearing. In fact, whatever the severity of the impairment, there is always something that can be done to make it easier to live with. This is the role of rehabilitation (often called rehab).

Rehabilitation helps someone to remain independent, regain or gain new skills, improve their quality of life and limit risk, and it provides emotional support.

Part of rehabilitation work is to help people use aids, such as magnifiers or hearing aids, in order to make the most of their remaining sight or hearing (see also Chapter 9). But rehabilitation work does not stop there: just as sensory impairment is not purely about finding it hard to read the bottom line on the eye chart or to hear the bleeps in the headphones, it also addresses the physical, sensory, emotional and social needs of the individual.

Who carries out rehabilitation?

Non-specialist staff working with older people carry out a great deal of rehabilitation work from day to day: they encourage someone to walk to the end of the drive each morning, help another to read their book by sitting near the window or a third to join in the daily bingo by sitting next to the caller. They are at the front line of care and play a significant role in rehabilitation.

Marcus Farley is a rehabilitation worker for visually impaired people. He confirms that, although specialist rehabilitation work itself requires training, there is a great deal that non-specialist staff can do. In particular, he suggests that staff always ask the impaired person what they want: for example, 'How would you like to be guided?', 'Do you mind if I take your arm?', 'Where would you like to sit?' In other words, it is extremely important to treat the person as an individual. Specialist rehabilitation work is based on this principle. (See also Chapters 10, 11 and 12 for further information on how to help people to make the most of their sight and hearing and to live full lives.)

Working with individuals

> 'No two people ever want exactly the same from rehab.' *Liz Duncan, Sense*

Everyone copes with a sensory loss differently, not just in terms of their emotions but also in the way that the impairment affects their senses. This is because we experience our senses through our brains, and no two brains are exactly alike. So we cannot know exactly how the impairment affects any one person's senses.

Whatever sensory loss a person has, they will automatically compensate, to a certain extent, using other senses or techniques. Some people find this easier to do than others, and some are more willing than others to experiment and to make mistakes in the quest for a better way of doing things.

> 'I've just had a lady in who is delightful, full of character. She can read the third line up from the bottom with one eye, although not with the other. She says "I can't see". But another lady I see who is partially sighted, and has less vision, says that she can see fine.' *Janine Sykes, Optometrist*

A number of factors influence people's ability to cope emotionally with sensory impairment. As described in Chapter 6, these include their personality, general health and previous life experience, and support by the family.

Specialist rehabilitation workers – what they offer

Rehabilitation has changed enormously over the years: in the 1970s, for example, the most rehabilitation that a visually impaired person could hope for was a social club run by a Blind Welfare Assistant, where people made wicker trays and pot holders:

> 'We've moved on since Mrs Wagham and her pot holders!' *Chris Cogdell, Social Services District Manager*

The main role of rehabilitation now is to provide specialist assessment and advice to people with a new sensory impairment. Ideally, someone will be assessed as soon as the impairment causes them problems, although often they are not.

> 'Successful rehabilitation depends, above all else, upon early intervention.' *(Willetts 2002)*

The rehabilitation officer works in partnership with the individual to identify that person's needs and functional difficulties and ways to address these. Most rehabilitation officers are specialists in either sight or hearing loss – rarely both, and rarely in multiple disabilities.

A typical rehabilitation worker for people with a visual impairment would expect to work with people on:

- orientation and mobility training;
- daily living;
- communications training;
- lighting;
- low-vision therapy;
- emotional adjustment.

> 'One woman came to the low vision unit who was dual sensory impaired. She used a Minicom [textphone] to communicate, but found it hard because she could not read the type. Staff helped her to reduce the type size – she had set it so big that she could no longer see a complete word at a time – and she was able to communicate again.' *Anita Lightstone, RNIB Low Vision Unit (an all-in-one low vision and rehabilitation unit)*

> 'Elsie was a 75-year-old woman with a severe hearing loss. She was referred because she was not wearing her hearing aid; the neighbours were complaining about the noise from her television and her family was worried that she seemed withdrawn.
>
> 'The earmould on her hearing aid was making her ear itch, so I arranged for her to have a new one made of a non-allergenic material that would be more comfortable. Even while wearing her hearing aid, Elsie was still unable to enjoy the television. I suggested that she use the subtitles and try a television device. She tried and liked the loop system the most. I arranged for her local social services department to provide and fit one in her lounge.
>
> 'Elsie felt that her loneliness was caused by her hearing loss. She said that she avoided meeting people, as she felt nervous asking

them to repeat things. I invited her to join our lipreading class to learn lipreading, communication tactics and assertiveness. She thoroughly enjoyed the class, especially meeting other deaf people and chatting over a cup of tea. One year later, she has started going to a local lunch club for retired people.' *Val Tait, Hearing Therapist*

Low-vision work helps people to make best use of their sight by providing aids such as magnifiers and training people in the use of the aids. A hearing therapist (possibly called a hearing specialist) covers many of the same areas but, in particular, also works on using hearing aids and on lipreading.

'In my opinion, almost all rehabilitation subjects are suitable for the elderly, at the right pace and with the necessary repetition.' *Sita Schipper, Sensis, Eindhoven, Netherlands*

This broad view of the scope of rehabilitation work is not, however, always achieved. Katia Gilhome Herbst found that, after issuing hearing aids, much follow-up rehabilitation work was limited to helping people to use their aids more frequently:

'... what the private sector has most to offer the hearing impaired is personal attention, which (for the severely deaf in particular) is probably as therapeutic as the aid they eventually buy.' *(Gilhome Herbst 1986)*

With regard to daily living skills, rehabilitation workers can often help people to use ordinary domestic equipment that they have at home. They may also recommend specialist equipment, and train the person how to use it. Local authorities vary in what they provide and what they charge for, and this may differ according to whether people are under or over 65.

Rehabilitation workers are a good source of information, both regarding the impairment itself and how to live with it and about local services and support groups. Some provide counselling; others refer on to social workers, specialist voluntary organisations, self-help groups or counselling services.

How specialist rehabilitation can help: a case study

The hospital eye clinic asked Marcus Farley, a rehabilitation worker with a local authority social services department, to visit Mrs Thomas. She is an 82-year-old widow who lives alone. She lost the sight in her right eye through glaucoma, and has a detached retina in her left eye.

He found that, although she had been issued with a hand-held magnifier, she still had difficulty using it for reading. She also had difficulty seeing to read the controls on her gas cooker, to make a drink, to read her watch, and to do the crosswords and puzzles that she used to enjoy. These problems, she said, were making her feel depressed.

'We talked about how additional lighting might make a difference, and about the use of large print and contrast. I established that she did not have glare problems and, before leaving after my first visit, I suggested that we remove her net curtains in her kitchen and lounge. She was reluctant at first but agreed for me to try. Once they were removed, she found that the increased natural daylight made a vast difference (an increased reading from 300 lux to 1500 lux). She was able to see her cooker area more easily, and to see more easily to make a drink. In addition, sitting with her back to the window, she could see more easily to read with her magnifier. This also proved that, in poor light conditions such as night-time, she would benefit from a fluorescent 'task' lamp for reading and strip lighting above the cooker area.

'These were issued on a later visit and dramatically improved her reading function and her ability to see to cook. I fixed fluorescent tactile markings to her cooker controls on the low, middle and high settings so that she could see more easily to judge the temperature of the cooker. In addition, I explained the importance of colour contrast. I got her to use different-coloured mugs for different liquids in order to increase contrast. For example, I persuaded her to use a red cup to pour milk into, instead of her existing white mug, a white mug for black coffee as opposed to her existing brown mug, etc. She was also issued with a large-print watch, and I told her where she could get large-print crossword and puzzle books.

'I could just as easily have given her talking books or tried to teach her Braille for her reading difficulties; given her a gadget that bleeps a warning that you are reaching the top of a mug when pouring; arranged for a home help to cook for her; and so on. But this would not have helped her to overcome her feelings of depression. What I did was help her maximise what vision she had rather than take it away and, by giving her back her independence, I helped eradicate her depression.'

Learning new skills

Many people with impaired sight or hearing discover techniques to help them use their remaining sight or hearing almost by accident. A trained rehabilitation worker, however, will be aware of a whole range of strategies and techniques, and can help the impaired person to learn and practise them.

For example, someone with macular degeneration will probably automatically realise that their peripheral vision is now essential to them but may not know how to make the best use of it. A rehabilitation worker might ask them to look at a vase of flowers on the table. By looking straight at it they will not see it, because they have lost their central vision. But if they keep their head still and try moving their eyes upwards, downwards and to left and right, they will see which part of their vision works best. They will find that they need to use a different part of their eyes to look at the ceiling or the floor. This technique is sometimes called 'eccentric fixation'.

This is only one of a range of skills that a trained sensory rehabilitation worker will be able to teach visually impaired people. Above all, the skills must relate to what the individual is actually going to do once back in their home environment:

> 'The most important thing is to put everything learned immediately into practice.' *Sita Schipper, Sensis, Eindhoven, Netherlands*

Beryl Palmer – Manager, Sensory Disabilities, of Kent Social Services Sensory Team – commented that rehabilitation workers are not generally trained to work with older people. Their training in this area needs to be increased and improved. They do recognise multiple impairment but not usually its impact on individuals and what to do about it.

The rehabilitation relationship

It would be all too easy for a rehabilitation worker to take control of the rehabilitation process, using their skills and knowledge. Liz Duncan, from Sense, feels strongly, however, that the rehab worker should 'give up active control of the rehab process and accept the choices made by the deafblind person'. She adds that 'this is vital if the process is to be of any real value to the individual'. Beryl Palmer confirms that it is crucially important to use a 'partnership' approach.

In her work with Elspeth, a deafblind woman, Liz Duncan found that the complex communication and information needs of a deafblind person made for a close relationship that was not always easy but which enabled them to work together as a team. As Elspeth herself said, 'We are a team – I learn from you, you learn from me, and we work together to get the best out of the system.'

Elspeth was asked what she felt she gained from the rehabilitation process. She listed:

- Increased self-confidence and self-awareness.
- Increasingly articulate.
- Being able to deal with paperwork.
- A better knowledge of what is available and therefore what I want.
- Being part of a team.
- Some good friends.

An important part of rehabilitation work is to motivate the impaired person to learn new skills and to feel positive. For example, whilst it is common for people to hide their impairment, it can help enormously for them to take a more assertive approach – to acknowledge their impairment and to tell others how best to help. When people do this, they generally find that others respond in a positive and understanding way.

> 'I just have to say to them I'm deaf – would you mind speaking clearly and loud and fairly slow.' *Ivy Cook*

A positive and motivated approach makes all the difference to how well someone adapts to their impairment. The only way to help this motivation is to build a relationship based on trust, which will take time, empathy, listening, encouragement and respect.

Where to find rehabilitation workers

Most people obtain rehabilitation services through either social services or the NHS. To be eligible for social services rehab services, the individual first must be assessed by social services. (For more on assessment, see page 232.)

Visual impairment rehabilitation services

Social services rehab workers for visually impaired people may work in all areas of rehabilitation, as detailed on page 75.

NHS rehabilitation focuses on low-vision work, and is provided by specialist optometrists. They may carry out their work in a hospital setting or in a low-vision clinic. Some make domiciliary visits. Referral to NHS rehabilitation services can be made by a GP, optometrist, eye clinic or hospital ophthalmic team, or by social services.

There are also freelance or independent rehabilitation workers for visually impaired people. Because there is no national network for these rehab workers, it can be hard to make contact with them. Try asking your local society for blind people. Individuals can pay for an independent rehab worker's services either privately or using Direct Payments.

Hearing impairment rehabilitation services

In the NHS, some Ear, Nose and Throat (ENT) departments employ hearing therapists. Their primary role is to help with the use of hearing aids and to teach communication skills; they may also issue other aids and devices, and offer counselling.

There are also a few independent hearing therapists across the UK. Contact them through the British Society of Hearing Therapists (address on page 277).

Social services may employ a Technical Officer for Deaf and Hard of Hearing People, who will assess for environmental aids and equipment.

Many technical officers also advise on communication techniques for individuals and their families and friends.

Some social workers for deaf people offer information, advice and support to people who develop a hearing impairment.

Links between the hospital-based services and other rehabilitation services vary enormously from region to region.

There is a national rehabilitation centre, the LINK Centre for Deafened People, in Eastbourne, where people who become profoundly deaf in adulthood can go for an intensive residential rehabilitation course. These courses help individuals to cope positively and successfully with profound deafness. They are run by a multi-disciplinary team of doctors, hearing therapists, speech and language therapists, and counsellors, alongside deafened peer educators. Families and carers participate fully in the programme.

An individual can contact the LINK centre direct, or their ENT consultant, audiologist, hearing therapist or GP may make the first enquiry on their behalf. Some health authorities and primary care trusts fund places at the LINK centre. Contact the LINK Centre (address on page 284) for more details about the referral process.

Dual sensory impairment rehabilitation services

A few authorities employ specialist deafblind workers. Many others jointly allocate rehabilitation workers and technical officers to assess and work with older people with dual sensory loss.

How to get the best out of your local rehabilitation service

The RNIB issues these guidelines, which are equally valid for hearing and dual impairment:

- Find out about your local rehabilitation service: Where is it? Who is eligible for help? How does someone get referred? What help are they able and not able to provide?

- Talk to a rehabilitation worker about the specific condition the individual has – they can explain what it means and what its effects may be.
- Ask other professionals to get involved, such as speech and language therapists and physiotherapists.
- Work with all these professionals as a team, swapping your skills and information.
- Keep a list of problems or questions – what makes Mrs Evans knock her cup over only when it is on her left?
- If you find it hard to get access to the service, find out why and get help in sorting it out.

9 Optical and hearing aids

Many people can be helped to make the most of their remaining sight or hearing by the use of optical, hearing or listening aids. This chapter describes the function of these aids, outlines the different types of aid and provides information on where to obtain them. It includes tips on how to help people to maintain and make the best use of their aids. In particular, the following areas are covered:

- Hearing aids
- How to obtain a hearing aid
- Being fitted for a hearing aid
- Getting used to wearing a hearing aid
- Making it easier to use a hearing aid
- Types of hearing aid
- The mechanics of a hearing aid
- Care of the aid
- Listening aids
- Induction loops and infrared devices
- Optical aids
- Choosing a magnifier
- Types of magnifier
- Using magnifiers effectively

Hearing aids

'It's very misleading to think that technology will help if people persist in talking behind the deaf person's back, or shouting.' *Brian Grover, Head of Product Technology, RNID*

Nevertheless, technology can help, and many people derive great benefit from a hearing aid. Hearing aids make sounds louder: they may not produce perfect hearing but they should make it easier to hear in many situations, and make conversation easier.

> 'Without the aid I tend to hear the wrong thing. I took it out once to have my hair washed, and asked if the hairdresser had family. I thought she said she had two gerbils and said "I don't know much about gerbils" – she was rather surprised, as she'd said she had two children!' *Rose Arthur*

Hearing aids tend to make all sounds louder – including the ones people do not want to hear, such as traffic noise.

> 'It's right loud and if they're all speaking then you're picking all the sounds up. It's gobble, gobble, gobble, like Donald Duck. If I go into the kitchen and they're all speaking, someone starts shouting and the dog barks, it goes through you. And that's why I don't wear it ... I think a hearing aid is dangerous when you can't see. Because you might have leaves or wind blowing and the noise of the traffic, even though you're only using one ear, and you're not right good in the other ear, you're better with your hearing aid out and listen for the quietness.' *Albert Way (using an analogue aid)*

Some digital aids can now cut out some types of background noise.

How to obtain a hearing aid

In the UK, people can either buy a hearing aid or obtain one free from the NHS. To obtain an NHS aid, the person needs to see their GP and be referred to the hospital for a hearing (audiology) test. If the test indicates that a hearing aid would be helpful, the audiologist will issue one.

An NHS aid is provided on loan. The batteries, earmoulds, repairs, tubing and adjustments are free. If the aid wears out, or the person needs a more powerful one, the replacement will also be free. If, however, they damage the aid through carelessness, they may have to pay something towards the cost of a new one.

Hearing aids last about five years. A replacement from the NHS will be free but if someone buys privately they need to budget for replacements.

Although the NHS offers a choice of styles, not all types of aid are available. If someone wants an in-the-canal aid, for example, they will have to buy it privately. It is wise to insure privately bought aids against loss, theft or damage.

Anyone wanting to buy an aid privately should choose the dispenser carefully. Dispensers are required by law to be professionally qualified and registered with the Hearing Aid Council, and are ruled by a code of practice. There are many good dispensers, but also some less reputable ones. Some private dispensers sell hearing aids on hospital premises but this is entirely separate from the free NHS hearing aid service.

When buying aids from a private dispenser, the user will sign a contract agreeing to buy the aids. It is important to read this contract carefully – ideally it should allow a 28 days' trial period and a money-back guarantee.

The NHS referral and testing process is described in Chapter 14, 'Testing for sensory impairment'. Someone who buys an aid privately will go through a very similar testing and fitting process.

Being fitted for a hearing aid

Once testing has established that someone might benefit from a hearing aid, they should be offered a choice of styles if more than one matches their hearing needs. They should also receive an aid for each ear if two aids will be more helpful than one.

Once an aid has been chosen, staff take an impression of the ear so that they can make a mould to fit. At the next appointment, staff set up the aids to give the best result. This may involve programming the aids with a computer. Staff will give advice on using and caring for the aids; if they are uncomfortable or irritate the ear, this should be corrected. Various materials can be used to prevent irritation.

Getting used to wearing a hearing aid

The key to success is to take it slowly. Encourage the new hearing-aid user to start out by wearing it once or twice a day for about an hour, in quiet situations. They should listen to everyday noises such as the kettle boiling or doors opening and closing to get used to how these sound. They can then try conversations with one person, in a quiet room, making sure that the other person sits facing the light so that the wearer of the aid can also lipread.

Next, the new hearing-aid user can try conversations with two people or in a small group. They should not expect to hear everything that is said but should try to follow the conversation.

When they have practised using their aid indoors, they can try wearing it outside – taking care not to have the volume turned up too high at first, as some outside sounds are very loud.

Finally, they can try using the aid somewhere with more background noise. This is probably the most difficult situation. They will not be able to hear everything people say, but this should become easier in time.

If someone finds it very hard to get used to a new aid or if they feel it is not working properly, they should go back to the audiologist, dispenser or hearing therapist who fitted it.

Making it easier to use a hearing aid

Many families and carers become extremely frustrated by a hard-of-hearing person's refusal to use their hearing aid(s). Brian Grover of the RNID gives five main reasons for people giving up wearing their aids:

1 Disappointment and false expectations:

'They think it will be like spectacles, which make such a clear difference immediately. But specs correct an optical defect by taking over what the lens should be doing – a hearing aid can't repair the damaged hair cells. The best it can do is redistribute sound to the remaining cells. The result won't be perfect because not enough information gets through.'

2 Physical discomfort – most people do not like the feel of an aid in their ear. This is made worse if the aid is a poor fit or if there is moisture in the ear. (But the audiologist will be able to help improve comfort.)
3 Batteries – some people do not remember to keep spares ready, so their aid is put in a drawer and forgotten when the batteries run out.
4 Inappropriate sound levels or sound quality – they may not have the most appropriate aid for them, or it may not be set up correctly.

   'Unlike spectacles, you can't produce a precise prescription for a hearing aid – you have to maximise sound without making it uncomfortable, possibly emphasising high tones.'

   (But the audiologist may be able to adjust the aid to suit them better.)
5 You have to learn to hear with a hearing aid.

Hearing therapist Alex Willoughby says that what does not work is constant nagging – 'any normal person will just resist'. She tells people that she knows a hearing aid will help, and then explains why. 'That can change their resistance, when they understand.'

People come up with all sorts of reasons for not using their aids, however:

> **'... what tends to distinguish hearing-aid users from non-users are the situations (including environments and partners) in which each group regularly participates.'** *(Erber 1993)*

In other words, if a hearing-aid wearer uses the aid most frequently for conversation in a quiet place with someone who speaks clearly, they will see the benefit of using an aid. If, on the other hand, they most often want to communicate in a large group in an echo-y place, they will see little benefit from wearing their aid.

Other factors that affect someone's willingness to use a hearing aid include the user's attitude and their ability to manage their aids. In a care home, staff should be able at least to help residents to manage and care for their aids. This will take time, particularly in the mornings when residents need help fitting their aids, and staff may find it all too easy to delay giving assistance while they deal with other work. But taking time to provide this help can make an enormous difference to the residents' quality of life – not only will they be better able to hear but they will also know that staff are taking their hearing impairment seriously.

> 'In my work as a GP [now retired], I often had to persuade a patient that they needed a hearing aid. Commonly they would respond how old it would make them look, how people would think them silly or of low intelligence, and so on. After leading them on to make more and more outlandish comments, I would respond "Of course, you know I use a hearing aid", which of course they did not know until I told them and showed them. Much embarrassment on the part of the patient, and admission that their previous thoughts were wrong.' *Dr Robert Newton*

According to the RNID, about 2 million people in the UK own a hearing aid, but only 1.4 million use them regularly. At least another 3 million do not have hearing aids but have enough difficulty in hearing that they would be likely to benefit from them.

Types of hearing aid

There are four types of hearing aid, classified according to where they are worn:

- **Body-worn** (BW) aids are relatively rare but are useful for people who find smaller aids too fiddly. They can also be extremely powerful.
- **Behind-the-ear** (BTE) aids are the most common. The earmould sits inside the ear and the aid itself rests behind the ear. (See Figure 9.3 for a diagram of this type of hearing aid.)
- **In-the-ear** (ITE) aids have their working parts inside the earmould, so that the whole aid fits inside the ear. They tend to need repairing more than BTE aids. (See Figure 9.4 for a diagram of this type of hearing aid.)
- **In-the-canal** (ITC) and **completely-in-the-canal** (CIC) aids are tiny; they fit in the ear canal itself and are almost invisible. Canal aids are not usually suitable for people with severe hearing loss or small ear canals.

Hearing aids can be either analogue or digital. Digital aids contain a tiny computer that is programmed to suit the individual user; from the outside they look just like analogue aids. Analogue aids are generally being phased out. Users of NHS analogue aids can ask to transfer to NHS digital aids. From 2005 in England, Wales and Northern Ireland they will all be digital. There is limited provision of digital aids in Scotland until 2007.

Aids for people with hearing in only one ear

There are two types of aid for people who have hearing in only one ear. The contralateral routing of signal (CROS) aids pick up sound from the side with no hearing and feed it to the better ear. BiCROS aids amplify sound from both sides and feed it into the ear that has some hearing.

Someone who has CROS or BiCROS aids will wear them in both ears. The aids are usually connected by a wire across the back of the neck. There are versions that are wireless and where one of the aids fits in the canal, but these are expensive.

Waterproof and water-resistant aids

These aids have a thin membrane to help stop water getting into them. Waterproof aids are suitable for swimming, and water-resistant aids can be used for other water sports. They are worn behind the ears.

Disposable hearing aids

Disposable hearing aids – which are in-the-canal aids – are now available on the High Street. The advantage of these aids (one model is called the Songbird) is that the user can avoid the high initial costs of buying an aid privately. So, instead of paying a large sum of money for a private aid, the hard-of-hearing person pays a fraction of this sum for three months' supply, which allows them the opportunity to try out a hearing aid at relatively low cost. This is probably best suited to someone with recent hearing loss that is not yet severe.

The mechanics of a hearing aid

A hearing aid, which is usually worn in or around the ear, makes sounds louder so that the user can hear them. Hearing aids come in different shapes, sizes and types but they all work in a similar way. As well as an earmould (the part that goes in the ear), tubing and batteries, all aids have a built-in microphone that picks up sound, which is then processed electronically. The resulting signals are then passed to a receiver or earphone in the aid, where they are converted back into sound for the user to hear. Figure 9.1 is a diagram of the controls of a typical hearing aid.

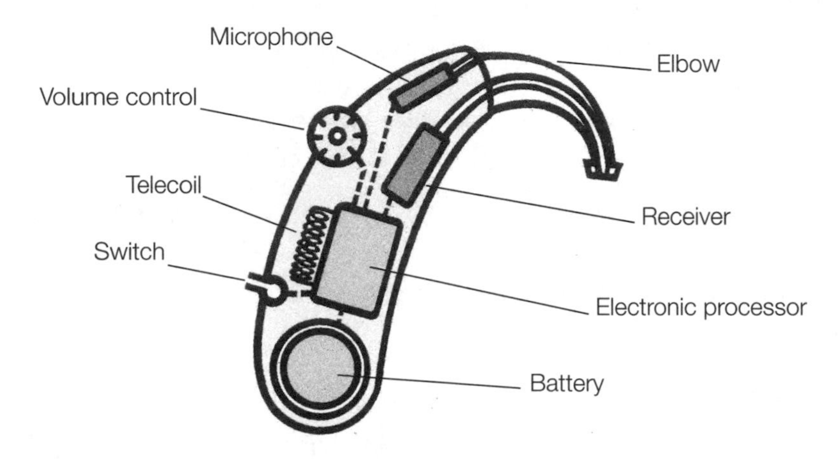

Figure 9.1 A typical hearing aid. (Reproduced by permission of RNID)

A new hearing-aid user will need to practise using the switches and controls of the aid in various environments.

Sometimes there is a volume control although in some aids the volume is preset. Some aids – especially those that can be programmed – have a remote control for changing volume, and have settings for different environments, such as parties or outdoors. Some digital aids change volume automatically according to the sound level they pick up.

Most aids have an on/off switch but others turn off when the battery door is opened. Some aids turn on automatically when put into the ear.

The T setting

The T setting enables the hearing-aid user to pick up selected sounds directly through a loop system (explained on page 97), sending the sounds straight to the hearing aid, cutting out background noise and room acoustics. Most aids have a T setting, although some do not.

Figure 9.2 This symbol means that a hearing-aid user can tune into a loop system by setting their aid to 'T'.

The symbol shown in Figure 9.2 is displayed wherever hearing-aid users can tune into a loop system by setting their aid to 'T'.

An aid with a T setting also enables the wearer to use a telephone with an inductive coupler inside (it will probably be described as hearing-aid compatible). These phones give the user a clearer sound. The hearing-aid wearer needs to practise holding the telephone earpiece in different positions to see which works best with their aid. Hearing-aid users can also use the T setting with some listening or conversation aids, which may be fitted with an inductive link, a device that works in a similar way to a loop system. Some aids have an MT switch – they pick up sounds from the aid's microphone and an induction loop at the same time.

Batteries

There are different sizes of battery to suit different types of aid. They cannot be recharged, so it is sensible for users and care homes to keep a stock of spare batteries. NHS users can obtain new hearing-aid batteries free of charge from the hospital audiology department in person or by post, or they may have been told about more local NHS centres where they can obtain the batteries.

To fit a new battery, peel off the sticker and insert the battery into the aid. The cross on the side of the battery must match the cross on the hearing aid battery door. The battery should fit snugly – if it moves around or you cannot shut the door, it is probably fitted the wrong way round.

Putting the aid in

The audiologist or hearing-aid dispenser should have shown the hearing-aid user how to put it in, and it is important to practise. The aid should be turned so that the opening in the earmould points towards the ear, and then put in. The wearer then needs to practise feeling for the switch and adjusting it.

Care of the aid

Sometimes a hearing aid will stop functioning properly and needs to be returned to the supplier for repair. Most audiology departments have a drop-in repair centre, where you may either wait while the aid is repaired or leave it to be collected later. They should also run a postal repair service.

However, most problems with hearing aids can be sorted out by the user or care staff: knowing how to fix basic problems with a hearing aid is a crucial skill for anyone working with older people, as having a functioning hearing aid makes such a big difference to their ability to communicate.

Anand and Court (1989) surveyed older people in residential care. Before interviewing them, they tested their hearing aids. They found that:

> 'Half of the hearing aids already fitted were not functioning, nine because of flat batteries and sixteen because of blockage by wax. Although eight of the twenty-four residents fitted with functioning aids required no action, ten needed a new mould or aid; the hearing aids of the remaining six needed minor attention such as new tubing.'

If you are unsure about caring for a particular aid, ask the audiologist or dispenser to show you how. Helping someone to care for their aid will enable them to maximise its use, and will keep the aid in good repair.

The RNID issues the following guidelines for the care of each type of hearing aid.

Body-worn aids

Wipe the aid all over with a cloth every time it is taken out. Wash the earmould at least once a week: gently pull the receiver off the earmould, put the aid (the part with the battery in), lead and receiver in a safe, dry place – *never* get these wet. Wash the earmould in warm soapy water, using a soft brush to remove any wax blocking the opening. Rinse and dry it carefully, then leave to dry overnight before clipping it back on to the receiver.

The lead from the receiver to the aid will need replacing from time to time.

Behind-the-ear aid (Figure 9.3)

Wipe the hearing aid and earmould with dry tissue every time it is taken out. Ideally, the earmould should be washed every night – at the very least every week. The aid (the part with the battery) should *not* be washed.

Do not unscrew the 'elbow' from the aid. Instead, gently pull the soft tubing off the elbow. Leave the tubing in the mould. Wash the earmould and tubing in soapy water and rinse. Blow down the tubing to remove the water and allow it to dry overnight. Once it is dry, push the tubing back on to the elbow.

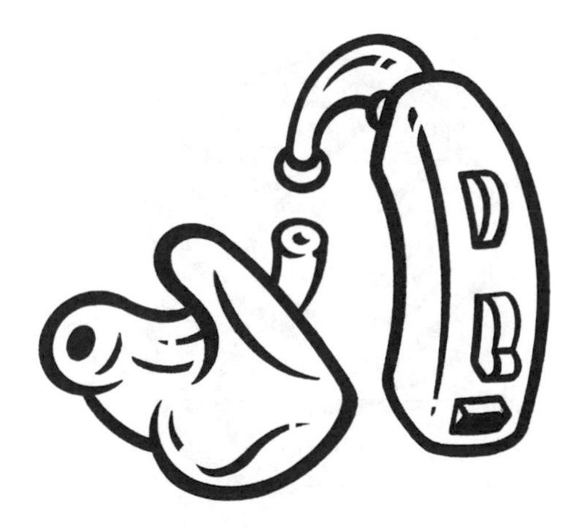

Figure 9.3 A behind-the-ear aid. (Reproduced by permission of RNID)

When the tubing begins to harden, the aid may not work as well, so the tubing should be changed. The hearing aid department or dispenser will supply the tubing and demonstrate how to change it, or will change the tubing themselves if the hearing-aid user finds it difficult, but this is something that care staff can easily learn to do.

Earmoulds eventually wear out – they become brittle or develop cracks. When this happens, ask the hearing aid department or dispenser to make a new one.

In-the-ear aids

There are two types of in-the-ear aid: custom and modular.

Custom ITEs consist of only one piece (see Figure 9.4). If an aid is bought privately, it is probably a custom ITE. It cannot be washed. It should be wiped dry with a tissue, and wax should be removed from the opening with a soft brush. A custom ITE may come with special instructions and cleaning tools.

Modular ITEs consist of an earmould attached to a hearing aid. To clean it, separate the earmould from the aid and wash the mould in soapy water. Wipe the hearing aid part with a dry tissue – *never* wash it or allow it to get wet.

Figure 9.4 A one-piece in-the-ear aid. (Reproduced by permission of the RNID)

In-the-canal and completely-in-the-canal aids

These aids cannot be washed. Wipe them with a dry tissue and use a soft brush to clean any wax from the opening. Special instructions and cleaning tools may be supplied with them.

Troubleshooting – when the aid does not work

You can often fix problems with hearing aids quite easily. If none of the solutions below works, seek help from the hearing aid department or dispenser.

WHISTLING OR SQUEAKING

Whistling or squeaking is caused by feedback. This happens when the amplified sound made by the hearing aid 'leaks out' and is picked up by the aid and fed back into it. This may happen if:

- the earmould has not been inserted properly – push it in gently to check;
- the wearer has too much wax in their ears – ask the doctor to check;
- the earmould does not fit the ear snugly enough – ask the audiologist about this;
- the volume is too high;
- in the case of a BTE aid – the earmould, elbow or tubing can become loose or split, and may have to be changed.

NO SOUND COMING THROUGH

If the aid does not seem to be working:

- check that it is not switched to the T setting by mistake;
- if the hearing aid has a volume-control wheel, make sure the volume is at the right level – it may have been turned down low;
- check that the battery is the right way round;
- try fitting a new battery;
- in the case of a BTE aid, take it out, pull the soft tubing off the elbow and blow down it to remove any condensation that may be causing a blockage;
- check that the tubing is not twisted, squashed or split;
- check that the earmould is not blocked with wax;
- in the case of a BW aid, check whether the cord or receiver needs to be replaced.

BUZZING SOUND

Buzzing noises may indicate that the aid is switched to the T setting by mistake. If not, it may mean that the aid has developed a fault and needs to be repaired.

Listening aids

If someone is diagnosed as having a mild hearing loss, they may be told that they do not need or might not benefit from a hearing aid. In either case, they may still find other listening equipment useful. In particular, they might like to use a listening or conversational aid. These are usually small, and are easy to use. They consist of a microphone to pick up speech or TV (or a lead to plug straight into the TV), an amplifier to make the sound louder, and equipment through which to hear the amplified sound (eg earphones or headphones). Other equipment includes amplifiers, amplified telephones and louder doorbells. Some of this equipment can also be useful for people using hearing aids. (See also pages 131–134, 164–166 and 168–169.)

At the RNIB care home at Wavertree House, they have a number of residents with both sight and hearing loss. Most manage to continue to communicate using speech. One man, however, lost so much of his hearing that this was no longer possible, so he used a pair of headphones and a microphone – he could put the microphone on the television, or give it to some who wanted to talk to him. He did not use it all the time, only when he wanted to talk or watch TV.

Erber and his colleagues (1996) visited care homes to investigate why people were not using their hearing aids. They found that many actually did not need a hearing aid, but did benefit from an amplifier in the form of a microphone with headphones. Most people conversed more easily with amplification – both interviewer and interviewee were more relaxed, the conversation was more fluent, and the hard-of-hearing person was better able to understand the subject of the conversation and so to stay on the topic.

It can be extremely useful for anyone working with older people to have available some easy-to-use listening aids that provide good amplification.

As we have seen, an effective method uses a pair of headphones for the hard-of-hearing person, attached to a box amplifier with a volume control, and a microphone for the person they want to speak to. It may have a switch to enable signals to be picked up from an induction loop system.

Induction loops

A major problem for most hearing-aid users is the way that aids amplify all sounds, including background noise. An induction loop helps people to hear better by cutting down that background noise, amplifying only the sounds that they do want to hear. It is useful for listening to the television, radio or music system or where there is a screen that makes hearing harder (eg in a ticket office or at a bank counter). Loops are also useful for hearing speech at a distance, as in a church or theatre or in meetings.

An induction loop is basically a wire that circles a chosen listening area, picking up sound within it and transmitting that sound to a hearing aid with a T setting, or to a 'loop listener' (usually either a small box with headphones or a device worn behind the ear). Because the user is listening directly to sound through an aid or listener, they can adjust their own volume without affecting anyone else in the room.

In the UK virtually all hearing aids supplied through the NHS, as well as many that are bought privately, have a T setting. A great advantage is that the listener is not wired to anything, so they can move around freely.

To use a loop system

If the person has a hearing aid with a T setting, they should switch it to T. If it has an MT switch (combined microphone and T), it can pick up sound through the loop and the microphone at same time.

Even if the person does not have a hearing aid, or the aid does not have a T setting, they can still use a loop listener.

NECKLOOPS AND EARLOOPS

A *neckloop* is a short loop of wire that the user wears round their neck. An *earloop* hooks behind the user's ear, close to their hearing aid. Both devices work with the T setting on the hearing aid and come with a lead that plugs into the headphone socket on a TV or stereo system, making it easier to hear them, or into a listening aid.

Someone who wears a hearing aid may well find it easier to use a neck-loop or earloop than headphones.

Problems with loops

A hearing-aid user may need to turn the aid's volume up when set to T, although this should be unnecessary if the loop has been properly set up. If they pick up buzzing noises on 'T', this may be a result of electrical interference from fluorescent lights, dimmer switches or electric cables. Moving to another listening position may help; or it may be possible to move or switch off the equipment causing the problem.

The loop signal can spill out into other rooms because it is not blocked by walls, ceilings and floors. So anyone else with a hearing aid on 'T' or who is using a loop listener will be able to hear – or be forced to hear – the signal, too. They may therefore pick up private conversations or TV sound in rooms on either side, above and below. You can resolve this by reducing the size of the loop – and hence the overspill – although you may need to rearrange the seating. Using an infrared system (discussed below) can also solve the problem.

Choosing and installing a loop

There is a wide range of loops available, from personal systems worn round the neck to ones for a whole room. There are also portable or temporary loop systems, which can be used in a room that does not usually have a loop system. This can be useful for one-to-one discussions or appointments, group meetings, training and special occasions.

Installation is usually straightforward and can be done by someone competent at DIY. When buying a loop system, make sure that the supplier gives you a money-back guarantee so that you can try it out at home. It should be VAT exempt. Some social services departments supply loop systems, usually for a charge.

Infrared devices

These provide good-quality cable-free sound from the television or radio. Unlike a loop, they can supply stereo sound, which can make listening easier and more pleasing. To pick up the infrared signal, the user needs an infrared receiver. This receiver can come with:

- a stetoclip (special earphones) – useful if the user does not have a hearing aid or removes their hearing aid;
- a neckloop – used with a hearing aid set to T; this is good for someone with a greater hearing loss;
- built into headphones – which must be those made specially for deaf people.

Infrared is blocked by walls, floors and ceilings, so there are fewer problems than from loops with sound spilling into other areas, which means that several infrared systems can be used in neighbouring rooms and are useful for private meetings. The sound quality may, however, be reduced by strong sunlight and dark wall coverings.

Choosing and installing an infrared device

Installation is very straightforward and consists simply of connecting a small infrared transmitter to the sound source. It works most effectively if nothing blocks the path of the infrared light from the transmitter to the user's receiver.

Infrared tends to cost more than an induction loop. Like a loop, it should be VAT exempt and a money-back guarantee should be supplied. Some social services departments supply infrared systems.

Do not buy a cheap infrared system in the High Street – they are not designed for people with a hearing impairment but are to enable hearing people to listen to music or television without disturbing others.

Loops and infrared devices in public places

Loops and infrared devices are most often provided in theatres, cinemas, places of worship, meeting rooms, conference halls, airports, banks, shopping centres, and bus and train stations. Provision of loops should become more widespread as a result of the Disability Discrimination Act (DDA) 1995, which stipulates that public places have to make reasonable adjustments to ensure equal access to services; this might include fitting an induction loop or infrared system. Loops are more common than infrared because users do not need a special receiver and may simply turn their hearing aid to T to pick up the signal.

Most places indicate that they have an induction loop or infrared system by displaying a sign or the T symbol. It is also worth asking, even where there are no signs. If the loop is not working, check that it has been switched on and is set at the correct level.

The RNID catalogue, *Solutions*, shows a range of listening aids (see page 289 for contact details).

Optical aids

The aim of providing an optical aid is to enable someone to make best use of their sight and to maintain or restore their autonomy and independence. For example, a magnifier may enable the person to read their own bills and correspondence again, and so to manage their daily life independently, with no need to ask someone else to read private documents for them.

A magnifier is often the only optical aid a person has, and is generally the most easily accepted. It can be useful for reading prices, oven temperatures, instructions and medicine labels, for looking at photographs, and generally making a whole range of activities possible.

Marcus Farley, a rehabilitation worker, described the difference that the correct use of a magnifier can make:

> Mrs Nainan is 86 years old. She has age-related macular degeneration in both eyes, with a dense cataract in her left eye and an emerging cataract in her right eye. She lives in sheltered accommodation and most daily tasks are carried out by her daughter, who visits three times a day. She referred herself to my team because her sight

had worsened to the point that she could no longer use her prescribed magnifying glass, and was having difficulty seeing to take her medication. She walks with a zimmer frame and, additionally, has severe arthritis of her hands and knees. Her resulting problems meant that she was housebound.

I visited Mrs Nainan and her daughter with a low vision colleague. My colleague assessed Mrs Nainan and found that she could read magazine print with a particular type of illuminated magnifier on a stand; he explained how she should position it and the objects she wanted to see.

Because of her general frailty, we agreed that Mrs Nainan would find it easier to work with a raised table pulled up to her chair. For reading, it would also help her to use a task lamp and a raised writing board on the table on which to rest her magazine. I supplied these.

For Mrs Nainan's medication, I issued a 'dosette' pill box with large-print letters placed over each compartment, indicating the days of the week. Her daughter filled this up at the start of the week and Mrs Nainan was then able to self-medicate by placing the pill box on her raised writing board and looking at it, and the pills, with her magnifier.

Choosing a magnifier

There are many different types of magnifier, so it is important to choose carefully and to seek expert advice. There should not be any need to pay for this advice – it should be available from a low vision unit, optician or local voluntary organisation for visually impaired people. A low vision unit or voluntary organisation may also provide magnifiers free, on loan.

Types of magnifier

Size is not a good indication of the suitability of a magnifier. Some are basic, some have quite complex lenses. Many people have more than one, using different magnifiers for different types of task.

The bigger the magnifier, usually the lower its strength. But while a small, strong magnifier may provide powerful magnification, its size may restrict how much the user is able to see at once – perhaps only part of a word at a time. Pocket magnifiers are useful for carrying around. For use at home, there are hand-held magnifying glasses and large, stand-held magnifiers – these are particularly useful if the user has a tremor or difficulty in holding things. Some magnifiers have built-in lights (illuminated magnifiers) to reduce the shadow that may be created by holding a lens close to an object.

Magnifiers may be mounted in spectacle frames, which leaves both hands free. The user has to hold objects very close to these glasses but this can be useful for tasks such as sewing, changing a fuse or doing the crossword. They generally use either very thick lenses or telescopic lenses. This can make them rather unwieldy and, because they make things look bigger than they actually are, they can be somewhat disconcerting.

There are also magnifiers for longer distances – just like opera glasses. These are good for the cinema, watching cricket, checking bus numbers, and so on. But they are not necessarily ideal for watching TV – it is better to sit nearer to the set. These distance magnifiers may be either monocular or binocular (for one eye or for both eyes).

Closed circuit television (CCTV) can be used to magnify things: the user places the text, picture or object under a special camera and it appears, magnified, on a TV screen, at a size that can be controlled. This is usually an expensive system. A cheaper option is a CCTV reader, which is hand-held and linked to a TV set. It is less flexible and the print size will depend on the size of the TV screen. CCTV readers are sometimes available to rent.

Using magnifiers effectively

- The user should shine a light on to the task.
- The user should take a break if the eyes tire, and try again later.
- If the person has more than one set of glasses, the magnifier will work best with one set in particular – the low vision unit or supplier should have specified which pair to use.
- Magnifiers make print bigger, but the user will see less of it – help them to use their finger to mark each line, moving the finger down only when they reach the next line.

- If the person brings both object and magnifier closer to their eye, they will probably be able to see more of the object.
- A magnifier has to be held steadily for it to be effective – this can be achieved by the person resting their arm on a cushion or the arm of a chair, or by supporting the material to be looked at on a cushion or stand on a table.
- Rather than moving the magnifier or the eye, some people find it easier to move the book from side to side when reading.
- If the reader is sitting in a chair, they can put the book or paper on a clipboard to keep it still and flat. A cushion or tray can be used for support.
- Keep the magnifier clean with lens cleaner or warm soapy water.
- The low vision service or optician should be able to help if someone is finding it hard to use their magnifier – they may need more training or a different magnifier.

It can, none the less, be very tiring and hard work for some people to use low-vision aids. They might prefer to rely on others to read written material to them.

Finally

This chapter does not cover the use of spectacles – it assumes that the visually impaired person has been properly tested and fitted with the correct ones. However, when someone has been prescribed glasses, it is crucial that they are kept clean. One of the most common obstacles to improved vision is dirty glasses. Staff working with visually impaired people can help them enormously simply by checking that their glasses are clean.

Our identities are constantly formed and confirmed by the way we interact with the people around us. Because a sensory impairment directly affects our ability to communicate, it can potentially undermine our entire sense of self, of identity. This is why communication is so important for people with a sensory impairment.

Think about your own identity. How do you know who you are? Would you be the person you are if you never spoke or heard or saw anyone else?

Communication and integration

> 'To live in a group setting, as in a residential care or nursing home, and be unable to hear can, paradoxically, cause greater feelings of isolation than those experienced by someone with a hearing difficulty who lives at home.' *(Counsel and Care 1993)*

Jill Nichols, who is dual sensory impaired, describes the isolation she felt, even when at the day-care centre:

> 'When I'd been going a time or two, I will admit I got a little bored because I took my knitting but I longed for someone to come and have a chat, or for me to go and have a chat with them.'

Although conditions at home may not be ideal – and not everyone has sympathetic people around them – those living at home are more likely to be communicating on a one-to-one basis with people who know and understand their impairment. In a care home or a day-care centre, much communication takes place in a group setting, which is more difficult for someone with a sensory impairment.

A local Age Concern day-care centre realised that, although they were providing for their clients' physical needs very successfully, a significant number of clients were unable to join in with activities and were effectively being marginalised. Staff simply did not have time to talk to these service users, many of whom had some sensory loss. So the centre decided to create a new position, which they called a 'social integration worker'. This person's job would consist entirely of providing communication support to those who needed it. She was strictly forbidden to help with any other task, as staff felt that she would soon find herself with no time to help with communication. Centre manager, Sandra Springett, said:

> 'It's very difficult to change the culture of a day-care centre. People come with physical needs – say, needing a bath – so we help them. And because we're so short of time, it's easy for people with bad sight and hearing to be left on the sidelines.'

It could be easy to assume that someone no longer wants to communicate if they seem withdrawn and unmotivated. In fact, most people want to communicate but have been unable to find a way to do so.

> 'I think that if I could hear I would probably take more interest. But I can't converse with people, you see, so there's no point is there? I mean, I don't know what they're saying.' *Peter Bradbury*

Communicating with someone who is hearing impaired requires patience and attention, and, all too often, the people around them are not willing to make that effort. Many hard-of-hearing people describe their frustration with those who, when asked to repeat, say 'Oh, never mind'. They *do* mind.

There is a common view that hearing impairment cuts a person off from people, while visual impairment cuts them off from objects. However, people with a visual impairment report that they too become isolated because they cannot recognise faces, so others may view them as being moody or rude. They also miss out on body language and other non-verbal cues: if they have a serious impairment, they may not even know someone is there unless they speak, and then the visually impaired person may prefer not to speak themselves for fear of interrupting. They may therefore find it hard both to start a conversation and to respond.

> 'Up to 70 per cent of communication is conveyed visually through a combination of reading body language, facial expression and signals. Many people nod their head instead of saying "yes", for example.'
> *Marcus Farley, Rehabilitation Worker*

> 'To turn away or focus on a distant object when addressing another person can be attributed to rudeness, shyness or guilt … eye contact signifies honesty, directness, attentiveness, respect …' *(Scott 1969)*

Non-English speakers

People with little spoken English can find group situations particularly isolating, and they rarely use day-care centres or care homes where only English is spoken. No doubt this is due partly to cultural norms but also to the knowledge that it will be impossible to communicate. Such isolation will be greater if they also have a sensory loss, and they will therefore need considerable support. If you have a service user who speaks little English, you could try to contact people from the relevant community who might be able to provide a volunteer to visit; you can provide talking books in a range of languages; and you can educate your staff and others about this user's culture.

Communication problems in practice: the health service

Whilst many people describe their experience of health care as being extremely positive and supportive, this may not always be the case. All too often, health staff fail to recognise the need for good communication skills when working with sensory-impaired people:

> 'The most distressing experiences I have come across have taken place in the health service.' *Beryl Palmer, Social Services Sensory Specialist*

Beryl worked with one dual-impaired woman who was diagnosed with cancer but knew nothing about the diagnosis because the doctors could not communicate with her. Another dual-impaired patient awoke in terror to find her genitals being scrubbed, with no explanation being given for this treatment because no one knew how to communicate with her.

These are extreme examples but, on a daily basis, patients may find that the care they receive is compromised because of a sensory impairment.

Many people report that, on the wards, food is put in front of a visually impaired person and then taken away again uneaten because the person did not know it was there. Hard-of-hearing people may find that doctors and nurses do not take the trouble to speak clearly to them, to face them or to write down important information.

> 'Because I'm my mother's chauffeur, I go with her to her hospital appointments and we've found that some doctors talk to me as if she was unable to answer for herself. In fact, one doctor told me to tell her afterwards what we were discussing. Deafness does not equal dementia.' *Lisa, Nora Dorman's daughter*

There can also often be a language barrier: sometimes the impaired person does not speak English, and no provision is made for an interpreter:

> 'We went to the hospital and she was totally confused as to what was happening. They did not have a single person on the staff who was speaking the language.' *Rakesh, relative of Zahra Khan*

In this situation, staff often depend on the family to translate, although this may not be appropriate if the problem is of an intimate nature.

Equally, if the doctor or nurse does not speak clear English, it is doubly hard for someone with a hearing loss to understand what is being said. This may not even be due to a language barrier: many people describe hospital staff as talking quietly, mumbling, covering their face or turning away when speaking to the patient.

This problem is reported extremely frequently and causes great anxiety: the patient does not doubt the doctor's ability but knows that, because they cannot communicate adequately, there is a significant chance of wrong or insufficient information being transmitted. The patient may also fear how their request for clear speech will be received:

> 'My husband was my ears. When he died, I was completely shattered but I knew I had to get used to being on my own. The first time I used the telephone after he died was to phone the doctor's surgery for my repeat prescription. The lady I spoke to was very quietly spoken and also spoke too quickly for me to make out what she was

saying. I asked very kindly if she would mind talking more slowly and a little louder as I was deaf. Her reply came back very quickly, which I heard most distinctly – "If you think I have nothing else to do but shout down this phone to you all day you're much mistaken" – and banged the phone down on me. Well, my reaction was one of horror, completely taken aback, and put me off the phone for many a day. My sister went for my pills.' *Jean McIntosh*

Verbal communication is not the only way to provide information: this chapter explores a wide range of communication strategies. In a health care context this might mean, for example, providing large-print labels on medicines, or recording instructions and information in audio format. It also means looking carefully at the quality of the printed information that is supplied – letters should always be in large print and in bold type.

'At a hospital appointment I wore my blue hard-of-hearing badge and was greeted very kindly, even being given a printed card telling me how to get to the appropriate clinic.' *Doreen Cammish*

This need to consider how information is provided is clearly important for ophthalmology, ENT and audiology departments, but is equally so for all other departments. Older people with sensory impairments often have multiple impairments or illnesses, and need to receive care and information for these conditions that is not limited by their sensory impairment.

Hearing aids and glasses in hospital

It is not unusual for medical staff to ask a patient to remove a hearing aid or glasses and then fail to recognise that the person can therefore not see or hear well. Incredibly, this often happens at hearing aid clinics – staff ask the person to remove their aid for cleaning, and then continue to talk, failing to note that without the aid the person cannot hear them. In eye clinics, too, staff often fail to take into account the fact that the patient may also have a hearing impairment and depend on lipreading – if they ask someone to remove their glasses or if they put equipment in front of the patient's eyes, the patient will no longer be able to lipread.

Staff on wards need to ensure that patients can remove hearing aids or glasses, for example to go to sleep, and have somewhere safe and accessible to store them. It is not unusual for these to become lost during a hospital stay.

Face masks

If someone relies on lipreading, they will be completely lost if staff wear masks over their mouth. This is a particular problem with dentists – but also with other medical staff.

Waiting rooms

Waiting rooms can be a great problem for people who are hard of hearing because clinics and surgeries often depend on audio announcements of the next patient's turn. One man described the embarrassment of seeming to queue jump when he misheard names and stood up out of turn. Hard-of-hearing people need visual clues, too. People with a dual impairment need a member of staff to tell them personally and sensitively when it is their turn.

> 'Last year I was in the ENT clinic – not about my hearing but about my nose. The specialist was kind and helpful and suggested I have a hearing test as I was in the right place. This was carried out and the nurse asked me to wait to see the specialist again. I waited and waited, everyone else was seen and went home. At last someone asked what I wanted, and I explained. She found that my name had been called in another room and, as I had not responded, they assumed I had gone home! I saw the specialist and he apologised for not ensuring that his staff made more effort with deaf patients. I received a letter very soon afterwards apologising again. I've never had an apology for such treatment before; it's always been seen as my fault that I can't hear, not theirs for not communicating properly when they know of a problem.' *Nora Cooper*

COMMUNICATING FACE TO FACE

How to communicate effectively: clear speech and consideration

A sensory-impaired person may blame themselves for a breakdown in communication – and non-impaired people may do so, too. But it takes two to communicate.

When there are difficulties, all too often the impaired person can see frustration on their partner's face or hear it in their voice – causing anxiety and an almost self-fulfilling fear of failure. They may respond to this by withdrawing or, in some cases, by becoming aggressive in conversation – they may dominate, control and interrupt so as to avoid the embarrassment of misunderstanding others' speech.

Most people with dual sensory loss find it extremely difficult to communicate with more than one person at a time. They prefer a one-to-one situation, which means that they often miss out on conversations between friends and family, and feel left out.

It is worth noting that, with older people who acquire dual sensory or hearing loss, it is almost always 'receptive' communication that is affected; 'expressive' communication is not usually a problem. In other words, most people will have no difficulty in speaking, but will find it hard to hear.

There is a great deal we can do to help people with any sensory loss to communicate more easily. The strategy described below involves the technique usually called 'clear speech' but effective communication is based entirely on common sense and courtesy.

Starting a conversation

- Attract the person's attention – make eye contact, smile – before you start speaking.
- Always tell a visually impaired person that you are there.
- Begin by asking the person what will make communication effective, and follow that.

Where to talk

- Place yourself about five feet away, on the same level – do not talk down to someone who is seated.
- Make sure they can see your full face – not just a side view – and do not walk around or turn your head from side to side.
- Good light is important – face the light so that they can see you well. It is important, too, to ask a visually impaired person where they want to sit – they may be affected by glare, for example.
- Avoid background noise – turn it off or move to somewhere quieter.
- Do not talk from another room.

Speaking clearly

- Speak clearly – whatever your accent, pronounce every part of every word.
- Speak a little slower, but keep the natural rhythm of speech.
- Speak just as you would to someone with good hearing – do not use pidgin English.
- Speak a little louder but do not shout. Shouting distorts your face, which makes you look angry and distorts the lip pattern.
- Try to make your lip pattern olear but do not over-exaggerate.
- Keep your face visible. Do not smoke, eat, chew gum, cover your mouth with your hand or wear sunglasses. Full beards can hide the lips, making it hard to lipread. Dangly earrings can be distracting.
- Keep focused on the person you are talking to. If you are using an interpreter, always talk to the deaf person direct, not the interpreter.

Help the other person to understand

- Repeat if asked, and then rephrase – different words may be easier to lipread. Do not repeat single words – whole phrases or sentences are easier to understand.
- Establish the subject from the start.
- Keep to the subject: if you talk about the train being ten minutes late, and then say that it'll rain in five minutes, the person you are talking to may be very confused. If you change the subject, make sure the other person notices.

- Support your speech with gestures and reinforcement, which can include block or deafblind manual, or rephrasing with verbal clues – 'I'll see you after church on Sunday' gives the person two clues about the day on which you will be visiting. Match your expression to what you are saying to give extra clues about it – deadpan is very hard to understand.
- Use movement and sound to make sure the person knows you are still listening.
- Pause briefly at the end of each sentence to give the other person time to work out what you have said.
- If what you are saying is important, check tactfully that they have understood. Some things, such as directions for taking medicine, are better written down, as are names, addresses and numbers, which are hard to lipread. Remember that their smiling and nodding does not mean that they have understood – it may just be a polite reaction to the fact that you have said something. Check back by asking what they think about the subject but not by asking 'did you understand?'
- Make sure you know what you are trying to say – vague half-sentences will not make sense.
- Convey information verbally when talking to someone with a visual impairment: they will not see you gesturing towards a chair, for example.

Include everyone

- If sitting in a group, make sure that everyone can see you clearly; sitting in a circle is often best.
- Only one person should speak at a time.
- If the deaf person is with a hearing person, do not concentrate on the hearing person; in a group, make sure the deaf person is involved.

Be considerate

- During conversation, always use their name so that they know you are speaking to them. When you leave, tell them you are leaving.
- Lipreading requires concentration and hard work – do not expect someone to maintain it for hours.
- Make the effort to communicate, even if you have nothing important to say – do not just say 'it doesn't matter'.

'People take the tips in, but forget in time – it's easy to forget to be "deaf aware" when you're familiar and relaxed with the deaf person – I do it myself.' *Barbara Godwin, Hi Kent*

> 'Many older people have noted that some of their partners are hard to understand, specifying soft voices, unclear articulation or rapid speech as potential sources of difficulty.' *(Erber 1993)*

Someone who takes trouble with their communication can make all the difference to a sensory-impaired person.

Recognising people

When you are aware of the problem, it is obvious that someone with a visual impairment will find it harder to identify people. Yet those working with a person with sight loss often forget this, which can make the person feel vulnerable and embarrassed.

Someone with macular degeneration may find it difficult to see faces as more than a blur, so they will look for other clues: body shape, hair shape, style of walk, voice. But they can use these clues only if they know the person well, and they are still not guaranteed to reveal someone's identity.

What helps most if you meet someone with a visual impairment is to introduce yourself straight away, using the person's name and your own so that there is no confusion about who is talking to whom. This is important, whether you know someone well or not, and is essentially basic courtesy. In unfamiliar surroundings, identifying yourself becomes even more important. Imagine lying in a hospital bed, being visited by an endless round of nurses in identical uniforms and with blurs for faces; then imagine the difference it would make if each nurse were to identify him- or herself as soon as they arrived.

Strategies for maintaining a successful conversation

Researchers Caissie and Rockwell (1994) visited care homes and looked at why conversations broke down between hard-of-hearing residents and staff.

They found that, when residents could not understand what was being said, they would use non-specific questions like 'what?' or 'pardon?' so that the speaker did not know which part of what they had said had not been heard. In addition, residents did not necessarily always know when communication had broken down, nor did they have the assertiveness or skills to ask for clarification. They found that staff often tried to repair conversations by partially or completely repeating what they said before. This succeeded only to a limited extent: paraphrasing works better but was used least often by staff.

They concluded that staff need to help residents to:

- identify and repair communication breakdown;
- be assertive;
- be effective in asking for clarification.

Staff also need to learn to paraphrase.

Visual language

Some people become very anxious about saying things like 'Did you see Edna last night?' or 'Just look at me – I'm a mess!' in case they offend a visually impaired person. In fact, because the non-visual meaning of the words is clear, they do not cause offence at all.

It is extremely easy, however, to use visual language unhelpfully without thinking. Imagine that you are bathing Mr Spenser, who has poor vision, and say, 'I've put the towel over here' – he will have no idea where the towel is, because 'over here' is an entirely visual reference. You need to tell him that the towel is on the edge of the bath, just to his right, and that it is blue.

Likewise, 'this' is a visual word: as you help Mrs Sutton to put her clothes away, how is she to know what you are talking about when you ask her 'Where do you want this?'

The effect of the environment on face-to-face communication

The tips above apply wherever and whenever someone with a sensory impairment needs to communicate. They are easier to remember when talking one-to-one in a resident's room but no less important when they are eating dinner or walking down the corridor.

One woman in a care home, who depended on two hearing aids, talked about how hard it was for her to give or receive information in areas of the home without a loop, such as corridors or the lift. These parts of the home became silent zones for her. Another resident was frustrated that many announcements in her home were made in the dining room, where she found it hard to follow them and therefore felt excluded.

Another effect of communal living is that any activity is likely to be conducted at quite a high volume. For example, one day-care centre found that, every afternoon, a group of service users would settle down to a game of bingo. The caller would have to read out the numbers loudly so that all participants could hear. Because the centre is based in one large room, this disturbed the people nearby who were talking and playing Scrabble. Both sides claimed that the other was making an unreasonable amount of noise and that this noise made it hard to hear because, with all their hearing impairments, they struggled to distinguish speech against a background of constant talking or bingo calling.

How could each group continue its activity without disturbing the others? Possible solutions might be for the clients to discuss and negotiate the time and duration of the bingo game, for movable screens to be used, or for a microphone and headphones or a portable loop system to be installed. (See also Chapter 12 for more information on the environment.)

Privacy

The staff of a day-care centre named loss of privacy as one of their main concerns about working with people who were hard of hearing. Because most activities are carried out in a communal environment, they felt that it was not always appropriate to speak in a raised voice in order to make themselves heard. This is particularly true when bathing service users, because the bathrooms have relatively thin walls; speaking clearly and slightly louder than usual to ask someone to lift their leg was not felt to be dignified for them. This day-care centre has a private room for counselling, and they try to use this wherever possible when talking privately with service users who have a hearing impairment.

The problem is even more acute in hospitals where conversations are likely to be of a confidential nature and usually only a curtain divides patients.

Lipreading

Most of us lipread automatically to some extent. But when someone loses their hearing they depend far more on their ability to lipread. It is a skill that needs to be learned and practised – people cannot lipread well straight away – and it is very hard work.

Alex Willoughby, a hearing therapist, gives top priority to attending lipreading classes in her list of communication tips for people with a hearing impairment. She finds that people often resist at first – 'they're always convinced everyone else will be brilliant'. If they really cannot face a class, she suggests they start off with one-to-one training or just sit in on a class to observe what happens.

Why is lipreading difficult?

Many words look similar on the lips; for example *boast*, *post* and *most* would look very much alike, because **b**, **p** and **m** look alike. So do **sh**, **ch** and **j**. Some sounds, like **k** and **g**, do not have a visible shape on the lips at all, because they are made at the back of the throat. This means that it is impossible to lipread every word, as some are invisible. A good lipreader therefore tries to get a general idea of what is being said, rather than trying to lipread every word.

> 'Lipreading is mostly guesswork, and it's a lot easier to guess a word if you know what the speaker is talking about' *(Hi Kent 1993)*

Another barrier to effective lipreading is that people often do not speak clearly, or have an unfamiliar accent. Nevertheless, many people do learn to lipread well and find it very useful.

Jack Ashley, a former Labour MP and now Lord Ashley of Stoke, was deafened in 1967. He decided to return to political life but it was not easy. He described his first time back in the House:

> 'After a few moments, I tried to lipread. I had not expected to understand much but the reality was a chilling experience. I understood very little of what was said and, to add to my discomfort, I had no idea where to look. By the time I had swivelled round to locate a speaker he would be halfway through his question; a brief one would be finished before I could start to make any sense of it.'
> *(Ashley 1991)*

Jack Ashley found that, although most people were friendly, his social contacts were hugely reduced because of the difficulty in communicating. But, crucially, some people stuck with him and made the effort to talk to him and include him. Although it was incredibly difficult, Jack Ashley once again became a fully active and involved MP.

If you are helping someone who lipreads, the general communication tips on pages 112–114 will be useful. In addition, encourage the lipreader to tell others that they lipread before starting a conversation. They should also:

- watch the speaker's whole face, not just the lips;
- watch facial expressions and gestures – they reveal a great deal about what is being said;
- keep pen and paper handy in case they need to clarify anything;
- stop the speaker as soon as they miss anything – they may not be able to catch up again;
- remember to blink regularly (if they're concentrating hard on someone's lips, they might forget to blink).

Lipreading classes

At a lipreading class, qualified teachers demonstrate the different shapes that sounds make on the lips so that the hard-of-hearing person can identify them. The teacher also explains how to fill in the gaps of speech that they cannot hear, and how to use clues from the context of the conversation. In addition, they provide information and support about hearing loss; for example, about hearing aids, equipment, and people and organisations that can help.

Many people find lipreading classes enormously helpful – not only do they learn a new and vital communication skill but also they often find that it boosts their confidence and gives them a chance to talk to other people with a hearing loss.

> 'I couldn't make out what my husband was saying. He has Parkinson's disease and his voice can be very weak and unclear. He didn't understand that shouting was not the thing to do. But then I discovered lipreading classes and now we both understand each other's problem.' *Mina Wilson*

> 'About three years ago, I joined a free lipreading class run by the Adult Education Centre in the village. My outlook on life was transformed. We had a marvellous teacher and a friendly class, and the effect was quite liberating, making me feel no longer a second-rate citizen.' *Doreen Cammish*

Classes are usually organised by a local authority adult education service, but may also be run by a hearing therapist or a local voluntary organisation. The cost varies and some are free. For information, ask at your library or education department, phone the RNID Information Line, or send a stamped, addressed envelope to the Association of Teachers of Lipreading to Adults (address on page 276).

It is also possible to learn to lipread at home using books or videos. The RNID and Forest Books (address on page 296) are good sources of material.

Lipspeakers

A lipspeaker repeats what a speaker is saying without using their voice, so that a deaf or hard-of-hearing person can lipread them. They produce the shapes of the words clearly on their lips, reproducing the natural flow and feel of speech, and using facial expression and gesture. They will also fingerspell (see page 123) if the deaf or hard-of-hearing person asks them. A lipspeaker can also help a hearing person to communicate by repeating what a lipreader is saying. Lipspeakers are useful at conferences and meetings, courses, hospital and GP appointments, for legal work and religious services. They are bound to keep confidentiality and must be qualified.

Because of the speed of normal speech, a lipspeaker will have to cut out some of it, although without losing the sense of what is being said. There are two levels of lipspeaking: level 2 and level 3. A level 2 lipspeaker works at up to 120 words a minute; a level 3 lipspeaker manages higher speeds. Ask for advice about the level you need when you book a lipspeaker.

When using a lipspeaker:

- prepare them with a little background information, particularly if specialist words or phrases will be used;
- the deaf or hard-of-hearing person should ideally meet the lipspeaker in advance to talk about how they like to communicate and to get used to the lipspeaker's lip shapes;
- the deaf or hard-of-hearing person needs to talk to the lipspeaker about whether to use finger spelling, how to interrupt the lipspeaker, seating, the best distance between them, and lighting;
- the lipspeaker also needs to confirm rest breaks and mealtimes.

The Association of Lipspeakers (ALS; contact details on page 275) can advise on choosing a lipspeaker. There are about 100 lipspeakers in the UK, so it is essential to book someone at least two or three weeks in advance. The Council for the Advancement of Communication with Deaf People (CACDP; contact details on page 279) and ALS both list lipspeakers.

COMMUNICATING WITHOUT SPEECH

Many people who are born profoundly deaf or become deaf when they are young use sign language to communicate – it may be their native tongue rather than English. But few people who become deaf in later life use sign language: most prefer to continue to use speech for as long as possible. Eventually, however, some will no longer be able to hear speech, and will have to learn a sign language to receive information, although they will continue to speak themselves. People with both sight and hearing loss experience the most extreme communication problems because a non-visual sign language such as deafblind manual is often, by its nature, slow and unwieldy, especially for a new user.

British Sign Language

The most widely used sign language in Britain is British Sign Language (BSL), the language of the Deaf community. It is a language in its own right, with its own grammar and syntax.

BSL is specific to Britain – Deaf communities in other countries have their own language; for example, Irish Sign Language. So a sign language user who has spent much time in another country, or who was educated there, may use a different sign language or use signs from that language in their communication. There are also marked regional differences in BSL within Britain.

BSL can be adapted for someone with vision problems by keeping the signs within their visual field, by making them close up to the person, or by the impaired person putting their hands over or under the signer's hands and following the sign that way.

If a deaf or hard-of-hearing person wishes to learn BSL, check that the course will be appropriate for them: some are designed for hearing people, with the tutor showing the sign and then using speech to explain it. BSL needs to be taught by a deaf person for whom it is their mother tongue.

Fingerspelling

Fingerspelling – which is also called the standard manual alphabet – uses the hands to spell out letters. Each letter of the alphabet is represented by a different shape on the fingers, as shown in Figure 10.1. Fingerspelling is easy to learn.

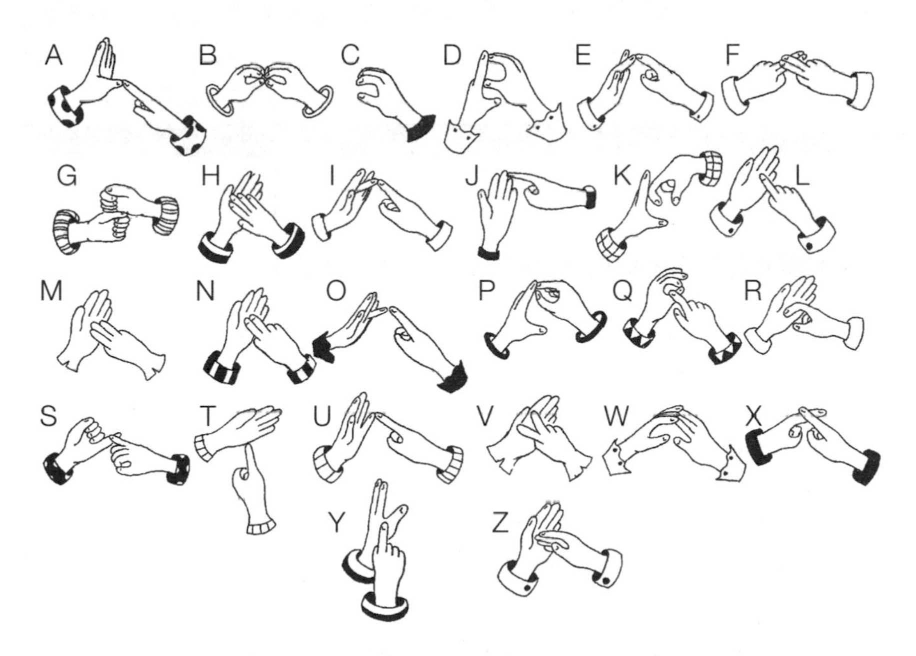

Figure 10.1 Fingerspelling (also called standard manual alphabet) can be used to spell out words on someone's fingers. (Reproduced by permission of RNID)

Deafblind manual and block

These are methods of writing on a person's hand. If someone loses all their sight or hearing, deafblind manual or block may be the only way of communicating. Neither is hard to learn.

Deafblind manual involves spelling words out on the person's fingers and hand (see Figure 10.2). It is easy to learn if the person is still open to learning a new language, but tiring to use: for example, one woman in her 80s

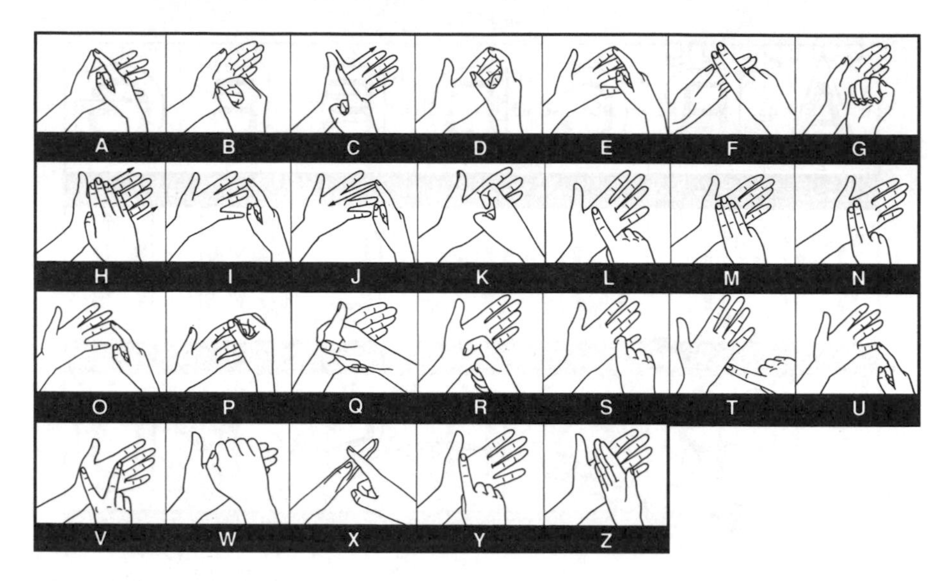

Figure 10.2 The manual alphabet for communicating with a deafblind person. (Reproduced by permission of the RNIB)

manages only three 15-minute sessions a day. Few older people use deafblind manual: out of 150 users of a day-care centre for older people with dual sensory loss, only one uses deafblind manual, despite the staff's willingness to teach them.

Block involves simply writing capital (block) letters with your finger on the palm of someone's hand (see Figure 10.3). It is therefore very easy to learn to produce block, although it takes more practice to read it. (If asking someone to spell something out in block, it is important to ask them to do it with their *finger* – one man asking a bus driver for information to be spelt on his palm ended up with ink all over his hand!)

Block can be a very useful addition to clear speech when precise information needs to be conveyed.

Both deafblind manual and block share some disadvantages:

- They may be hard to use for people with arthritis, stroke or diabetes or any other illness that affects their ability to feel or that causes them pain in their hands.

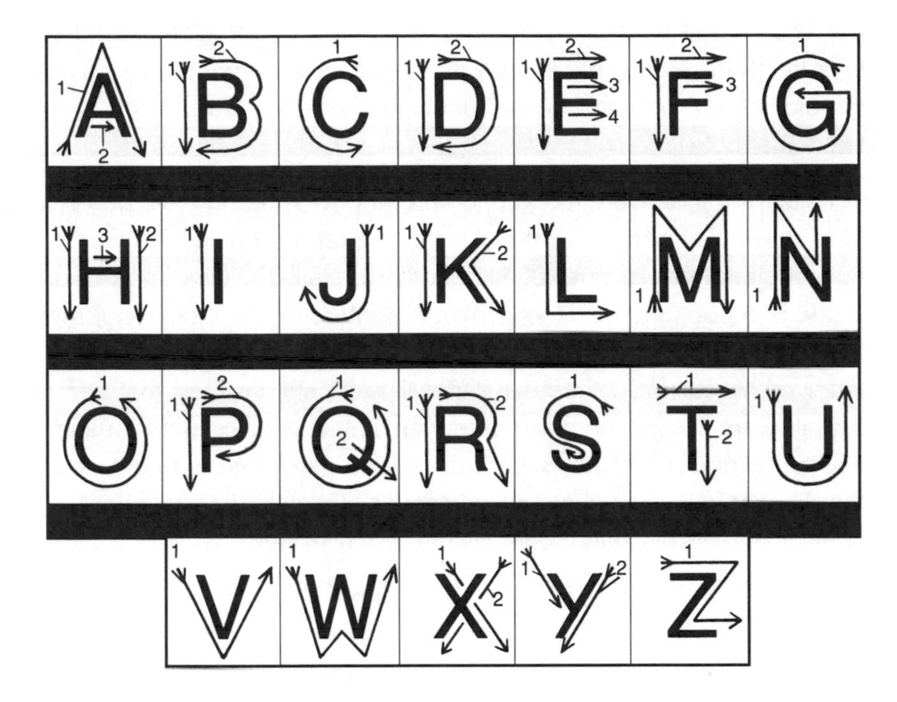

Figure 10.3 How to write letters on the palm of a deafblind person's hand. The lines show the direction and sequence of strokes on the palm. (Reproduced by permission of the RNIB)

- Users need to be literate and able to spell.
- Some people do not like being touched, perhaps for cultural reasons; this may affect some Muslim women's willingness to use these methods, for example.
- Related to this, some people are simply uncomfortable about having their personal space invaded, which is necessary in order to be close enough to write block or deafblind manual.

Ria Wijnhoven, a communication therapist in the Netherlands, tells the story of Mr Wolff, a 95-year-old man living in residential accommodation. His sight and hearing had both deteriorated badly in the last six months and staff were no longer able to communicate with him. She describes first seeing him:

'Mr Wolff sat at a table in the living room from morning to night. He was put there. He did not know with whom he was sharing the table. He did not know what his surroundings were like. He did not dare leave the table.

'Mr Wolff's hands were rough and stiff, and he made it clear that he did not want to communicate with them. Staff had held his head to nod or shake yes or no. But Ria gently persisted over a number of visits. She put some relief letters on the table, until curiosity got the better of him and he reached out to feel them. She then traced the letter on his palm. At the next visit, Mr Wolff still insisted that hand signals were for deaf people, not for him. But when a member of staff walked by and put some food on the table, he wanted to know what the draught was, and what he could smell. He relaxed a little after Ria spelt it out on his hand. She visited twice a week, and gradually established a relationship and helped him to build his confidence – even to begin to find his way around.

'Staff had to learn, too: when Mr Wolff needed his hair cutting they had taken him in a wheelchair to the hairdresser's, where someone cut his hair. Mr Wolff became angry and aggressive because he had no idea what was happening. Ria taught them either to spell out "hairdresser" on his palm, or to get him to feel his hair and then to give him a pair of scissors.'

It is hugely important to find a way of telling people what is happening, to reduce their feelings of fear and helplessness. This can be very simple: if you are going to give a deafblind resident a shower, you could give them the shower head to feel, or spell it out. If they need to wait in bed for a doctor's visit, you could give them a stethoscope or write 'doctor' out big in black marker pen so that they understand the change in routine.

'Learning to cope with deafblind people means gathering new knowledge and skills but also, just as importantly, getting out of the habit of thinking or deciding what you think the client would want.'
Ria Wijnhoven

Other sign languages

Apart from BSL, other sign languages in use in the UK include: Sign Supported English (SSE), a form of English with key signs added; Paget Gorman, a sign system that reflects normal patterns of English; and Makaton, a system for people with speech and learning difficulties. For more information, contact the RNID.

Other people may have developed their own personal system of signs, which may be known to only a few people close to them. This is known as 'home sign'.

Other ways of communicating

Sometimes communication becomes extremely difficult and none of the strategies discussed above will work. So professionals have adopted a flexible approach, exploring all the means available to find a way to keep communication going.

At a recent conference of people working with dual-sensory-impaired people, the following suggestions were put forward. One deafblind person uses plastic letters on an anti-slip surface. Another is afraid that this will look childish, so she has had wooden letters made, which she can spread out on a tray over a soft cushion. The letters have Velcro on the back to stop them slipping. Yet another support worker writes with the deafblind person's hand on a cushion on their lap.

These methods take time – it is crucial to build up a relationship before developing the communication system. In one home where staff turnover is rapid, there isn't time for staff to build up a relationship with a deafblind resident. Their method of communicating basic information – a compromise – is to use a set of cards, where the first in the pack means 'Time to ...' and the worker then chooses an appropriate card saying 'bath' or 'eat', and so on.

It is also useful to establish a sign or symbol to tell the person that you are going away.

> 'With one lady we put two fingers in the palm of her hand to say that we are leaving. When we arrive, we put a fist in her hand. She lives in a care home and often has other people in the room, so she gets easily confused about the number of people with her, so it's important for her to know who is there. When we've put a fist in her hand, she asks who it is and we tell her, using manual.
>
> 'With someone else, I use a rubbing motion on my watch. With another, I do a quick cross on him – anywhere that's non-threatening and non-intrusive: maybe his back, or arm or shoulder.
>
> 'The sign can be anything at all, as long as you agree it and everyone uses the same sign. Sometimes the sign just evolves but sometimes you really need to think – perhaps the person has arthritis or problems discriminating between different types of touch.' *Liz Duncan, Sense*

These methods clearly fall short of meeting the individual's need to have meaningful communication and interaction. But they do at least ensure that people are safe and physically cared for.

Interpreters

Failure to communicate with the outside world can mean loss of access to all basic activities of life as well as health care, benefits, social services and independence. For this reason, many people with hearing and dual sensory impairment need support with communication. This can take several forms:

- They may need an interpreter, who may translate the spoken word into BSL, deafblind manual or block.
- They may need an interpreter who translates unclear speech into clear speech. This is called 'speech relay'. It can be useful where a speaker is unclear – perhaps they have a strong accent or speak very fast – or to help two deafblind people to communicate.
- They may need more general support and reassurance, especially when it comes to explaining to a professional that they have a hearing

or dual sensory loss and that they need that professional to speak clearly and to follow the communication guidelines set out on page 112. For example, they may ask the professional to write down any important information, and suggest a shorter meeting than usual, because it is so tiring for the impaired person to communicate for any length of time. Such support may also be very valuable during a potentially stressful journey to an appointment, where the advocate or interpreter can provide reassurance and information.

Under the Disability Discrimination Act (DDA), if someone cannot communicate with medical staff, they can ask the hospital to provide a qualified interpreter (for more about the DDA, see page 247). Although interpreters are in short supply, the hospital should be able to supply one when there is advance warning of an appointment. They should also, of course, provide one in an emergency.

It is crucial that a BSL/English interpreter be fully competent and qualified. It is not enough to have a little BSL – the individual needs to be absolutely sure that they are getting the correct information. If you are not a qualified interpreter, you may make a mistake, perhaps by misunderstanding a medical term or an instruction, and the consequences can be extremely serious. Even those experienced in working with people with sensory loss would not expect to interpret except in an emergency.

Turning to the family may not be the best solution either, as illustrated by this 80-year-old woman describing her hospital appointments:

> 'My husband usually takes me to the hospital. But he won't tell me what's going on while we're there, or write it down – he waits till we're home. So I don't know what's going on when the doctor's talking about me. And I'm sure he misses things out.'

Similarly, if you are responsible for assessing someone who does not speak English well, you should ensure that you have a professional interpreter present to establish how that person wants to communicate.

The need for an interpreter is not limited to medical appointments and social services assessments and reviews. Hearing- and dual-impaired people also have problems communicating with benefits staff, solicitors and court staff (for example, if they need to discuss probate of a will), and a whole range of other professionals. In all these situations, they can ask for an interpreter under the Disability Discrimination Act. It may be difficult to get an interpreter but it is certainly worth persevering.

Speech to text

Another way of interpreting is for a speech-to-text reporter to transcribe speech for the deaf person to read, either on paper or on a screen. The deaf person needs to be comfortable reading English at high speed for long periods – perhaps up to two hours – for this to be effective. The reporter can keep up these speeds because they type phonetically on a special keyboard and their typing is then converted into English. Stenograph and Palantype are commonly used systems.

Electronic notetakers

Electronic notetakers type a summary of what is being said, which can then be viewed on a screen. They are likely to use special software called RNID SpeedText®. Because the notetaker provides a summary, there are fewer words to read than with speech-to-text reporting, but the report will be slightly less accurate.

Finding an interpreter

There is a national shortage of interpreters but you should still be able to find one. You can try one of the following:

- RNID has Communication Service Units around the UK, which provide BSL interpreters, deafblind interpreters, Sign Supported English, video interpreting, lipspeakers, electronic notetakers and speech-to-text reporters.
- The Council for the Advancement of Communication with Deaf People (CACDP) has a directory of interpreters.
- The Royal Association for Deaf People has a directory of interpreters.

(See pages 288, 279 and 290 for contact details of all three of these organisations.)

It is best to book at least four to six weeks in advance. However, if you need an interpreter urgently, it is always worth trying. Video interpreting (where the interpreter works on video rather than in person) can usually be booked at shorter notice. You need access to a videophone and an ISDN line to use a video interpreter.

When you book an interpreter, tell them:

- what kind of assignment it is (a meeting, interview or conference);
- how many people will be involved;
- how long it will last;
- any background information you have.

The cost of an interpreter depends on which service you use: fees are about £90 an hour (2004 figure) although speech-to-text reporting is more expensive. You will probably need to book a minimum of two hours. Video interpreting may cost less if you book for a shorter time.

COMMUNICATING AT A DISTANCE

Telephones

The telephone is a lifeline for most people. It keeps them safe – they can call for help – and in touch with the rest of the world. When someone develops a hearing loss, they may find an ordinary phone hard to use.

> 'I returned with my budgie from the vet – at this time, I was able to hear a little – and I had to contact a friend. My husband was ill with bronchitis; he usually makes my phone calls for me but, so as not to worry him, I thought I would try to phone. All went well, until she asked "How's your hubby?" Brightly, I replied, "I've just come back from the vet with him. They scraped his nose, so he can breathe much better now."!' *Betty Clarke*

To make it easier for someone with a hearing impairment to use the phone, speak clearly – using the clear speech skills described on pages 112–114. Do not shout or hold the phone too close to your mouth, because this causes distortion. When you phone them, give them time to adjust their hearing aid before launching into a conversation. When you set or leave an answerphone message, keep it at a steady pace and keep it short. Do not speak too quietly; repeat any telephone numbers.

If someone finds it hard to hear the phone ring, check to see if you can turn up the volume of the ringer or change its pitch. Placing the phone on a hard surface will make the ring sound louder. If this is not enough, you can add an extension bell or a flashing light in one or more rooms.

If someone finds it hard to hear the person speaking to them on the phone, check to see whether they can turn up the volume of incoming calls. If not, they could try a telephone amplifier. There are different types of amplifier: one is attached to the earpiece of the handset, another fits between the phone and the handset. Some phones have an inductive coupler in the handset. This should enable someone with a hearing aid with a T setting to hear more clearly and with reduced background noise.

Cordless phones can be either digital or analogue. Unfortunately, digital phones can cause severe interference to hearing aids. Encourage the person to try different phones to see which one works best for them.

If a hard-of-hearing person finds a standard phone very difficult to use, there is a wide range of special phones. These phones have various features, including volume control, amplification, T setting facilities, loud ringers and flashing lights. And remember that on most modern phones the volume and tone can be adjusted to suit the individual's needs. There are also care phones with preset emergency numbers, and hands-free phones for people with dexterity problems. People with a visual impairment can use a phone with large number pads.

There are answerphones with a volume control or a T setting capacity, although it may be easier for a hard-of-hearing person with a BT line to use the BT Call Minder service so that they can use their own telephone handset.

BT provides several services for people with sensory impairments. These include free directory enquiries for visually impaired people (call 195) and a range of text-based phone services for deaf or hard-of-hearing people.

RNID Typetalk

This is a national telephone relay service, run by RNID and funded by BT. The deaf or hard-of-hearing person uses a textphone to type in messages, which are relayed by an operator to a hearing person on a standard phone. The operator then relays back spoken answers by typing them in as text.

BT TextDirect

BT TextDirect links textphone users with other textphone and voice telephone users (via the RNID Typetalk relay service). It is available to all fixed line phone users, whether they have a BT line or not. To use it, a textphone user dials the prefix 18001 and then the number they want. A voice telephone user dials the prefix 18002 followed by the textphone number they want. To reach the emergency services, a text user should dial 18000.

Textphones

Textphones (sometimes called Minicoms) allow deaf and hard-of-hearing users to communicate through the standard phone network. They have a small display screen and a keyboard so that the user can type what they want to say and read what is typed in reply. Some textphones also have a voice telephone handset, and others are designed to be used with a separate voice telephone.

Detailed information about the different types of phone and textphone can be found in the RNID catalogue or on its website.

Mobile phones

A mobile phone can be particularly useful for sending SMS text messages to other mobile phones. This is an increasingly common way of keeping in touch. A mobile phone can also be handy in an emergency, although it is not completely reliable, as messages do not always get through. Mobile phones have a variety of ring tones, and an adjustable ringer volume. Many also vibrate when they ring, which is very useful.

All mobile phones in the UK are now digital. Unfortunately, this can cause severe interference with some hearing aids. A hearing aid user should therefore try out a new mobile phone before buying it. A way round the problem of interference from a mobile phone is to buy add-on listening accessories such as neck loops and ear hooks. The RNID has a useful factsheet on mobile phones.

Mobile communicators

At the time of writing, the Nokia 9210 is the only product that can be used as a mobile textphone. The user can have textphone conversations while they are out and about.

Home-based SMS systems

A number of products enable people to send an SMS message from home without having to buy a mobile phone. However, at the time of writing, only the BT Diverse 4010 phone allows the user to both send and receive SMS text messages.

Other technology

Fax machines have long been used by deaf or hard-of-hearing people to communicate. More recently, videophones and webcams have also been introduced. A videophone is not cheap but it can help someone who communicates through sign language to stay in touch. A webcam can be a cheap addition to a modern PC – it enables the user to chat with friends through text while watching them through the webcam. (See also page 138 for more information about PCs.)

Information

> 'Information is now widely recognised as the key to helping dependent older people and their carers to improve the quality of their lives in the community.' *(Tester 1989)*

Most sensory-impaired people have some sight or hearing, and there are many ways for them to receive information. All that is needed is some commitment – both on their own part and on the part of the people around them – and sometimes a little imagination.

When running a day-care centre or a care home, it is very easy to forget to provide information about daily activities and procedures in all formats. However, everybody needs to learn about mealtimes, fire procedures and so on; they will also want to have the information to keep, so that they can remind themselves and refer to it when they need to.

Other service providers also need to remember the needs of people with difficulties of sight or hearing. For example, many GPs encourage older patients to have a flu vaccination, using an advertising poster on the surgery notice board ... which a visually impaired person will not be able to see.

When providing information, any service provider should check that it is:

- user friendly;
- in an appropriate range of formats (large print, Braille, tape, BSL, video, disk, etc);
- provided at key points in time (eg on initial contact with a service);
- easily accessible (eg at local information points);
- in ethnic minority languages.

You will probably find that many people who cannot read print prefer to receive their information on audio cassette, but you should ask each person how they would like the information provided rather than making assumptions.

Printed information

> 'Three out of four people with a visual disability can see large print and well over half (58 per cent) are able to read it comfortably.' *(Williams 1994)*

In 2001, the RNIB asked visually impaired people which information they most valued. The most common response was bus numbers and medicine labels, closely followed by food packaging, personal mail, medical letters, forms and bills, prices, magazines and loudspeaker announcements. Most of this information is supplied in print – print that is too small for people with visual impairments.

> '86 per cent of people attending eye clinics – often because of serious sight loss – receive their appointment in a print size they can't read.' *(McBride 2001)*

What is large print?

Most visually impaired people have enough vision to read printed material if it is sufficiently large and bold. 'Large' print is basically anything over 16 point. A size that works well is 18 point, but 20 point is too big to be practical. Arial is a good font because it is clear and plain. It works best in bold.

> **This is what Arial 18 point in bold looks like.**

Many people find it easier to read black print on yellow paper, because there is less glare from yellow than from white paper.

When producing large print, never use capitals – they are much harder to read than upper and lower case letters. Typewritten text is almost always easier to read than handwriting. If you need to write by hand, use a thick, black felt-tip pen on white or yellow matt paper.

Where to find large-print materials

The most obvious source of large-print materials is the local library. You can also contact the publishers of large-print books direct for a catalogue (see the 'Audio-visual aids' section on pages 295–298).

Big Print News is a weekly large-print newspaper, which includes TV and radio listings. Large-print Christian materials are available from the Torch Trust (see page 298).

Making reading easier

For almost anyone with a visual impairment, reading will become harder, and may eventually become impossible. But most people with a visual impairment can and do still read if text is appropriately formatted, although they may need to learn new reading techniques to overcome the effects of their impairment.

> 'It's going along the line, then finding my way back to the next line again. Sometimes I miss a line or go back on to the same line ... Then, after a while, my eyes start running and I get fed up with doing it.' *Simon Carter*

The following guidance helps to make reading easier:

- Use an adjustable lamp.
- Obtain the material in large print – anything can be photocopied to make it larger: recipes, letters, music, and so on.
- Use a magnifier.
- Put the book or newspaper on to a clipboard to keep it straight.
- Use a stand or cushions, perhaps on a table, to prop up the reading material.
- Use a ruler or 'typoscope' to keep the focus on one line (a typoscope is a piece of card with a slot cut in it through which you read one line at a time).
- Use a mini-scanner such as an Eezee Reader. When passed over printed material (eg books, medicine labels, newspapers), it transmits the text through a cable to a standard TV screen, where the print is enlarged.
- Bear in mind that shiny paper can be hard to read because of the glare.

Increasingly, local libraries have reading machines that either magnify print or read it aloud. Users can wear headphones for privacy. The machines can read personal documents, too.

Making writing easier

Many of the tips for making reading easier also apply to writing. Probably the most important is to ensure that the person is working in good light – an adjustable lamp is best. (See Chapter 12 for more on lighting.)

If a visually impaired person has any keyboard skills, they may find it much easier to write on a typewriter or computer (although they may not find it easy to correct what they have written). If they need to write by hand, one of the biggest problems experienced by visually impaired people is seeing what they have written. They will probably find it easiest to see black felt-tip pen on white or yellow paper. A mini-scanner is useful here, too. They may also have problems in finding where they are on a page. To solve this you can make or buy guides of various kinds. A *signature guide* is a black card with a slot in which the person writes their signature. A *page guide* has a page-sized hole crossed with horizontal lines that the writer can feel, so that they can write in straight lines. It may have a slight protuberance just before the end of each line to warn the writer that they are running out of room on that line. Banks also issue cheque book templates and larger cheque books to visually impaired people.

Computers and email

An increasing number of older people are computer literate, and computers can provide great help to people with sensory impairment. People with poor hearing can find email, the Internet and chat rooms a lifeline, giving them access to the worlds of news, information and shopping, and allowing them to maintain communication and contact with a wide range of people.

People with a visual impairment can also find IT extremely useful. For example, they can use the computer to present material in a way that is easier for them to read: changing type into a bigger size, a simpler font or better-contrasting colours. There is also software that magnifies text or that reads text back.

In setting up a computer for someone with a visual impairment, position the screen in even light and avoiding glare. If someone finds it hard to see the keyboard, there are large-print stickers and overlays to help identify the keys.

Audio materials

When someone cannot read print, the best way of supplying information may be in audio format. This can be on tape, CD or DVD. Audio can be used not only for information but also for spoken books and newspapers, and instead of letters – both formal and personal. Audio materials give the reader access to information when they want it: a visually impaired person can listen to the tape several times over if they wish, with no need for a human reader.

You can help someone to use their tape player by sticking raised markers on to the key switches or by painting those switches in different colours. You may need to help insert the tapes in some machines. There are special cassette players that are designed to be easy for people with vision loss to use. They are available from the RNIB.

If you are making a recording, use good-quality equipment in a quiet place. Alternatively, you can use a transcription service (eg the Sense Transcription Service; see page 297), which will produce a professional quality recording.

Talking books and newspapers

BOOKS

A range of books is available in audio format. The RNIB Talking Book Service produces many unabridged audio books. This is a subscription service, which provides a special tape player on loan and a straightforward system for choosing books. Some local authorities will pay a visually impaired person's subscription to the Talking Books Service.

'Mrs Vermeer is 82 years old; she is blind and hard of hearing. She spends most of the time in her room. She is not able to walk alone. Listening to a book on tape was one of her favourite activities. She could not hear it any more so staff asked us for help. We replaced the tape recorder with one with speed control and a button to regulate the high and low sound. With it she was able to "read" her books again. I visited her the next week, to ask how things went. She was still reading the same book. I asked her if

> there was something wrong. No, the tape recorder was excellent, she said but she needed the nurses to change the tape. Help can't stop at the moment you deliver a new aid.' *Ans Huvenaars and Ria Wijnhoven, Kalorama, Netherlands*

NEWSPAPERS AND MAGAZINES

Most national newspapers, many magazines, the *Radio Times* and the *TV Times* and, in many areas, the local paper are recorded on to tape or CD. The main organisation for this is the Talking Newspaper Association.

Producers of audio-visual aids are listed on pages 295–298.

Braille

Relatively few people use Braille but, if you need to provide information in Braille, the following tips may help:

- Make sure that the content has been checked.
- Store it on its side, and not flat, so that the dots do not become flattened.
- Give the person time to read it – it may take longer to read than standard print.
- Check with the person whether they need the whole document, and all of the diagrams or pictures transcribed.
- Allow enough time for the transcription – it probably cannot be done straight away.

The National Library for the Blind (address on page 286) has a huge Braille collection, which is available to individual readers.

Transcription services

There are organisations, both nationally and locally, that specialise in putting information into a range of formats, from tape, to CD, to large print, to Braille. In the first instance, try Sense's transcription service. Charges vary according to what is needed. For example, at the time of writing (2004) Sense charges £20 per hour (minimum £5). In addition to this:

- £1.50 per cassette for audio transcriptions;
- 20p per A4 sheet to transcribe from disk into large print;
- 35p per A4 sheet to scan text for transcription into large print.

Sense usually needs about five days to transcribe 20 pages. Shorter documents, such as letters or short leaflets, can be transcribed in 48 hours.

Some services are cheaper than Sense, but you may find that they are also slower. Others are more expensive.

> 'There are more and more hospitals coming to us. They've asked for transcriptions of leaflets, and have been good lately at putting their information into ethnic languages – though hospitals do tend to lag behind organisations such as banks and building societies.' *Gavin Griffiths, Sense Transcription Service*

The British Deaf Association (address on page 276) can make information available in BSL on video, DVD or CD-ROM.

11 Quality of life

Older sensory-impaired people are often encouraged to restrict their activities and become dependent on others. This practical chapter suggests ways to help people to maintain independence and control over their own lives. It includes:

- Loss of independence
- Giving back control
- Understanding the effect of the impairment on the individual's life
- Skills training, equipment and support
- Being organised
- Tailor-made solutions
- Personal care
- Preparing and eating food
- Mobility
- Getting out and about
- Leisure
- Time
- Safety and alerting devices
- Money
- Voting
- Equipment and equipment suppliers

This chapter needs to be read in conjunction with Chapter 12, The Environment, as it covers issues such as lighting and décor, which can directly affect personal care. For example, a visual impairment in itself does not prevent someone from getting up out of bed independently. But poor lighting may do so – if they cannot see where to put their feet, or where the door is to visit the bathroom in the night, they will be dependent on someone else to help them get up.

One of people's greatest fears, when they are told that they have a sight or a hearing loss, is the impact it will have on their ability to carry out their normal activities. They may find it hard to cook and to eat without spilling food and drink, they may have to give up the car, stop singing, give up reading, painting, going out with friends. All these things are part of the person's life and their understanding of who they are and how they fit into society.

> 'One of my most painful experiences is that, as a previous music lover, I now find it impossible to detect any melody, however well known it is. It's a jumbled distortion, which greatly reduces the cultural quality of life.' *Eric Moore*

It is easy to forget how much we use our senses to orientate ourselves and interact with the world. For example, if someone cannot see well, shopping becomes incredibly difficult – it can be an enormous challenge to travel safely to the shop, find the products and choose them, check prices, and find the correct money. The same trip for someone who is hard of hearing presents a whole new raft of problems: buying a ticket for the bus, hearing traffic, understanding the shop assistant, all make a once simple chore into an extremely stressful one.

People are adaptable, and most people with a sensory loss will find new ways of carrying out their daily tasks in the home, especially if given help and support. Adapting to the outside world can present far greater problems because it is so much less predictable and controllable. This can mean that a sensory-impaired person begins increasingly to stay at home. As their impairment develops, they may similarly give up activities that require the use of their impaired sense.

Loss of independence

A sensory-impaired person may give up activities partly because others insist on taking them over. For example, a woman asks friends round for tea, as she has done for years. Because they are worried that their hostess cannot see to pour the tea, her friends offer to pour it for her. This well-meant gesture may, however, undermine the woman's sense of confidence and may reinforce her dependency on others: she may begin to see herself as more dependent than she really need be. And she may realise also that her friends fear their own embarrassment if she spills the tea, so she may allow them to take over in order not to jeopardise the tea party, and the friendship. Eventually she may stop inviting them.

It is a fine balance: we must allow people to do things for themselves, and to take risks, but both the impaired person and those around them must also recognise that we all depend on others to a certain extent, and that the sensory-impaired person will have to depend on others in order to perform certain tasks. This can be very hard, and it is not unusual for people to feel, at the same time, grateful for the help they receive and reluctant to depend on others for that help:

> **'Well, really, what else can you do? I would prefer to do it myself, you know. I'm grateful but it means you are beholden to that many people.'**
> *Maud Jenkins*

Jean Shorten has had macular degeneration for some years now: she can see my face but not my features. A couple of years ago, she was knocked down by a car and badly injured. She lives in residential care because she can no longer do everything for herself. Nevertheless, she still goes out alone and uses public transport. In fact, she was late for our appointment because she had missed the bus home from town. She is fiercely independent – despite her frailty, all she will say is 'I could do with some manual help sometimes'. She commented to me that she enjoys using the exercise bike in the home, although 'it's a bit of a stretch with my little legs'.

On paper, Jean, aged 95, with very poor vision and badly damaged legs from her accident, might seem to need very high levels of care. Far from it – she knows exactly what help she does need, and is determined to get it, but is equally determined to do as much for herself as possible. It is crucial never to prejudge someone's needs.

Giving back control

> 'Being done "to" rather than "with" can cause helplessness, and reinforce dependency.' *Beryl Palmer, Manager, Sensory Disabilities Services*

All too often, we decide what help people need without consulting them, and sometimes without even telling them. Carrying out tasks for someone without telling them what you are doing can be counter-productive, as in the case of Mrs Smit. She is 82, partially sighted, deaf, and has arthritis:

> 'The nurses complained that she was rebellious in the mornings and at night, at the times when they had to help her. I suggested they use pen and paper more and tell her what they are about to do: she needed to be informed. They needed to give her time to react, and to check if she understands.' *Ans Huvenaars and Ria Wijnhoven, Kalorama, Netherlands*

It is only too easy for staff working with older people, let alone older people with an impairment, to take over and do things themselves rather than letting the individual try. It may seem quicker, or safer, to take control. But the result is a terrible undermining of the older person's autonomy, dignity and self-esteem, and eventually their ability to live as independently as possible. It can therefore be counter-productive for staff too, who will eventually create greater dependency on them if they always intervene.

Take the case of a woman who has entered a care home, and who has a visual impairment. She is finding it hard to dress, and is always late for breakfast. The easy option might be for a care assistant to choose her clothes for her and to help her to put them on. But perhaps the problem is not her ability to choose, or to put the clothes on, but rather that she cannot find her clothes because she cannot see them. When staff help her to establish a system for storing and finding her own clothes, she regains her confidence and her ability to control her own appearance.

A similar and common situation in care homes is finding people who have a visual impairment using a wheelchair, although they have no problems with mobility: the staff's fear is that they might fall, so they are put in a wheelchair for safety. Imagine how that feels to the person concerned – not only are they losing their sight but also they cannot even decide where and when they should move about. It is perfectly possible for someone with a visual impairment to retain full independent mobility but, by putting them unnecessarily into a wheelchair, staff have started them on the way to true loss of mobility, and a real risk of falling.

Understanding the effect of the impairment on the individual's life

Providing care for someone with an impairment of any kind means enabling them to retain as much independence as possible, and making sure that they are the ones who decide what they need. It means listening to them to find out why they are having problems in carrying out particular tasks. Planning how to provide help for someone with a sensory impairment can only be done, therefore, alongside that person.

An important element of that discussion is listening to how their impairment actually affects them and their life. While you may be able to predict that they will have difficulty in reading the cooker knobs if they have macular degeneration, they may not feel that this is a problem if their spouse always cooks for them. On the other hand, being unable to do the crossword each day may be a source of great loss – so by putting them in touch with a low vision unit, and helping them to find the best place to sit to maximise light, you could make an enormous difference to their quality of life.

Skills training, equipment and support

Although social services departments are supposed to provide the same quality of service to all people, no matter what their age, it is still the case that in many areas younger impaired people tend to receive training in daily living skills, whilst older impaired people tend to be given a care package. Because the provision of training to sensory-impaired people of all ages is also extremely erratic, very few older sensory-impaired people receive any training in daily living skills.

> 'Only 9 per cent of blind and partially sighted people surveyed [RNIB/Office of National Statistics Survey 2002] had been offered training to help them cope with daily living skills and tasks like cooking, shopping and mobility.' *(Vale and Smyth, 2003)*

All too often, statutory support is limited to the provision of a narrow range of gadgets, only some of which are useful.

> 'There was a social worker who was very good at coming round. I think he was on commission for what he sold. Packs of cards, dominoes, thing for slicing bread, no use nor ornament to us. We used to take it back. We buy sliced bread.' *Janet Way, Albert's wife*

Gadgets can, of course, be useful: writing guides, dots to mark cooker dials and so on can make a real difference. But help should not stop with the provision of a gadget – so much more can be achieved towards maintaining independence simply by helping an impaired person to find new ways of carrying out their daily tasks.

Take, for example, Mrs Brown's glass of water on the table. Her visual impairment means that she finds it hard to judge depth and distance. This has many effects but one is that she cannot tell how far away the glass of water is, so she often knocks it over when reaching out to pick it up. This is incredibly frustrating for her and upsets her – every time she does it she is reminded of her impairment once again, has to find a cloth and clear up the mess, and pour out a new drink. But, by observing how she picks up her glass, you see that she knocks it over when her hand is waving in the air to find it. So you encourage Mrs Brown, instead of reaching out for her glass of water, to gently slide her hand across the table until she reaches the glass: she is far less likely to tip it over this way. This may seem a minor step, but learning this new skill will make a difference to Mrs Brown's quality of life.

Often, then, by using our knowledge of the effects of a particular impairment, we can help simply by finding a new way of carrying out a task. The use of contrast is a good example of this.

Using contrast

All the experts talk about using contrast to make life easier for people with a visual impairment. They talk about painting doors and walls in contrasting colours, and so on. These are key changes that anyone working with older people can make to their environment, and they are described in Chapter 12.

There are also simpler ways of using contrast in daily life. Nicolette Ringgold (Ringgold 1991), an American woman who developed macular degeneration in late life, described one of her most useful accessories: a piece of black card. She used it to provide a background against which she created contrast: almost any colour other than black or very dark blue would show up on it well. On it she would place notepaper when she wanted to write a shopping list – so that she could see the edges of the paper. She could place an envelope on it and write an address without half of it going on to the tablecloth, and stick the stamp down in the right place. She used it to sort coins, to find pens, paper clips and jewellery.

She used contrast, too, with more distant objects: to see if her daffodils were faded, she held them against the distant background of a dark door, and saw them more clearly. She chose two-coloured pens, so that there was less chance of losing them against a matching background. She used pins with light heads for dark fabric, and dark heads for light fabric. She learnt to place easily lost objects such as pens, pencils and needles against the angle of a pattern so that they would not blend in.

Nicolette Ringgold was an unusually determined woman but she showed that, by using common sense, a basic understanding of the effect of macular degeneration and the fact that contrast would make things easier to see, she was able to devise ways of carrying out daily tasks and remain independent, despite her impairment. Helping the people we work with to find similar methods that work for them is probably one of the most positive ways we can contribute to their general well-being.

Providing care

Sometimes an impaired person needs more than training and gadgets – they really do need help with some tasks. All too often, we assume that this will involve personal care but, in fact, we may be able to find new ways for them to carry out personal care tasks with little or no daily help.

Where they may need help is with tasks such as washing curtains, window cleaning, or gardening – although these are rarely identified as a priority by service providers. They are none the less significant – dirty curtains and windows restrict the amount of light that reaches indoors; an untidy garden is full of obstacles that may trip up someone with impaired vision or mobility. In addition, the psychological effect of knowing that your home is not being looked after should not be underestimated.

Being organised

People with visual impairments – and those around them – need to be extremely organised. Those with good vision can usually put their hands on whatever they need at home without any trouble. For someone with impaired vision, this is not the case. If they take their gloves off when they come in and then answer the phone before they put them away in the glove drawer, it can take a long and frustrating hunt through the whole house to find them again before being able to go out next time. A visually impaired person's need to be organised can be seen as obsessional tidiness – especially if they get upset when things are moved. But it is a survival technique.

If you work with people with sight loss, therefore, it is crucial that you always put things back exactly where they belong. This is another example of how thinking about the true effects of a sensory impairment can enable us to find ways of helping.

Tailor-made solutions

Clearly, it is not possible to describe solutions to every problem associated with daily living in this book. Nor is it desirable: each solution should be worked out to suit the individual concerned. It needs to take into account what they want to achieve, where they are coming from, what their cognitive ability is, whether they can use their hands easily, and so on. But we do hope that the daily living solutions outlined here will help you to find ways of helping sensory-impaired people you work with to live a better quality life.

Personal care

The need for help with personal care varies from person to person, and will depend largely on whether they have other disabilities and how adaptable they are. When you plan someone's personal care, you must look at whether they need help in bathing, washing and dressing, cooking, treating feet, getting up and going to bed. You need to establish whether they can accomplish these tasks independently if you give them appropriate training and support.

Dressing

Being able to dress oneself is an important aspect of personal care, because the inability to do so means that the person is dependent on someone else for an intimate and personal task. People care about their appearance, and worry about whether they are clean and tidy – they know that, if they cannot keep themselves smart, others will quickly assume that they are no longer competent to look after themselves.

> 'There is no protocol about who tells a person that their clothes are dirty – so they may go around looking terrible and not realise it – and then be really upset when they find out.' *Gill Levy, RNIB*

Wearing dirty or odd combinations of clothes is a common sign that someone is developing a visual impairment. You may need to talk to them tactfully to establish whether they have had their eyes tested, and, if they do have an impairment, to work with them to find ways of keeping their clothes clean and organised.

Thinking back to the resident who found it hard to dress herself in the morning (page 145), when you ask her, she says she cannot find her clothes. Why? Is it because they are always put back in a different place? If so, look at your system for distributing clean laundry – if putting it away is the job of a care worker or laundry worker, do they simply put it all into one drawer unsorted? They could be shown how to put it away correctly. If it is a task carried out by the resident, you can make sure they have a care worker present to help them.

If the resident is having problems because they cannot identify the clothing correctly, you could try the following solutions:

- Section off the wardrobe or chest of drawers into different colours or types of clothing.
- Put whole outfits together on the hanger.
- Sew different-shaped buttons into the clothing to indicate colour – so perhaps square buttons indicate black, round ones blue, and so on. This can be adapted by sewing a ribbon or safety pin into the left sleeve to indicate one colour, into the collar for another, and so on.
- Always make sure the clothes are stored in the correct place.

If the problem derives from a member of staff – such as the laundry worker not sorting the washing – give them training in sight loss, so that they understand what a particular eye condition means for the person concerned, and can think of solutions to daily living problems for themselves.

The bathroom

In Chapter 2, we saw how the provision of a plug chain enabled a man to wash himself rather than rely on a member of staff to help him. Most people with a visual impairment can wash and toilet themselves without help, as long as their environment does not conspire against them. For example, if you always ensure that lids are put back on bottles, they do not spill if they are knocked over (flip-top lids are harder to lose). Other common-sense tactics include buying coloured toothpaste, if possible, so that a visually impaired person can judge how much paste is on their brush, and providing coloured soap, as it is easier to find against a white sink or bath.

A man with poor sight may be accused of dirty habits if he misses the toilet when urinating. Make sure the toilet rim is visible (use contrast), and explain to staff why he has this problem.

If someone has other impairments, they may need help to carry out personal care tasks, in which case it is of course important to help people to retain as much dignity as possible. A hearing impairment can present a particular challenge here, especially as the impaired person will need to remove their hearing aid before a bath:

> My dad is deaf so I'm kind of used to it; I'm used to repeating. In the end if you want them to, say, raise their arm, you have to raise their arm. But it's not very dignified.' *Care Worker, day-care centre*

When bathing someone who is hard of hearing, it is easy to forget to face them. But this is crucial or they will not be able to lipread; nor will they be able to do so if they have removed their glasses – or if they are steamed up. Although it can be tempting, do not raise your voice too much – quite apart from the fact that shouting does not help the person to hear, bath time is personal and private, and they probably will not feel comfortable about fellow residents hearing you shout out, 'Lift your left leg now, Mrs Mackenzie!' (See Chapter 10 for more about communication.)

In the next chapter, we look at the room itself – how its bright shiny surfaces, often all white, can create problems for people with sight or hearing difficulties, owing to glare, lack of contrast and poor acoustics.

Medication

Taking medication can be a challenge for a visually impaired person if they cannot read the labels on the bottles nor see the dispensing spoon. This is where gadgets can be useful. You could try using:

- large print on medicine labels;
- colour-coded dispensers and pill organisers;
- plastic cap dispensers;
- syringes that draw up the exact amount of medicine from a bottle;
- eye drop dispensers;
- talking thermometers.

These are all available from the RNIB.

Preparing and eating food

The kitchen

'Mrs Hempelman is 86 years old, hard of hearing and blind. The first time we visited her she only wanted us to take her to the nearest railway station – so she could jump in front of the train. "What is life worth living for, if you can't see or hear?" she said. I started to visit her once a week for one hour. I asked her about old times and she started talking. She lived in Indonesia, a good time to think about but she was glad it lay behind her. Cooking was one of her specialities. But losing her vision also took away her enjoyment of cooking. I asked her if she would like to teach me how to cook Indonesian recipes.

'Every week she gave me recipes that I cooked at home. She asked me how the results were. When things went wrong she gave me information for the next time. Our contact gave her something to think about, something to care for. Together we cooked in her apartment: I cooked and she helped me. Afterwards she was surprised about the things she was capable of without seeing.' *Ans Huvenaars and Ria Wijnhoven, Kalorama, Netherlands*

It is common for people with vision loss to do less and less in the kitchen – due, in part, to their anxiety about the high potential for accidents. But careful planning can enable anyone to retain their independence in the cooking area. If you can encourage someone with low vision to follow the rules listed below, they will be more likely to retain their independence, especially if their kitchen environment has been adapted with their impairment in mind (see Chapter 12).

- Never put anything tall in front of anything low.
- Turn all pot handles, and utensils in pots, to the back.
- Glass is especially hard to see – use glass with strong patterns, or put it against a dark background (paint the back of the glassware cupboard; use coloured coasters).
- Try to provide contrasting containers: for example, it is easier to see coffee if it is being poured into a cup with a pale inner surface.

- Serve soups and sauces with a ladle.
- Always close a bottle straight away in case it is knocked over.
- If it is hard to see which way up the sharp edge of a knife is, put a notch or small piece of tape where the thumb goes.

The most common accident in the kitchen is spilling – it is sensible to have a good supply of kitchen towels in any cooking area used by someone with poor vision.

Eating

Sighted people may complain about a visually impaired person's table manners. Although this is understandable, it is extremely upsetting to the visually impaired person, so staff need to explain to sighted people why they should show tolerance, and to help the visually impaired person to eat more easily.

The most helpful thing you can do when serving food to someone who is visually impaired is to ensure that they have a chance of identifying what is on their plate by using colour contrast. Try to serve food of different colours – in other words, avoid serving cauliflower, mashed potatoes and creamed chicken together. And serve the food on a plate whose colour will contrast with the food. Staff can help the visually impaired person by telling them not only what is on their plate but also where it is. It is probably most useful to describe it in terms of a clock face; for example, 'There are potatoes at two o'clock, beef at six o'clock and cabbage at ten o'clock.' It is also helpful if you always present the food in the same place on the plate so that, for example, the meat is always at six o'clock and the vegetables at two o'clock and ten o'clock.

If the visually impaired person finds it hard to manoeuvre their food on to their fork, it may be helpful to offer them a spoon. Some food is easier to handle than others. Lettuce is particularly hard – it should be torn into small pieces before being served. Meat on the bone, such as lamb chops and chicken legs, is a real challenge if you cannot see it. Staff should watch out to see which meals on the menu seem to present problems, and should talk to the cooking staff about either not using that food or presenting it differently.

If someone finds it hard to take an offered cup – perhaps because they need to judge its weight – either put it down on a table near them or suggest that they use both hands. They may be less likely to drop or spill it this way.

If food is presented buffet-style, hygiene can be an issue, because a visually impaired person would need to lean over close to the food in order to identify it, and so will breathe over it. If food must be served this way, keep it covered or identify verbally each food to the visually impaired person.

Mobility

Mobility is often affected by sensory impairment. In the RNIB/Office of National Statistics Survey (Vale and Smyth 2003), a fifth of visually impaired people over 75 had not been outside, even in their own garden, in the week before the interview. Seven per cent had not been out in the last year.

It is easy to understand how finding it hard to see makes it difficult to move about safely, but hearing impairment also affects mobility because it may affect balance and because we rely on our hearing to warn us of danger, particularly when we are out in traffic. Rose, who is both visually and hearing impaired, was knocked down outside her day-care centre by a car reversing round the corner – she did not see it, and could not hear it coming either until it was too late.

> 'Impaired vision and hearing are important risk factors for imbalance and perhaps falls and injury.' *(Gerson et al 1989)*

Someone with poor vision is almost twice as likely to fall than a sighted person. This means not only that they may injure themselves – broken hips being a very likely outcome – but also that they may rapidly lose confidence in their mobility. They may give up moving around or going out, for fear of falling again. Falls are often cited as a significant factor in someone's decision to move out of their home and into residential care. Given the links between sensory impairment and falls, it is clearly imperative to take mobility extremely seriously.

> 'Mobility is a major issue for older blind and partially sighted people, with six in every ten never going out on their own.' *(RNIB/ Health Promotion England 2001)*

One reason for sensory-impaired people losing mobility is the unpredictability of their environment. Providing a safe environment is looked at in Chapter 12.

Exercise

Exercise is a key factor in preventing accidents and loss of independence, because it increases mobility. It can help to maintain bone density, muscle strength, flexibility, balance and coordination.

Lack of mobility leads to greater frailty, and thus even less mobility – so the impaired person enters a vicious circle. People with a sensory impairment are very likely to reduce their activity level because of their fear of falling and because of their dislike of going out, which means that they need to be encouraged to take part in activities and to exercise if they are to keep safe and independent.

There is no reason why a person with a sensory impairment cannot exercise – it just needs to be carefully planned, in consultation with the impaired person, and it should take place in a safe, well-lit environment. Any teacher must give clear verbal and visual instructions, and must help people by touch if they cannot see or hear well enough to receive these instructions.

Gill, senior carer in a care home, described one resident's enjoyment of an exercise-to-music group that she runs:

> 'She used to sit there oblivious, and always refused a hearing aid. But recently she's asked for one so that she can join in our movement class.'

Guiding

When working with someone with poor sight, you may need sometimes to help them to find their way by guiding them. Untrained people may be worried about guiding someone properly, so it is best if every member of staff receives training in guiding techniques. Below are the basic rules to good guiding.

- Always ask the visually impaired person first, to see whether they would like you to help.
- Stand slightly in front of them and ask them to grip your arm just above the elbow. If they are sitting down, do not pull them up but allow them to stand up themselves.
- Keep your arm by your side, and walk at a normal pace.
- In a narrow space, you will need to walk in single file: ask the person to walk behind you with their arm out straight so that they do not trip over your feet (see Figure 11.1).
- To change sides, first stand still. Ask the person you are guiding to move across behind you, keeping in contact with you until they can hold your other arm.
- Going through a door is easier if the person you are guiding stands next to you, nearest to the hinge. Open the door with your guiding arm, and let the person you are guiding feel along your arm for the door so that they can hold it with their free hand.
- When you need to go up or down stairs, pause before you start and tell the person you are guiding whether the stairs go up or down. They need to be on the handrail side, and you need to help them to put their hand on it. Set off, keeping one step ahead. (Figure 11.2 illustrates the procedure.) At the end, pause and tell them that was the last step.
- When crossing a road, pause briefly before stepping on and off the pavement.
- When helping someone to a seat, put your guide hand on the back of the chair and let the person you are guiding slide their hand down to feel the chair and then the seat. Never push someone down on to a chair.
- Before getting into a car, tell the person you are guiding which way the car faces. Put your guide hand on the door handle so that the person can feel down for the handle themselves. If they then find the roof with their other hand, they can open the door, duck their head and find the seat themselves, and sit down, swinging their legs after them. They may need help finding the seat belt.
- When you leave someone after guiding them, make sure they know where they are, and say goodbye.

(Thanks to the Kent Association for the Blind for these guidelines.)

Figure 11.1 When guiding someone in a narrow space, you should lead; if they keep their arm straight out, they won't tread on your heels. (Reproduced by permission of the Kent Association for the Blind)

Figure 11.2 When guiding someone up or down stairs, you should keep one step ahead. Take your time, and tell the person when you reach the last step. (Reproduced by permission of the Kent Association for the Blind))

Guide dogs and hearing dogs

Although relatively few people have a guide dog or a hearing dog, an assistance dog can transform a person's life. There is no upper age limit for having a dog, although it is important to be physically active – the dog needs to go out every day – and to be able to look after and work with a dog.

Guide dogs help a blind or partially sighted person by leading the way, stopping at kerbs, dealing with traffic, and helping their owner to avoid obstacles. A hearing dog alerts its profoundly deaf or severely hard-of-hearing owner to sounds such as the doorbell, telephone or alarms. A guide or hearing dog can also give its owner the confidence to leave the house without help from others – this is especially useful if they live alone.

> 'I see a chap who stopped going out because his hearing is so poor. He's getting a hearing dog, which will enable him to overcome his fear and go out.' *Alex Willoughby, Hearing Therapist*

If you meet someone with a working dog, do not pat or offer titbits to the dog when it is working (it will be wearing its harness), as this will distract it.

Rose, who is blind and hard of hearing, is getting a semi-trained hearing dog, because her own dog has gone deaf like her. Proper hearing dogs learn not to bark, but her semi-trained one failed the course and barks, which is what she wants – it will tell her when the doorbell rings.

Canes

> 'Carrying a white cane can be helpful to a person with low vision. However, it is understandably a major decision for a person to make.' *Ann Lewis, KAB*

A visually impaired person may use a cane, either to identify themselves to others as visually impaired or to help them find their way. Some people refuse to use canes, however, because of the stigma they associate with them.

There are several different types of cane:

- Symbol cane: a 1 metre long, folding, white cane, which alerts others to someone's visual impairment.

- Walking stick/support cane: for people with less mobility. Some people will not use a support cane for fear that it makes them look vulnerable.
- Guiding cane: a folding cane, used to feel the way. It provides no support; it indicates that the user is visually impaired, and is usually used by people with some useful residual vision.
- Long cane: often used by people with active lives and good mobility. Other people generally move out of the way for someone with a long cane; the user moves the cane to scan a body-width in front of them while they walk; users can walk quite fast with them. It is possible to train people who are less mobile to use a long cane.
- Red and white cane: for people with dual impairment. Not many are issued, and, although recognition of them is in the *Highway Code*, few people know what they mean.

Not all local authorities automatically provide white canes free of charge, and training to use them is not always available. The RNIB/Office of National Statistics Survey (Vale and Smyth 2003) found that only 12 per cent of blind people surveyed had lessons in how to use a cane.

> 'I phoned up the Society for the Blind and someone just came and gave me a white stick and I stood at the kerb and I thought cars would stop if they saw a person with a white cane, but they didn't ... They didn't say what you had to do with it or anything. They just gave it to me and that was that, and I thought well, this is no good to me.'
> *Belinda Longhurst*

Getting out and about

One of the most significant effects of any sensory loss is on people's ability to get out and about. Travelling easily depends, in our society, on being able to see bus numbers, to hear station announcements, to cross the road – innumerable skills, in fact, which are affected by sensory impairment. Increasing numbers of older people also travel regularly, whether on holiday or to visit friends and family – and many of them have a sight or hearing impairment.

'Travelling by train is fraught with dangers. I was travelling with my sister and we got on the train and sat down. The train didn't move. An announcement was made to the effect the train had broken down – my sister translated this for me! If my sister had not been with me I wouldn't have had a clue what was going on, and would have missed my train home and been unable to tell them where I was.' *Nora Cooper*

Planning ahead

Travel information is notoriously difficult for sensory-impaired people to access: timetables in small print, arrivals boards high up, distorted announcements, announcements of platform changes made only verbally so that deaf or hard-of-hearing people do not receive them, and so on. There are countless horror stories, but also many tales of success. If at all possible, the key to a stress-free journey is to plan ahead, buy tickets in advance and warn staff that the traveller will need help. For a longer journey, the traveller should also, ideally, have a hearing or seeing companion with them.

To find out times of trains, buses and coaches, there is a telephone and web information service, Traveline (see page 294). On the other hand, if someone regularly uses a particular service, they may find it useful to enlarge the relevant timetable on a photocopier.

En route

When asking for information in a station or on a bus or train, it can be useful for a deaf or hard-of-hearing person to take a pen and paper for place names, times and prices. If a sensory-impaired person cannot see their stop or hear it announced, they should ask to be told personally, making it clear that they cannot hear or see general announcements.

Taxis and community transport

If public transport is completely impractical – or does not exist – some people turn to taxis, which have the advantage of providing a door-to-door service. They are, however, much more expensive than public transport, especially in rural areas. Neither are they ideal for trips to hospitals and clinics: it would be extremely expensive to ask them to wait but, equally, there is often a long wait for another taxi on the return journey. For this reason, many local authorities and voluntary organisations provide a community transport service.

Rose needs to go to the local hospital regularly to see the specialist about her eyes but, as it is on the edge of town, it is hard to get there. The buses often drop passengers off on the other side of a busy road, so she started going by taxi – expensive, but at least she was delivered to the door. Her doctor has now referred her to a local organisation that takes her to the hospital and then waits to bring her home again.

If someone is in a care home and needs to visit the hospital, the hospital should provide transport.

Discounts

Fare reductions vary from place to place. In some areas, all older people are given free or discounted bus and train passes. In others, fares are reduced for blind and partially sighted people, or for all people with a disability. Some sensory-impaired people may be eligible for a Disabled Person's Rail Card. It is always worth finding out.

Accompanying someone with a sensory impairment

If you accompany someone with a visual impairment, perhaps to go shopping or to the dentist, remember that they will not be able to find you if you become separated: it is up to you to find them.

Local authorities run 'Blue Badge' schemes, which offer parking concessions to passengers who are registered blind or who have great difficulty in walking.

Leisure

Wavertree House is a care home that caters specifically for people with a visual impairment. Yet the activities it offers residents are varied and wide ranging, and include painting, wood carving and exercise classes. They have been carefully thought out – painting can be done freehand or with stencils, and woodcarving is a tactile activity for which vision is barely necessary.

Any care home or day-care centre needs to ensure that it offers a range of activities, and that all residents are encouraged to join in, no matter what impairment they have. This section looks briefly at three popular activities, to show the kinds of adaptations that can be made to make them accessible to everyone: sewing and knitting, painting and television.

However, while it can be rewarding to continue a lifelong activity – such as sewing or painting – despite a visual impairment, some people do not wish to carry on once they cannot see. If they previously worked to a high standard, or level of complexity, they may be disappointed by the results now, or they may find working at a very simple level extremely dull.

When setting up many of these activities you will need to provide good light. This is covered in Chapter 12.

Sewing and knitting

It would be only too easy to take over the task of sewing from someone with a visual impairment but, if they have some residual vision, they may well still be able to carry out simple tasks such as sewing on a button or taking up a hem.

Using contrast is essential: before starting work, suggest that the person puts a blanket over their lap that contrasts well with the fabric and materials they are working with, so that they can see them and locate any dropped items.

Threading a needle is probably one of the hardest parts of sewing for an older person with a visual impairment – especially if they also have arthritis or other problems with their hands. Fortunately, a special needle-threading device is available. It is best to use large needles for both sewing and knitting.

Measuring tape can be marked off with staples at useful intervals, perhaps one every inch and two staples to mark every foot. Pins should have coloured extra-large heads.

Knitting is more difficult, because of the challenge of counting stitches by feel. A skilful knitter may well be able to do this, however, and may benefit from using brightly coloured needles that contrast with colour of the wool.

Painting

Although it can seem strange, it is entirely possible for someone to paint despite a visual impairment. They may, however, need to adapt their technique or change their subjects.

It is easiest to choose subjects that remain static so that the painter does not have to keep refocusing – working from a photograph can be a good option. It is also easier to work in a medium with good contrast such as charcoal on white paper, or acrylic paints, which have strong colours, and to use a large canvas and brushes.

Some people work with a magnifier to enlarge their work, or even CCTV (see Chapter 9).

Television

People with sensory impairments often find watching television particularly frustrating. Their difficulties can make them feel cut off from entertainment, from information and news, and from sitting watching together with their family or friends. There are, fortunately, many ways of making it easier for people with sensory impairments to enjoy television.

Everyone needs to watch television in good light, which must be even, with no glare or reflections from lights or windows. It is better not to watch in the dark, as this creates too much contrast. Someone with a visual impairment should try sitting as close as possible to the television – it will not do any harm. They should also try changing the position of the chair they sit in to watch television, as they may find they can see more from some angles than from others.

It is worth experimenting with the colour and contrast buttons on the set to find the best picture. Some people find it easier to watch in black and white because of the contrast. One lady even found it easier to wear dark glasses – they seemed to cut out many of the confusing patterns and colours, so that she could make out the basic outlines of people. It can also be useful to use talking Teletext and easy-to-see remote controls.

> 'We have a video afternoon several times a week where we all go into the lounge with popcorn and all that. You can always tell the ones who can't hear because they're looking around. We just turn the volume up.' *Gill, Senior Carer, care home*

Gill's solution, however, is not ideal. It is true that, for many of us, the first sign of a hearing impairment is needing to turn up the volume on the radio or television. This may work to some extent, but can be extremely annoying to other people. A far more effective way of enabling both hearing and hard-of-hearing people to enjoy the television and radio is to use a loop system or other listening device. These are described in Chapter 9.

SUBTITLES

For people who are hard of hearing, one of the greatest frustrations is the level of background noise and music in almost all TV programmes, which makes it hard for them to follow speech. For this reason, subtitles are very popular. There are various ways to access them, depending on whether you have analogue or digital TV, and whether you use terrestrial, satellite or cable digital TV. For up-to-date information, including how to record subtitles, ask the RNID for the factsheet 'Subtitles on television, DVDs and videotapes'.

> 'Recently we lost the sound on our main TV. As I was virtually the only user of this set, I decided I would use subtitles. Well! What a difference – I must have been missing most of the dialogue on TV for years and years.' *Garry MacDonell*

VIDEO CAPTION READERS

Many prerecorded videos carry the caption symbol (Figure 11.3), which indicates that it has close-caption subtitles added to help people with hearing difficulties to follow the film. A video caption reader enables a standard video player to read these captions.

Figure 11.3 Video films that have closed captions added display this symbol.

Many DVDs also have subtitles; details are given on the DVD box. You do not need special equipment to see subtitles on a DVD.

VIDEOS AND DVDS

Audio-described videos are recorded with a spoken description of what is happening on the screen, alongside the dialogue. These are available to buy or rent. RNIB Customer Services (contact details on pages 288–289) will send a home video catalogue. Some audio-described DVDs are also available from ordinary retail outlets. The audio description is accessed via the on-screen menu, which might not be easy for some visually impaired people to use.

BBC LICENCE

Anyone who is registered blind can get a 50 per cent reduction on their BBC licence – they just need to take their registration certificate to the post office when they pay for a new licence. Anyone over 75 is eligible for a free licence.

LISTINGS

Both the *TV Times* and the *Radio Times* are available on tape from the Talking Newspaper Association (see Chapter 10). Some networks also provide their listings by phone.

Telephones, reading and writing

These aspects are covered in Chapter 10.

Time

A problem commonly experienced by visually impaired people is that of keeping track of the time, and some can become quite disorientated without this ability. It is therefore well worth considering ways of keeping visually impaired people you work with aware of the time.

Someone with hearing difficulties has no trouble keeping track of the time, as long as they are awake – their main problem is not hearing the alarm on a clock. To solve this problem, there are flashing alarms and vibrating alarms, which have a pad that goes under the pillow.

There are many watches and clocks available. They are mentioned briefly here so that you are aware of the kinds of equipment that may be useful to the people you work with, and which you may feel would be worth obtaining, either privately or through social services.

Clocks

Talking clocks can be very useful, although it is worth remembering that they are usually powered by the mains, and tend to revert to midnight if the power is interrupted – which the visually impaired person may not be aware of. A striking clock is an excellent way to help visually impaired people keep track of the time, and they may also find it a useful sound by which to orientate themselves in space.

If you are choosing a new clock for a public space, look for one that has a large face and clear numbers that contrast well with their background, and place it somewhere that people can easily get close to. If you do not already have a chiming clock, this would be a good option, but avoid having several of them – this will make orientation hard for visually impaired people and will irritate deaf or hard-of-hearing people.

Watches

There are special watches whose face can be opened so that a visually impaired person can feel the dial. This may be useful, although bear in mind that the person you work with may not have enough sensitivity in their fingers to do this. They may find a regular watch with a large face and black numbers on a white background easier to use.

Vibrating watches work like standard watches but have a vibrating alarm for people with hearing problems. Some have timers that vibrate at set intervals, which can be useful for reminding the wearer to take medication.

Safety and alerting devices

Smoke alarms

People who cannot hear well may not be alerted to the danger of fire by a standard fire or smoke alarm. Specially designed smoke alarms use a range of methods for alerting people: these alarms may be connected to flashing lights, a loud audio alarm or a vibrating pad (useful for night-time and for dual-impaired people). Social services and some local fire brigades provide and install smoke alarms for deaf people over 65.

Under the Disability Discrimination Act, service providers must ensure that users or residents who are deaf or hard of hearing will be warned of danger.

Doorbells and phones

People who are hard of hearing may not be able to hear the doorbell or phone. You may be able to help them to hear it by installing a louder bell or by adding extra bells in different rooms. If this does not help, a system linked to a table lamp, flashing strobe light or pager might be more helpful. These systems may be wired or wireless; in the latter case, they use radio signals.

Pagers are directly connected to doorbells, telephones, smoke alarms or alarm clocks. They may vibrate and/or give a visual signal, or may produce a loud audible alert. Pick-up systems work like baby alarms (some actually were designed as baby alarms): the user places the transmitter close to the doorbell or whatever they want to hear, and will then be able to hear it ring or see it flash through the receiver, wherever they are in the house or garden.

Some doorbells cause the house lights to dim or flash when the bell is rung. Some can be used with door entry systems, such as those used in communal entrances.

Social services may provide doorbells and phones for people with sensory impairments.

Money

Being able to manage one's own money is a crucial part of maintaining one's independence. You should therefore be sensitive and patient while someone deals with their own money. Someone with a visual impairment may need to learn some new skills, with the help of staff.

When it comes to cash, UK coins and notes are all of different sizes and shapes and, in the case of coins, of different metals. This makes it easier for visually impaired people to sort, although it may be a time-consuming process.

It may be worth helping someone to practise counting money, to give them confidence in their ability to do it. They may find it useful to use a coin sorter. It can also make things faster and less worrying if they develop the habit of folding each note in a different way, so that they can be confident that they are giving the right money, and perhaps carrying a small dark cloth on which to sort their money.

Continuing to manage their own finances is extremely important to most people. While they have some vision, they may find large-print statements useful – they might also find it useful to enlarge letters and accounts using a reading machine, or by photocopying them (see Chapter 10). Cheque book and pension book templates are also available, which make it easier to fill in and sign in the right places.

Voting

People who are registered blind can vote by post or by proxy, or can be helped at the polling station. The local town hall should have information about this.

Equipment and equipment suppliers

Many day-to-day problems resulting from a sensory impairment can be addressed without recourse to specialist equipment, and in fact often should be. It is all too easy for workers with sensory-impaired people to supply them with gadgets rather than taking the time to listen to what they really need.

> 'It is often mistakenly assumed that everyone with visual disabilities needs special equipment. In fact, its use should normally only be considered after a rehabilitation worker has assessed a service user's potential for adapting to new ways of tackling everyday tasks, preferably using his/her own familiar equipment and utensils.' *(Williams 1994)*

> 'Older people may be issued with a cane or loop but given little guidance and training in their use.' *Beryl Palmer, Manager, Sensory Disabilities Services*

However, some special equipment can be extremely valuable, and is mentioned in the relevant sections of this book. This section sets out how and where to find it. There is no need to look for equipment specifically designed for care settings: something designed for domestic settings is generally suitable.

To find out about equipment:

- visit a low-vision or hearing clinic;
- visit a resource centre, perhaps run by social services or a local voluntary organisation;
- contact social services – individuals can refer themselves.

Gadgets can be cheap – an eye drop dispenser, for example, may only cost a couple of pounds. But some equipment is expensive and beyond the means of many individuals, although it may be available on loan from social services. Before being issued with social services equipment, the individual will need to be assessed. If they have a visual impairment, they may have to be registered blind before becoming eligible for assessment.

Social services departments vary enormously in what they can provide to people with sensory impairments, and their list of available equipment changes constantly. The assessment process is described in Chapter 16.

Ageism is very evident in this area. Older people tend to receive little equipment – as a standard, someone with a visual impairment might receive a white cane, a magnifier and a teapot tipper. In many parts of the UK, there is a rigid cut-off point for eligibility for certain items – so someone with a hearing impairment may be eligible for a flashing alarm clock until they become 65, but, from then on, they are deemed no longer to need one.

Because older people are often on a low income, they may not be able to afford additional equipment. Voluntary organisations for people with vision or hearing difficulties may be able to lend equipment, or it may be possible to find funding from a source such as the Royal British Legion or other ex-servicemen's organisations. Whether people in care homes are eligible for equipment loans from social services varies from area to area but it is worth asking. If they are not eligible, they and the care home are responsible for bearing the cost of any equipment they need.

If a sensory-impaired person is of working age, it may be worth investigating the government's Access to Work scheme, which helps with the cost of equipment, communication support and adaptations to the working environment. Access to Work is administered by local Disability Service Teams, which can be located via the JobCentre.

Service providers need to be aware of the provisions of the Disability Discrimination Act. This sets out their responsibility for ensuring equal access to all services by all users. This might include, for example, providing a loop system for hard-of-hearing users. The Act is covered in more detail in Chapter 18.

Summary of sources of equipment

- Local social services may be able to lend equipment.
- Local voluntary organisations for people with vision or hearing difficulties may lend equipment, or have a range to inspect before buying.

- The RNIB and the RNID both have extensive catalogues of equipment to buy.
- Commercial suppliers – talk to your local organisations for recommendations; some suppliers also rent out equipment. There are local and national loop installation companies: the RNID has a Directory of Services, which includes a list of loop installers; this is available on their website and from their Information Line.

12 The environment

This chapter outlines the effect of the physical world on sensory impairments, and suggests practical ways to improve our environments for all users. In particular, the following areas are covered:

- Meeting everyone's needs
- Simulating sensory impairment
- The environment and hearing impairment
- The environment and visual impairment
- Size
- Lighting
- Contrast
- Planning ahead
- Orientation
- Obstacles and other hazards
- Doors, floors and windows
- Handrails and steps
- A room-by-room assessment of your environment
- Gardens and outside

When we plan spaces for older people, few of us give any thought to how these plans might affect those with a sensory impairment. Yet the colours we choose, the furnishings, the lighting and the layout all have an impact on our senses.

One group of residents with dual sensory loss reported that they found it extremely difficult to tell where they were in their care home, at least partly because it had such long featureless corridors. They were enormously relieved when a crack appeared in the wall, providing a much-needed clue to their whereabouts.

Many older sensory-impaired people also have problems with mobility. It is not unusual for them to stop going out alone at all. This is especially the case if they have a long-term illness or other disabilities.

> 'I can't go out, of course; I never go out. I think that's mostly due to old age. I can't walk, you see. All the same, the sight and the hearing don't help. I won't dare go out by myself ... I can't go to the length of the garden now and I can't get around the room without a stick. You can't have a stick in your hand all the time, so I pull myself around the furniture.' *Ivy Cook*

Impaired vision and hearing are important risk factors for lack of balance, falls and injuries. Falling can be frightening and, although the fall may not cause injury, it can lead to a significant loss of confidence. For example, Martin Trevor, aged 89, is now both visually and hearing impaired, and suffers from confusion and depression. His wife says: 'He spent three weeks in bed before Christmas, because he had two falls. He didn't hurt himself but it frightened him.' He will now no longer leave the house.

When planning an environment for older sensory-impaired people, therefore, we must, above all, make it safe and easy for them to use.

Meeting everyone's needs

Sometimes there can be a conflict of interest between users of an environment with different needs. For example, while it can be effective to use sound clues to help visually impaired people find their way, too many sound clues will create uncomfortable levels of background noise for people with a hearing impairment.

Dementia can add another dimension to a sensory impairment. For example, someone with a visual impairment might welcome a contrasting floor surface to warn them that they have arrived at the top of a staircase. But if they also have dementia, they may be unable to interpret what they are seeing and become confused or even scared by what might appear to them to be a hole or a pool of water. (See also Chapter 13.)

Generally speaking, however, an environment that is designed in the interests of sensory-impaired people will also be accessible and pleasant to most other people.

Most of this chapter focuses on visual impairment, because a visual impairment makes it harder to interact with the physical environment. It is none the less also important to bear in mind the needs of users with a hearing or any other impairment when planning your environment.

Simulating sensory impairment

To help you to imagine or investigate what it is like for someone with a sensory impairment to use your service, you can simulate their impairment. You can do this using Simspecs (a range of spectacles that simulate various eye conditions; supplied by Visual Impairment North East, contact details on page 295) and muffling headphones. You can buy these, or perhaps borrow them from a local voluntary organisation. Put them on, and then try to carry out all the normal tasks and activities in which users participate in your environment. This should enable you to see where some changes can be made – many of them as simple as not leaving the chairs out from the table after a meal, where someone with glaucoma will almost certainly walk into them.

Although we can simulate a sensory loss, we can never replicate it fully – and we certainly cannot replicate the way an individual experiences the impairment, either physically or emotionally. Before you make any changes, ask the person with a sensory impairment what needs to be altered or rearranged. They know, from first-hand experience.

The environment and hearing impairment

Few environments are ideal for someone with a hearing loss but some are better than others. Unfortunately, it is rare for a day-care centre or care home to be designed with hearing impairment in mind. Particular problems commonly include:

- a location in a busy area with considerable traffic noise outside;
- poor sound insulation against outside noise;
- poor acoustics inside, with little use of acoustic tiles, carpets and curtains to baffle noise;
- poor lighting (makes lipreading difficult);
- noisy machines such as extractor fans and washing machines near to areas used by service users or residents;
- architecture involving high ceilings and bare walls that produce echo and resonance;
- 'magnetic noise' from electrical equipment, which can cause interference on hearing aids set to 'T'.

While you can do nothing about a noisy location, there is plenty that can be done to minimise noise and make hearing easier inside. Solutions might include measures to improve the acoustics such as acoustic tiles, carpets and curtains; insulation against outside noise; relocation of noisy equipment or of activities near to those machines; and provision of aids to listening such as induction loops (see also Chapter 9).

Acoustics

All shiny, hard surfaces make noise bounce around and echo, which makes it difficult for a hard-of-hearing person to make sense of the sounds that they hear. Unfortunately, many communal environments for older people feature polished floors and tables and bare walls, so their acoustics are often terrible for hard-of-hearing people. Bathrooms are especially bad. You may have noticed that a particular user is happier in one bathroom rather than another – this could be because of its acoustics.

The answer to this problem is to use non-reverberant materials such as carpets, tablecloths and curtains on most surfaces, with a degree of caution. Rarely, overuse of such surfaces has muffled sound to an uncomfortable extent, even though it produced a better environment for hearing speech.

Shared accommodation

A feature of communal living is, of course, communal rooms – living rooms and dining rooms in particular – where noise levels tend to be high. To some extent this cannot be avoided because the very nature of these rooms means that they contain a large number of people, and often televisions, radios and stereos as well. This can, however, make them a very difficult environment for people with hearing impairments, who suffer particularly from high noise levels and find it hard to distinguish speech against background noise.

Staff should automatically adjust televisions, radios and stereos in such rooms to the lowest useful level and then make sure that hard-of-hearing people have access to systems, such as induction loops (see Chapter 9), that enable them to listen at a volume that suits them; those without aids can be encouraged to use specialist listening aids. This environment will, however, still be too noisy for many hard-of-hearing people to comfortably hold a conversation. Ideally, therefore, there should be a quiet room or area set aside where people can sit and read or talk quietly without other activities, television or music.

The environment and visual impairment

If you have used Simspecs to mimic the effects of a visual impairment, you will have realised how hard it can be for a visually impaired person to find their way around your environment and to participate easily in the life of their community.

There are four main ways to make your environment more visible:

- Make things larger.
- Improve the lighting.
- Use strong contrast.
- Use clear bright colours.

Each of these techniques is explored below.

Size

Clearly, the larger something is, the easier it is to see. We can make things bigger, for example by using large print on our menus, signs, calendars, phone dials and clocks. We can also help people to make things seem bigger by using magnifiers and getting up close to things. For example, we can encourage people to move closer to the television, and we can move clocks, signs and so on down to eye level so that people can get close to them.

Lighting

Good lighting is absolutely essential for good vision – without light, we cannot see. Older people often need more light than younger people, and people with a visual impairment need even more. They also find variations in light and glare hard to deal with.

Light not only enables us to see – it can help establish where we are, especially when used with decoration to provide good clues. Lighting should therefore be central to all your environmental plans.

Light levels

Lighting needs to be suited to the task, and carefully considered throughout a building. You may be able to identify problem areas simply by observing the people in them: for example, does someone with a visual impairment walk more confidently into the dining room in the mornings than in the evenings? Could it be the result of poor lighting levels in the evening?

Many people with low vision find that it takes them a while for their eyes to adapt when they move from bright to dark places – they need the level of light to be consistent throughout the building. It also needs to be appropriate.

Bright light is ideal for task work such as writing a cheque, chopping carrots, ringing the doctor or plugging in the kettle. However, because older eyes often find it harder to adjust to changes in lighting levels, beware of providing excellent task lighting but leaving the rest of the room in relative darkness. Watching television – itself a very bright light source – is often done in near darkness to reduce reflection; it is important to light the rest of the room, too.

Good ambient lighting is best achieved not by high power but by bouncing the light off surfaces such as walls, ceilings and tables. If people want less light, it is better to use dimmers and change the overall light level than to turn off overhead lights, leaving only side lights, as this creates uneven light levels.

Do not forget to light the corridors and stairs as well as the main rooms: leaving a well-lit bedroom to go down dark stairs could spell disaster. Ideally, there should be a switch for the light at both the top and the bottom of any staircase. Note that the light on stairs should highlight the treads, not the risers, so that people can see where to put their feet. Open-tread stairs are terribly hard for a visually impaired person to see.

Lighting contrasts cannot always be avoided: they occur whenever we look into a bright patch of light on the lawn, come in from the night into a lit room, or face any kind of glare – on a mirror, a piece of cutlery or a white shirt. But to someone with a visual impairment, such contrasts can be uncomfortable, or even painful.

Glare

Glare is caused either by light coming from many different sources at once or by light being reflected on a broken surface. It may cause particular problems to someone with cataracts: the effect has been likened to that experienced when driving in bright sunlight with a dirty windscreen – the light is shattered by the specks of dirt, and makes it impossible to see. But if the car enters a tunnel of trees, the light from above is cut out, and the driver can again see clearly. This might explain why some people say they see better when wearing a hat. A peaked or brimmed hat can help someone who finds the light outside too bright – often it is light from above or the sides that causes discomfort.

Many people, particularly those with cataracts, need diffused light to help them see more comfortably. Good shades on lights will help reduce glare and will be far more comfortable than bright bare bulbs. The light source should also be behind people, unless they need to look closely at something.

When assessing your environment, look out for surfaces that might cause glare, such as shiny floors, mirrors, tiles, polished table tops and gloss paint. It may be possible to cover or repaint them.

Table lights, standard lamps and adjustable lamps

Table lights and standard lamps rarely give enough light for close-up work such as reading or sewing, and cannot be adjusted. If you do use standard or table lamps, try to use shades with a white lining that will reflect more light on to what needs to be seen. For close work, however, you are better choosing an adjustable lamp that can be pointed towards the required area.

The best position for an adjustable lamp is between the person and the object they want to look at. It is important that the light be near to the task, but take care that the shade does not become too hot or the person may burn themselves when adjusting it. There is no need for a 100 watt bulb – it will probably give off too much heat and be expensive to run – 60 watts is plenty.

Bulbs

Different types of bulb produce different types of light. They also use different amounts of electricity, and some stay cool while others become extremely hot.

FILAMENT BULBS

Filament bulbs are the most common. They are usually balloon-shaped. Their brightness depends on the number of watts – the higher the number, the brighter it will be. Filament bulbs become very hot and use more electricity than do fluorescent bulbs. For safety reasons, never use a higher wattage bulb than the light fitting or shade can take.

Bulbs may be made of clear, frosted, white or coloured glass, which also affects their brightness. Clear bulbs can be uncomfortably bright, whilst frosted and white bulbs provide a light with softer shadows, lose very little light and are more comfortable. Blue bulbs (which are more expensive) give off a particularly white light, called 'daylight', which some people prefer.

FLUORESCENT BULBS

Fluorescent bulbs are more expensive to buy than filament bulbs but have many advantages: they are cheaper to run, they do not get hot and they last up to eight times longer and give off five times more light than filament bulbs of the same wattage. They are also available in daylight colours.

HALOGEN LIGHTS

Halogen lights are very bright, which can be useful. However, they are expensive to buy, use a large quantity of electricity and become very hot.

Daylight

During the day, it is worth making the most of the sun through a window – move chairs so that light comes in over the shoulder of the person and on to their work or book. Ideally, this should be a permanent arrangement – it is not practical to have to change one's position according to the time of day in order to see adequately. Beds and televisions should also face away from the window. Ensure that you have not placed someone with their back to a window but facing a mirror, as this will reflect glare straight into their face.

In the daytime, keep the curtains open to make the most of the light – use lightweight nets if you need privacy, and keep them clean. Keep windows clean, too, and paint window frames and walls a light colour.

Contrast and colour

You may have noticed the effect of contrast without realising it: perhaps one of your clients always reaches out for the bright green cup as opposed to the white one, or prefers the chair with a multi-coloured cushion. It could be that they choose these because they can see them better, because they contrast with their background. Figure 12.1 has an example of good contrast and poor contrast.

Figure 12.1 The white spot shows up much more than the grey spot.

What about the room itself? If all your walls, doors and door handles are white, a visually impaired person will probably find it hard to tell them apart. If, on the other hand, your doors are white but the frames and handles are dark blue, the contrast between light and dark makes it far easier to see the door.

Contrast, therefore, is an extremely effective way of helping people to make the most of their sight. There are two elements to contrast: colour and tone. This means that, although a dark green door in a dark red frame provides colour contrast, it does not provide any tonal contrast – it would be more effective for the door to be pale and the frame to be dark, or vice versa. Pale or pastel colours are also difficult to distinguish from each other. Visually impaired people find clear and bright colours much easier to tell apart.

As part of your rolling programme of maintenance and redecoration, it is well worth incorporating contrast. Although you might only decorate one room at first – perhaps the living room, or the bedroom of a person with a visual disability, you should be aiming eventually to create a consistent system where colour and contrast are used in the same way throughout your environment. So you might plan ahead for all toilets to have the same coloured door, for example. This consistency of approach should apply to all aspects of the environment, so that, ideally, stair handrails should not only all be of the same colour but should also use the same tactile clue to mark the start and finish of steps.

Where to start

If you want to improve a room without total redecoration, you could start with the doors, light switches and sockets.

You can either paint the whole door to contrast with the wall, or just the frame. The best light switches and sockets are coloured ones with a matt finish, available from a specialist supplier. As a cheaper (although less effective) alternative, use shiny coloured ones, available from DIY stores. Alternatively, and cheaper still, buy coloured fingerplates to identify where the switch is, or use coloured masking tape (although this will eventually peel off), paint a border round the switch, or remove the switch to spray it.

Planning ahead

When you next plan to redecorate a room, think about why it is decorated the way it is, and the effect this has on its users. Although white or magnolia paint are popular because they make rooms feel bright, white walls can also cause glare – use pale colours instead. It is also easier to distinguish walls, doors, skirting and ceilings from each other if they are in contrasting shades. A border can help to make the walls stand out.

Many care homes and centres use floral print carpets and soft furnishings but these create a difficult background for people with a visual impairment. Objects contrast better against a plain background or subtle pattern. To create interest, you can use colour or pattern on small items such as cushions.

In fact, when Sandra Cronin, of the RNIB, talks to home managers about redecoration in a way that is friendly to visually impaired people, she sometimes finds that it is not money that stops them changing their look but a concern that reducing pattern and using contrasting colours will make their home look garish, odd and institutionalised. However, when they have made changes, they have found that environments that incorporate good use of colour and contrast look stylish and attractive.

Designing for sensory impairment in practice: orientation

While colour and contrast can provide vital clues to location for a visually impaired person, there are also other techniques that can help.

Texture

An attractive way of providing a landmark for people with visual impairment can be to use an embossed wallpaper border halfway down a wall, for people to trail along with their hand. It can also be useful to change the texture of flooring to indicate location. For example, a change from carpet to lino at the top of a flight of stairs can warn people that they need to find the handrail.

This change in texture can be useful for people with a vision or a hearing loss: they will either be able to see the change or to hear the change in the sound of their footstep. If the texture change is sufficiently great, someone with a dual impairment will be able to feel the difference.

Sound clues

We can use sound to help people find their way. But sound clues need to be consistent – if a radio can be turned off or moved, it is not a reliable clue. Similarly, whilst the sound of a television set or a telephone ringing can help people to orientate themselves, this can be confusing if there are several of these in different places. Better clues might be a grandfather clock that ticks or a water feature that is always turned on.

Signage

Good signage is an essential feature of any communal environment – it is the main means of enabling people to find their way around an unfamiliar space, and also the way that news is posted. People need accessible signage everywhere, showing everything from fire exits and room directions to general information. Good signage uses the same principles of good design for visual impairment as we outlined above: size, lighting, contrast and colour.

Signs and notices should be big enough to see, using large print in upper and lower case rather than all capitals, and positioned at shoulder height, without any obstruction, so that people can get up close.

Signs need to be well lit, but designed to prevent glare. They should be on a matt surface, without a glass case. Contrast is vital again – white lettering on a black background works best and the sign should also contrast with the wall.

You also need to take into account your users' information needs. If they cannot read, because of loss of vision or mental faculty, you can try tactile signs or clear symbols in addition to large print – for example a knife and fork symbol next to the words 'Dining room'. Photographs can also work well – a familiar photograph from home on the door of someone with dementia can help them to recognise it. Users with no useful vision can find talking signs especially helpful if they are positioned where routes cross, to help them orientate themselves.

Keeping it simple

When we are at home, we probably barely use visual clues to find our way around: most of us can move around such a familiar environment with our eyes shut. Away from home, this is much harder, but people still learn non-visual clues in rooms and routes to help them to move about. If they use a particular room often, look at what routes they need to learn in order to get to and from it, and work with them to learn those routes. Ideally, each room will have a single function, so that it is easy to identify a room by what is going on in it. However, if a room is multi-functional, or is used for different things at different times, make sure that staff explain the changes. This is particularly important if the person also has dementia.

Creating a safe environment: obstacles and other hazards

When you plan your environment, it is essential that you remove all potential obstacles that a visually impaired person might trip or fall over, or walk into. Having planned your safe environment, you need to train all of your staff, service users and residents to keep it that way.

Some of the most common obstacles are:

- doors and windows left ajar;
- rubbish bins or bags;
- boxes and briefcases;
- fire extinguishers – these should be recessed into the wall;
- radiators that are too hot to touch – people may burn themselves, and cannot use them for orientation (it can help to use a radiator cover);
- radiators sticking out into a corridor;
- electrical and extension leads over floors;
- furniture that has been moved without notifying the person with a visual impairment;
- furniture that is hard to see – low stools and coffee tables;
- mats and rugs with edges to trip over.

Watch out for anything that overhangs – if it is higher than about 300mm, anyone using a cane will miss it. Likewise, someone trailing to find their way will not be aware of objects at head height.

A shadow can be an obstacle to someone who is visually impaired: they may find it very difficult to distinguish between that and an object lying across the pavement, or a big crack. They will have to treat all shadows with great caution until they have identified them.

Creating a safe environment: doors, floors and windows

Doors

Visually impaired people have two main problems with doors: identifying and using the correct door, and not walking into one by accident. The following hints can help:

- If doors swing open, for example on a cupboard, put a contrasting strip on the inside or outside edge of the door so that people can see when it has been left open.

- Doors should not open out on to corridors, passageways or hallways – people may walk into them.
- Hang all doors on the same side – so people can guess which way they will open, and can find their handles easily.
- Glass doors can be hard to see, whether they are open or closed. To make a closed door visible, attach a coloured transfer design at eye level – it should be at least 150mm square.
- Handles should be in a contrasting colour to the door in order to be visible.
- Identify doors using large print or other signs, and tactile clues such as a rubber band on a door handle or an adhesive Velcro patch on the door itself.

Floors

The main problem with floors for people with sensory impairments is that often they have a shiny or gloss finish. This not only creates glare and disturbing reflections but can also be mistaken for water, which is especially confusing for someone with dementia. Acoustically, a high gloss finish produces echo, and can also distort the sound reproduction of loop and infrared systems.

Windows

For someone with a visual impairment, the ideal window is clean with a pale frame, to let in as much light as possible. It will have blinds that keep out glare but do not block valuable light. If a window also has curtains, they should be in a contrasting colour to the wall – to help a visually impaired person find them – and should be distinctive – to help them to identify which room they are in.

Where a window is at the end of a corridor or passage, glare can cause a problem. In this case, use tinted glass or a blind. South-facing windows suffer worst from glare, but windows facing east and west will get low light in the mornings and evenings.

Windows left open are hard for visually impaired people to see, so they may easily bang their head on them or drop objects out of them by mistake. Try to ensure that people can see out of windows when they are sitting down, and that sills are kept clear.

Creating a safe environment: handrails and steps

Stairs and steps can be particularly dangerous for people with visual impairments, because they are often poorly lit (see also 'Lighting', page 178) and visually impaired people then find it difficult to see where the edge of each step is. The solution is to provide good lighting and to mark the edge of the step with paint or nosing that is in a contrasting colour and texture to the rest of the step (see Figure 12.2). This edging must be tough and non-detachable.

People not only need to be able to distinguish each step; they also need to know when they have reached the top or bottom of the stairs. You can indicate this either by providing a different type of flooring at the top and bottom or by an indicator on the banister rail.

Figure 12.2 A stairway with good contrast and clues for visually impaired people. (Reproduced by permission of the RNIB)

The handrail should be in definite contrast to the wall behind it and to wallpaper borders and dados. Ideally, it will have a long horizontal run at the top and bottom of the stairs, which gives the visually impaired person longer to anticipate the beginning and end of the stairs. A handrail should also return to the wall at the end of this run, but many do not. Rather than replace the rail, you can instead mark the end of the stairs on the handrail by attaching an upholstery pin to the inside of the rail so that a visually impaired person can feel it. Alternatively, you can use a coloured or textured tape.

A room-by-room assessment of your environment

Walk through the environment you work in, and check how it can be improved to help someone with a sensory impairment. Assess each space in your own environment according to the principles listed above, and watch your service users or residents as they move about. Then decide with them how you can improve their environment to minimise the effects of their impairment. Below are suggestions for particular areas of a building but they are far from comprehensive: you will probably come up with solutions of your own that work far better in your own environment.

Corridors

Corridors are often forgotten when planning an environment that is friendly to a sensory-impaired person. As always, you need to check for adequate light, whether it is natural or electric. Fire alarms and fire exits must be highly visible, and at eye level.

People use corridors to get from one location to another, so orientation is particularly important. You can help people to locate rooms by using colour and contrast on doors, and good signage (see Figure 12.3). You can help totally blind people by providing other indicators; for example, using only horizontal door handles for toilets, vertical handles for bathrooms, and so on.

Figure 12.3 A well-designed corridor. (Reproduced by permission of the RNIB)

Whilst you should avoid putting obstacles in corridors, a long one without features can be difficult for a visually impaired person to orientate themselves along. It is therefore helpful to provide clues along the way, such as a dado rail, signage, different materials on the wall or on a handrail, sound, flowers, ticking clocks, pot-pourri, or changes in air movement.

Halls and public waiting areas

Halls and public waiting areas are often large and disconcerting for someone with a visual impairment: they may find it hard to know which door is the toilet, which is the lift, and where they should go to make themselves known. If your reception area is large, you could try separating it into smaller sub-areas, using different light fittings, furniture or flooring in each. Department stores and hospitals use the same principles, often using different flooring and colour schemes to guide people through to key areas.

Lifts

Can your service users or residents find and use the controls in your lifts? Can they check which floor they are on? The following points are worth considering:

- Use the principles of good signage to create clear markings for the controls and to show which floor the lift is on.
- If possible, install a voice box that announces the floor number.
- Mark the floor of the lift and the floor of the entrance in contrasting colours, to help people to know where to step.
- Set the door-closing mechanism to allow people plenty of time to get in and out.

Bedrooms

Unlike other areas, which must serve a variety of needs, a bedroom can be tailored to the needs of a specific person. Work with that person to assess how you can improve their room. First of all, can that individual locate their own room? How do they identify it? Can they find the door, and the way to the toilet – especially at night?

Lack of lighting can make a continent person incontinent at night if they cannot easily get to the toilet. Low-level lighting (or a plug-in night light) is often the best way to help someone get up in the night without their eyes having to cope with significant light/dark adaptation. You could use a night light near the bed, another by the door to the corridor, and leave the toilet light on. If the person uses a bedside light, check that they can find the switch and turn the light on themselves from the bed.

The bed should colour contrast with the floor and walls, so that it can be located easily. Ideally, bed linen should be plain, with no large prints or colours, so that dropped objects can be found easily.

Furniture needs to be carefully chosen, and positioned so that people do not bump into it constantly. It should therefore be in a contrasting colour to the walls, and should have rounded edges. Furniture should never be moved unless at the resident or user's request, or in consultation with them: a visually impaired person relies largely on their memory to avoid walking into things.

Check that task lighting is provided, and ensure that the mirror is positioned so as not to reflect light from a bulb or sun from the window.

Bathrooms

We have seen how a bathroom with shiny surfaces creates poor sound quality (see page 176). Another effect of those shiny surfaces is glare. Because so much sanitary ware is white, it is also very likely that there is little contrast in a bathroom. Therefore bathrooms often need the most urgent attention to make them safe and comfortable for people with a sensory impairment.

The following points may be helpful to consider when designing and adapting a bathroom (see Figure 12.4):

- Use paint with a matt finish.
- Choose toilet-roll holders and towel and grab rails that contrast in colour to the walls. Alternatively, you can fix contrasting tiles behind these items.

Figure 12.4 A well-designed bathroom. (Reproduced by permission of the RNIB)

- When you buy new toilet seats, basins or tiles, choose colours that contrast with the fittings near them. For example, a black toilet seat works well on a white toilet.
- Choose bars of soap, toilet rolls and other toiletries in a contrasting colour to the walls, basin and toilet.
- Position mirrors so that people can get up close, and do not fix a shelf above the sink: it stops people reaching the mirror, and they are likely to bang their head on the shelf as they bend over the sink.
- Can people identify the emergency cord? It needs to look and feel different from the light pull. You could use a different shape and colour knob, and a thick cord to make it easier to see and grab.
- Tie brightly coloured material or ribbons to pull cords to make them easier to find.

Dining areas

Dining rooms can be particularly challenging for people with sensory impairments, as they are often noisy, crowded, cluttered with furniture and illogical in layout. These difficulties can be minimised, to make eating a pleasant and sociable event for all users, by taking the following into consideration:

- Keep the room well lit, with no glare: use tablecloths rather than leaving polished tables bare, and avoid shiny flooring.
- Avoid all shiny surfaces, to reduce the amount of unpleasant clattering noise for users who are hard of hearing.
- Ideally, each table should have its own additional lighting, such as a pull-down light.
- Use small tables – this enables users who are hard of hearing to sit close to those they would like to talk to, so that they can understand more of what their companions say, and to lipread more easily.
- Set out tables in a logical way, using a regular pattern. There should be enough space between the tables for a visually impaired person to pass with their guide (allow 1.2m for this).
- Use contrast – tables and chairs that contrast with the décor, coloured cushions that contrast with the chairs, napkins that contrast with the tablecloth, and place mats with a variety of different surfaces.
- Keep tables uncluttered, laid only with items needed for that meal.

- Choose cutlery that is easy to use with a visual impairment – for example, knives with an easily identifiable blade side.

Living areas

In any care setting, the majority of users will spend a large proportion of their time in communal sitting areas. In spite of this, such areas are rarely designed for the comfort of many of those with a sensory impairment.

In order to make your living areas good places to relax and socialise in, use the same principles as throughout the rest of the house. Start by assessing your living areas:

- How big is the room and what are the acoustics like? Can people hear?
- Is there continual background noise – is the television always on?
- Is the lighting even and without glare? Is there adequate task lighting?
- Can people find their way around the room easily and safely?

Just as for dining areas, you need to choose furniture that contrasts with the décor, and place it carefully and logically so that your users can find their way. As in the bedroom, you should never move the furniture without telling the users first. You should, as always, avoid clutter and other obstacles that people could trip over – this includes not choosing low furniture such as coffee tables, which are invisible to anyone with tunnel vision. See Figure 12.5 for an example of a well thought out living area.

Kitchen

If you work with people in their own homes, or in a care home where residents prepare some of their own food, you need to help them to create a safe environment. The tips listed below can help:

- Provide plain work surfaces – these are easier to use. They should contrast in colour or shade to the walls, floor, furniture and objects placed on them – especially those that may be hot, such as kettles.
- Cover shiny surfaces, for example with a tablecloth.
- Use paint or tape on the edges of surfaces and shelves to make them easier to see.
- Make sure that there is adequate room to put out equipment and use it safely without knocking other things over.

Figure 12.5 A well-designed and laid out living area. (Reproduced by permission of the RNIB)

- Provide easily identifiable objects – for example, avoid choosing a very modern design of kettle that an older person might find hard to recognise – especially if they have dementia as well as sight loss.
- Kitchens need good light, which should ideally be positioned near the work surface rather than on the ceiling – use clip-on spotlights or add under-cupboard lighting. Lighting needs to be especially good over the cooker.
- Avoid bare bulbs (including fluorescent strip lights) – these cause glare. If there is a central strip light, use a cover (a diffuser) to remove glare and spread the light more evenly.
- Avoid high cupboard doors that overhang the worktop – people walk into them when they are open. Take the doors off – this also makes it easier to see the cupboard's contents.

- Do not use glass shelves – they are difficult to see. But glass jars are useful for helping people to see their contents.
- Be aware of the special gadgets that are available, such as coloured chopping boards: use a dark one for chopping potatoes and a light one for green cabbage, for example. The RNIB catalogue lists many such gadgets for the kitchen.
- Fix stick-on markers to dials ('bump-ons', from the RNIB) to make appliances easier to see and feel, or attach labels written with a thick black marker pen. Some manufacturers provide specially adapted controls.

Gardens and outside

The same principles that you have applied to planning your interior environment are just as relevant and important to the outside. You need to ensure that everyone has safe access to the front door from the street, and that they can use the garden despite their impairment. Obstacles should be removed, and provision made for safe and visible surfaces to walk on, using contrast and other clues for orientation.

Gardens and other outside areas vary enormously, so you will need to make your own assessment of what is needed to make the most of yours. The hints below may help:

- Keep all pathways clear of obstructions such as hoses, flowerpots, weeds and potholes.
- Keep paving firm, even and level. It should not be cambered too much, as this affects people's balance and may disorientate a visually impaired person.
- Define the edge of the path using contrast, such as grass or gravel, rather than a low wall or edging. A handrail can be very helpful.
- Avoid gravel for the path itself – it is impractical for people in wheelchairs or with walking difficulties.
- Keep drain grills off paths and make sure that they are flush with the ground. The gap between grill bars must not be too be wide, and should be at right angles to the direction in which people walk, so that canes do not slide into them.

- Keep trees, shrubs and bushes cut well back – if they overhang a path, they can scratch people and push them away from a wall that they could use to orientate themselves.
- Position garden furniture so as not to overhang pathways: set it back from the path. Colour contrast furniture with the background; for example, use a pale wooden bench if there is dark vegetation behind.
- Provide clues for orientation: consider laying a grass verge next to every path. While different textures underfoot (pebbles or cobbles, for example) could be useful for orientation, they are not helpful for people with poor mobility.
- Plant some areas with strongly scented flowers and herbs. Raised flowerbeds can be helpful if placed strategically, but remember that plants change through the year and that beds will not provide consistent clues about orientation if they all look the same.
- A water feature is pleasant for people with a sight impairment to see, and is useful for orientation.
- Be aware of the garden layout and exit points: is the garden route circular so that people automatically return to the starting point? The exit should be easily identifiable and accessible – as should the way back in again. Is there any danger that someone might mistake a gate or door and walk out on to the road or other danger?
- Make sure there are no prickly shrubs around the door or gate that could stop people finding their way in easily.
- Consider the accessibility of the building – do people have to cross a car park to reach it? Can they find a safe route?
- Provide sufficient lighting at night.

Finding out more about improving your environment

You can find more detailed information, to suit your particular set of conditions, by seeking expert advice. Try your local social services department's sensory team, a local voluntary organisation for vision or hearing loss, a low vision unit, or the RNIB, RNID, Sense or other national body.

13 Illness and multiple disability

Many older people have multiple illnesses and disabilities, which need to be taken into account when supporting their sensory impairment. This chapter briefly describes how these multiple problems can affect a sensory-impaired person, and looks in more detail at the relationship between dementia and sensory impairment. The following areas are discussed:

- How illness and multiple disability affect people's response to sensory impairment
- The relationship between sensory impairment and major illnesses
- Dementia

As we age, we become increasingly likely to develop major illnesses or long-term conditions such as dementia, arthritis, heart conditions, mobility problems and diabetes.

Because many older people have more than one health problem, this has several effects:

- It may be harder for them to get to a hospital or clinic for diagnosis or treatment.
- It may make it harder for them to find ways of dealing with their impairment – for example, arthritis may make it hard for someone to learn deafblind manual.
- A condition such as arthritis may also make it hard for them to manipulate and care for aids and equipment such as hearing aids.
- They may be taking a range of drugs, which may react with each other.
- They may become sensitive to some common drugs, including those used to treat Parkinson's disease and strong pain-killers, tranquillisers and antidepressants.

How do illness and multiple disability affect people's response to sensory impairment?

Because sensory impairment is often experienced alongside other impairments or illnesses, it may be seen both by the affected person and by those around them as relatively insignificant. Indeed, it is not unusual for older people to feel that any impairment is what they should expect to experience as a normal part of ageing.

This could be seen as an effective way for an older person to cope with the major illnesses and impairments that often seem to come with increasing age. On the other hand, this attitude of passive acceptance lowers people's expectations of what they might be able to achieve, and of the support to which they are entitled. Their quality of life may therefore be much lower than it could be.

It can also mean that they do not seek proper diagnosis of a condition, assuming – perhaps wrongly – that their problems or symptoms are merely the result of ageing. This can have serious consequences, for example, if headaches are misattributed to poor vision when they might actually result from a brain tumour. Conversely, if an older person seems to be confused, disorientated and unable to answer questions quickly enough, medical and care staff all too often assume that the person has dementia, when in fact their problems derive from a sight or hearing impairment.

The relationship between sensory impairment and major illness

The range of illnesses that older people experience is wide, so their relationship to sensory impairment varies enormously. Some illnesses can lead directly to sensory impairment. Sometimes, damage to the eye or ear is the first sign of disease. Sensory impairment may mean that the person fails to notice symptoms, or misattributes them.

Other conditions can exacerbate the effects of sensory loss or make it hard to diagnose. It is shockingly common to hear stories of people with dual sensory loss being assumed to have dementia because they seem confused. Equally shocking is the tendency to ignore the effects of sensory impairment on someone with a major illness – too often the sight or hearing loss is seen as something minor or incidental, not worth spending time on. Helping someone to cope with their sensory impairment may well enable them to cope much better with other illnesses and impairments.

Diseases that cause sensory impairment

DIABETES AND STROKE

The two most common illnesses that lead to sensory impairment in old age are diabetes and stroke. The effects of these two illnesses on vision are described in Chapter 4.

OTHER DISEASES

To present a comprehensive list of diseases that might result in sensory impairment would be impossible in this handbook. However, you may encounter the following:

- multiple sclerosis, which causes inflammation of the optic nerve (primary optic neuritis);
- an over- or under-active thyroid, which affects the eye's ability to focus;
- rheumatoid arthritis, which can cause very painful inflammation of the iris (iritis) and needs immediate treatment with drops;
- AIDS or TB, both of which cause eye disease;
- hormone imbalance, which may cause dry eyes.

Sensory impairment as a symptom of disease

Symptoms in the eye may be the first indicator of a major illness – indeed, this is a very important feature of the testing carried out by optometrists, who are often the first people to notice signs of disease. For example, a number of disorders, such as high blood pressure or leukaemia, are likely to show up first in the retina. Someone who is experiencing headaches needs to be checked by their optometrist to see if the cause is in the eye or elsewhere, as does anyone with cancer, to check for secondaries in the eyes.

A hearing problem is less often the sign of a major illness, but it is none the less important to seek a proper diagnosis in order to be sure of its cause.

Failure to diagnose an illness because of sensory impairment

A visual impairment may mean that someone is unaware of symptoms such as skin problems, or bleeding (eg rectal bleeding in the faeces) and so fails to seek a diagnosis. Someone with a hearing impairment, on the other hand, may be well aware of their symptoms but can find it extremely hard to communicate them to the doctors.

It is also common for someone with a sensory impairment to wrongly ascribe symptoms such as headaches or balance problems to the cause of that impairment. So, for example, they may attribute headaches to tired eyes, when in fact it is perhaps migraine, glaucoma or, rarely, a brain tumour.

Diseases that make sensory impairment harder to diagnose

Sensory impairment may make it harder to diagnose a disease. Some diseases, however, such as those that cause dementia, make it harder to diagnose the impairment. It is none the less entirely possible for someone with dementia to be properly diagnosed, and absolutely essential that this be done.

The optometrist may be the first to see the signs of dementia: perhaps someone has been complaining of having difficulty reading, of dancing print and of difficulty in recognising faces or in finding the way. If, upon testing, the vision is found to be normal, dementia is a possible cause of these problems. It is very likely, however, that someone with dementia will also have an eye disease: 43 per cent of people with Alzheimer's will also develop visual problems.

Dementia

If someone is confused through dementia, the problems associated with a sight or hearing impairment will increase the practical difficulties their dementia causes. A person with dementia and a sensory loss is likely to have problems finding their way, identifying people and objects, dressing themselves, and so on. It may also increase their confusion, fear, distress or depression.

It also seems likely that the reduced sensory input that results from impairment can make someone more confused in the early stages of dementia (Cullinan 1986). When Anand and Court (1989) surveyed the effects of hearing loss on older people in residential homes, among their interviewees they found five people who were confused. They referred them to audiology: 'and their mental state noticeably improved with the use of personal amplifiers'. This underlines the importance of correct diagnosis of the sensory impairment no matter what other health problems someone has.

Whilst people with both dementia and a sensory impairment have many of the same needs as sensory-impaired people without dementia, there are some features of their care that should be given particular attention. For example:

- People who are confused may no longer be able to interpret sounds effectively, including speech. They may be distressed by noise that makes no sense to them.
- If the person has sight problems, they may not be able to pick up clues such as gesture and pointing at things.
- Shadows made by poor lighting can create disturbing images that may seem real and frightening.
- It is extremely important to be consistent in all things, including guiding techniques, room layout and people's names.
- If a standard technique does not suit an individual, all staff must consistently use the adapted technique.
- Someone whose first language is not English may remember only their original language.
- If you use prompts to help someone with dementia to understand questions, make sure they reflect their impairment – someone with a dual loss could be given a cup to ask if they would like a drink, for example.

- Learning and understanding new things can be hard for someone with dementia – they may therefore find it especially hard to adapt to a sensory impairment.

Finally, it is important to think about what is causing a particular problem, and to discuss it. Is someone incontinent because they cannot find the toilet due to their visual impairment? Could they have an infection? Perhaps they can see the way but are too scared to go alone?

The environment and dementia

For the most part, someone with both a sensory impairment and dementia has the same environmental needs as sensory-impaired people without dementia. However, each individual should be observed to see how they respond to their environment, as no two people with dementia are affected in the same way. The points below indicate the areas where particular attention may be needed:

- If the lighting in rooms changes significantly from day to day, this will change the appearance of the room and a confused person may become disorientated.
- If the person with dementia controls the lighting, the controls must be easy to find and use.
- Contrast is even more important when someone has dementia, to help them distinguish things around them. Imagine the confusion of entering a room where the walls and all the objects in it are white and so effectively almost invisible – not unusual in a bathroom.
- From the point of view of someone with vision loss, it is helpful to highlight the position of a door using contrast. However, if you want to discourage someone with dementia from, for example, walking out into the street, you can use lack of contrast to disguise the door. So, if the hall is painted white, you could paint the front door white also, but paint the living room door green, to encourage the person with dementia to go into the living room rather than outside. You can also use a curtain across an exit door.
- Leaving a window or door open can be seen as invitation to go out and explore – as well as being an obstacle that someone with vision loss might walk into.

- If you use contrasting texture on the floor – perhaps to indicate the top of the stairs – you may find that some people with dementia and a sight problem are confused. They may see the new flooring as an obstacle or a hole – shiny flooring can look like water, a shiny edging strip may look like a trip wire: so watch out for signs of distress that might indicate that the person fears falling, tripping or getting wet, and think carefully about tone and colour.
- Mirrors and other shiny surfaces can be confusing and distressing to someone with dementia. Lifts are often clad entirely with mirrors or polished steel.
- People with dementia tend not to look at things above shoulder or head height. Bear this in mind when positioning pictures and signs, for example.
- Good signage is important for everyone. People with dementia need signs that are clear and unambiguous. Staff should check that each individual understands the signs and symbols used.
- To help someone identify their own room, you can use a photograph of someone who is important to them on the door. Make sure it is of good quality, with contrast in tone and colour, so that they will still be able to use it if their vision deteriorates.

Assessing the vision of someone with dementia

Just like anyone else, a person with dementia needs to have their eyes professionally tested by an optometrist. Even if they cannot read letters, or even cooperate, the optometrist will be able to tell a great deal. The RNIB's Multiple Disability Service has information about the tests that can be useful.

After the test, ask the optometrist what the person can see, and pass this information on to everyone who might find it useful, such as fellow workers, volunteers and family members.

If it is not possible to obtain a test from an optometrist, you can still make a useful assessment of the person's functional vision – how much they can see in order to carry out specific tasks. You may be able to arrange for this assessment to be carried out by a specialist rehabilitation worker. You can also add your own observations. (See also Chapter 8 for more information on rehabilitation and Chapter 14 for more information on testing.)

14 Testing for sensory impairment

This chapter describes the importance of proper testing and diagnosis of sensory impairment. It also outlines the testing procedures for investigating sight and hearing problems:

- Eye tests
- Hearing tests
- Delivering the diagnosis
- After the tests

There is more information about the work of sensory specialists in Chapter 16.

Eye tests

Even if you are not concerned about the vision of anyone you work with, it is crucial that you ensure that everyone has their eyes tested at least once a year by a qualified optometrist.

Without regular eye tests, it is likely that someone you work with will have an undiagnosed eye condition. Undiagnosed, the condition cannot be treated or managed. This may mean, at best, that they are unable to enjoy as full a quality of life as possible or, at worst, that they experience severe, but preventable, sight loss.

It is not always easy to persuade people to have an eye test:

> **'A lot of the clients could do with eye tests and hearing tests, but you can't make them.'** *Jo Marks, Age Concern Day Centre*

But gentle encouragement and a certain amount of peer pressure can help, as can seeing someone else's life changed by the acquisition of new glasses or a hearing aid. Even just asking 'How well can you see?' can be a step to breaking the taboo of discussing sight – although be aware that the reply 'Oh, I can see fine' may be a useful defensive tactic that neatly avoids and closes the issue.

Paying for eye tests

NHS eye tests are free to anyone over the age of 60. If someone you work with has a family history of glaucoma, they will have been eligible for free testing since they were 40. Tests are also free to anyone with diabetes or who is registered blind or partially sighted.

However, some optometrists have recently begun to charge for some parts of the test that are not covered by the legislation for free eye tests, including eye pressure testing, which is used to detect glaucoma. It is therefore sensible for individuals to check the likely fees before choosing an optometrist. If the test is free, the optometrist will ask them to fill out an NHS Sight Test Form.

If cost is preventing the person you work with from getting the full range of tests, they will be referred to the hospital, where the tests will be carried out free of charge. There will, however, be a waiting list for these tests, which may delay essential treatment.

People on a low income (including many older people), or who need complex or powerful lenses, can also apply for vouchers to help pay for their glasses, using a form available from their optometrist.

Arranging eye tests

Ideally, an eye test should be carried out at the optometrist's clinic, where the lighting will be specially designed for testing and all the equipment is to hand. If, however, a person you work with is unable to travel, you need to arrange for a home visit by an optometrist.

Your regular optometrist may be willing to visit but, if not, there are specialist mobile optometrist units. You may find it more convenient to arrange for one of these firms to visit you and to test all the people you work with. Your GP should have a list of domiciliary optometrists. Although these are private firms, they can claim expenses back from the NHS, so you should not need to pay them.

Who carries out the eye test?

There is a certain amount of confusion about the difference between an optometrist and an optician. *Optometrists* are professionally qualified to test sight, look for eye conditions and to dispense lenses. *Opticians* are qualified to dispense lenses but they cannot test eyesight. Dispensing lenses is a highly skilled job, because lenses and eyes must be matched perfectly.

Although optometrists may identify an eye condition, they cannot diagnose or treat it. They must refer the person to a GP, who will, in turn, refer the patient to the hospital ophthalmologist for diagnosis.

At the hospital, the patient will see an ophthalmic specialist. This hospital visit may be very worrying as it can be the first step to realising that they have something wrong with their eyes. They may find it reassuring to take someone with them who can support them and make a note of the diagnosis and any other information. (See also Chapter 16 for more information on testing.)

What the optometrist's test should include

The most basic eye test should include:

- Eyesight test: how well can the person read letters on a chart?
- Checking the outer eye: by shining a light on the outer eye, the optometrist checks its health, and how well the eye reacts to light.
- Checking the inner eye: the optometrist shines a light into the eye to check its health, and asks the person to look in different directions.
- Checking the eye muscles: how well do the muscles that control eye movement work?

The test should also include checking the field of vision and the eye pressure, and possibly using dilating eye drops so that the optometrist can better see the back of the person's eye. A thorough test will take more than 15 minutes – insist that the whole range of tests is carried out.

If the person needs glasses, the optometrist will work out the exact prescription. This prescription can be used at any dispensing clinic to buy glasses: there is no obligation to buy glasses from the optometrist who carried out the test. It may be useful, particularly if you are working with people in residential care, to ask for a note to keep on file about their prescription and eye condition, if the individuals are in agreement with this. This could include details of glasses they need to wear and any medication or eye drops they should take.

Keeping your own notes

While there is never any substitute for a proper and thorough vision test by a qualified optometrist, you may find it useful to keep your own notes on the functional effect of someone's visual impairment, based on your observations of their daily life. You could note what they find hard to see and what helps their sight by asking questions such as, 'Is it easier to see these cards if I turn this light on?'

The following questions may provide useful guidance for observing the level of someone's visual impairment:

- Can they find food on their plate? Can they choose it from the serving dishes?
- Can they still read?
- Do they recognise people and objects?
- Can they find their own way around?
- Do they trip?
- Do they see well in dim light, bright sunlight, well-lit rooms?
- How do they best see things? For example, you could note that Mr Seddon sees dark blue numbers about 10 cm high on a white background best.
- Can they see and understand symbols and signs? For example, can Mrs Arkwright see the ladies' toilet symbol, and understand it?
- Are they surprised when someone approaches from the side?

- Does anything else affect their vision – such as time of day, use of medication, health or tiredness?

If you combine this information with what you know about their impairment, you have a good foundation of understanding on which to build a personal care plan for that individual.

Hearing tests

If you suspect that someone you work with has a hearing loss, ask them how well they are hearing. Be specific: 'Can you hear the television at the moment?', 'Do you hear the doorbell when it rings?', 'Can you follow conversation at the dinner table?' If they confirm that they do indeed find it hard to hear, encourage them to visit their GP. Before the visit, help them to write a list of when they have problems hearing and how this affects their daily life.

Who tests hearing?

The GP may be able to carry out simple hearing tests at the surgery, but usually they will refer someone with a hearing problem to the audiology clinic or the Ear, Nose and Throat (ENT) department at the local hospital. People over 60 are normally referred straight to audiology unless their GP thinks they need an ENT specialist's opinion first.

Some audiology departments have made special arrangements with GPs for patients to go straight to audiology without needing a formal referral from their GP first. If someone needs a home visit, the GP will tell the audiologists, who should provide one.

Some GPs may be reluctant to refer older people for hearing tests. If you encounter this attitude, you should insist that the person you are supporting needs a proper assessment, that their hearing loss is affecting their quality of life and that they need to find out if there is any way to help them with the hearing loss.

> 'If I come across someone whose GP has sent them away with "what do you expect at your age?" I would encourage them to go back to the GP to ask for a referral for a hearing assessment.' *Jacqui Jackson, Assessment Officer, Hi Kent*

When the person goes for their hearing test, they may prefer to take someone with them for support, whether or not they have problems communicating. If they have particular communication needs, you should tell the hospital in advance.

What does a hearing test involve?

At the hospital, a specialist called an *audiologist* will carry out tests. First they will look into the ears using an otoscope. Then they will carry out hearing tests (audiometry), which will last about 20 minutes. They will ask the person they are testing to put on headphones and to listen to a series of bleeps at different pitches in each ear. Each time the person hears a bleep, they should press a button – the bleeps get gradually quieter to find out at which level they become inaudible. They will get louder too, to see when they become uncomfortable. If the test reveals a hearing loss, the audiologist will ask the person being tested to put on a headband with a vibrating pad. This transmits sound through the bones of the skull to the cochlea. Comparing results from this test with the headphone test shows up any problems with the eardrum or middle ear.

There may also be a test that involves listening to sentences or words and repeating them. This shows how much the ears are distorting words.

The audiologist will explain the test results and give the person tested their audiogram. This is a chart of their hearing loss, if they have one: Figure 14.1 is an example. An audiogram shows how loud a sound has to be, and at what frequency, before the person being tested can hear it. When someone has a hearing test, they will be given two audiograms – one for each ear. Dots are used to mark the results for the right ear and crosses for the left.

The frequencies on the audiogram go from 125Hz (very low tone) to 8000Hz (very high tone). The hearing levels are shown from –10dB (very quiet) to 120dB (very loud). Someone without a hearing problem is able to hear sounds as quiet as 20dB and even lower.

As well as preparing an audiogram, the audiologist will also say whether a hearing aid will help, and whether further tests or treatment may be needed.

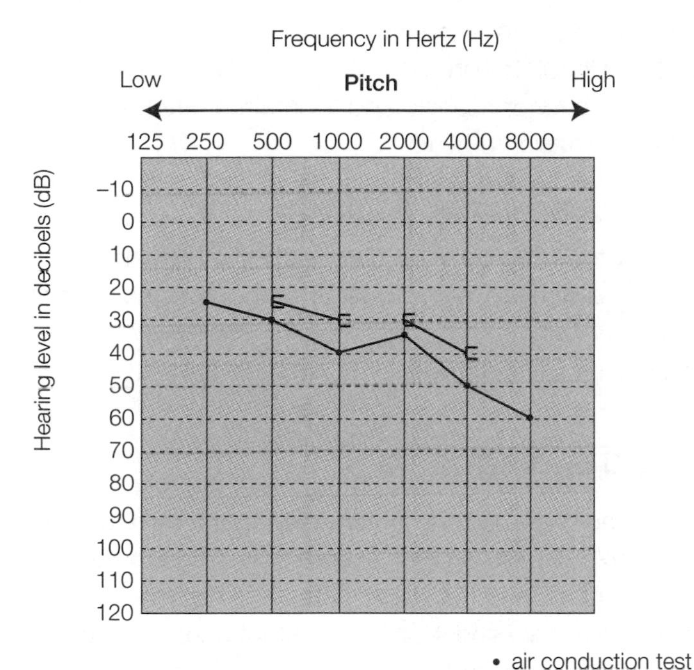

Figure 14.1 A typical audiogram for someone with sensori-neural deafness in the right ear. Both the air conduction and the bone conduction tests give broadly the same result.

Generally, people visit the audiology department three times: once for the assessment (this is when the tests are carried out, as described above), and then twice more for the fitting of hearing aids. Many audiology services take an impression of the ear during the first visit, as this reduces the wait for a hearing aid. The assessment and first hearing-aid-fitting visit should each last at least an hour. The fine-tuning appointment and any follow-up visit should last at least half an hour. As part of the hearing assessment process, the person should be told verbally and in writing about what happens next, other services and equipment, and given contact details.

Keeping your own notes

As with visual impairment, it can be extremely valuable to keep notes about the way that someone's hearing impairment affects them when they are in their home environment. These notes could cover:

- what the person finds easy to hear;
- what they find difficult to hear;
- rooms that are good for hearing, and rooms that are bad;
- which voices are easier to hear;
- times of day when hearing is hardest;
- how well they hear the television and radio;
- how effectively they can communicate with other people;
- any particular difficulties they have in using hearing aids or other equipment;
- tips for what seems to help overcome such difficulties.

Delivering the diagnosis

When someone receives medical confirmation that they have a hearing or visual problem, this can be a great shock, even though they may have been experiencing problems for some time. The diagnosis should therefore be delivered with care and sensitivity: to that person it marks the start of their being officially 'impaired'.

While no one doubts the desire of hospital staff to help their patients, they are often pushed for time, and can seem unaware of the effects of the way that a diagnosis is delivered.

> **'Our ophthalmologists are excellent but often they don't have time to explain things fully. Lots of people come back to us once they've had the diagnosis, somewhat confused about their condition and requiring further explanation.'** *Janine Sykes, Optometrist*

Very often at diagnosis, the person will only be told the name of their condition, and the fact that this means they are now impaired. Whilst someone with a hearing problem will probably be sent to have hearing aids fitted, often no such provision for aftercare is provided for people with visual impairment. Indeed, it is very common for an eye consultant to state that 'nothing can be done' – entirely accurate from a medical point of view, perhaps, but quite misleading in terms of the support that may be available to help someone make the most of their vision.

As far as visual impairment is concerned, often the only hospital provision for aftercare lies in the registration process, which gives access to social services support (see page 216). It is the consultant who certifies someone as blind. This means, however, that he or she may deliver the diagnosis of, for example, glaucoma, and follow it by telling the patient that they will be registered blind. The logical – but incorrect – conclusion that many patients draw from this is that their eye condition will lead irrevocably to total blindness. The trauma this causes is often enormous.

After diagnosis

Some audiology and ophthalmology departments recognise the importance of follow-up care after the diagnosis of a hearing or eye problem. They employ trained staff to talk to patients immediately after they are diagnosed, to reassure them and to provide them with information about their condition and about the support services that are available to them.

This provision of support is extremely inconsistent, however, and varies from hospital to hospital. Support staff are categorised under a range of titles, and may be members of the medical team, part of social services, or may be supplied – paid or unpaid – by local voluntary organisations.

The two main hospital-based support services that employ qualified staff are *hearing therapists* for hard-of-hearing people, and *low vision units* for visually impaired people.

Hearing therapists

Some audiology departments employ hearing therapists, who are trained in the rehabilitation of people with hearing problems. They help people to use their hearing aids and provide training in lipreading and communication skills, and counselling.

> 'ENT don't have the time to spend with the patients that I do. It's good that I'm here to help with support.' *Alex Willoughby, Hearing Therapist*

There are only 120 hearing therapists across the UK, however, so most hard-of-hearing people never meet one. Until recently they were not consistently regulated or trained, so in some areas they are not well respected by the rest of the medical team, whilst in others they are key members of the audiology team.

Referral to a hearing therapist may be through ENT, audiology, a GP, social services, a voluntary organisation or a teacher of deaf people.

Low vision units

The main function of a low vision unit is to help people to maximise the vision that they have. They assess people for magnifiers and supply them, and can advise on lighting. This work is described in Chapter 8, 'Rehabilitation'.

In some areas the low vision unit works in tandem with social services rehabilitation services, carrying out joint assessments and provision of services. This means that a rehabilitation worker can draw on the expertise of the low vision team when planning care, and that there is less duplication of effort.

Linking hospital and other support services

Ideally, hospital staff will be able to tell a newly diagnosed sensory-impaired person not only all about their condition but also where they can turn to for help once they leave the hospital. They should be able to refer them to social services so that rehabilitation workers can assess the impaired person, and to tell them about local specialist voluntary organisations and support groups.

Some hospitals employ staff precisely to provide this information – an eye clinic liaison officer will fulfil this role, for example. Others have given space in their clinics to voluntary sector organisations that provide support, so that patients can make contact with them as soon as they are diagnosed.

All too often, however, hospital staff seem to know little or nothing about the support network that exists outside the walls of the hospital, so many patients leave with no information at all about where they can turn to next.

15 Benefits and registration

This chapter provides an overview of the key benefits available to older people with a sensory impairment. In particular, it discusses:

- Registering blind, partially sighted or deaf
- Benefits

The benefits system in the UK is complex and it would be unwise, if not impossible, to try to explain it in detail in this handbook. If you need advice about benefits, you should contact the Benefits Enquiry Line or one of the national organisations representing older people or those with sensory impairment (see the 'Useful addresses' section for contact details). Age Concern, RNIB and RNID have many factsheets, updated regularly, with useful information about state benefits.

However, it is useful to outline here the main benefits that are available to older people with sensory loss, and to describe the registration system.

Registering blind, partially sighted or deaf

Registration is covered in the same chapter as benefits because visually impaired people must be registered as blind or partially sighted before they can receive state benefits relating to their impairment. This is not the case for hard-of-hearing people, whose eligibility for benefit is not dependent on registration. Visually impaired people do not always therefore receive financial help as soon as they need it: someone's poor vision may affect their life before it has deteriorated enough for them to be registered.

Registering as blind or partially sighted impels social services to assess a visually impaired person and to provide support. It may take up to a year for the first social services visit, however, and the RNIB recently found that 40 per cent of those who were registered waited over six months for a visit from social services. Without a systematic registration system for hearing impairment, it seems to be a matter of luck whether or not deaf or hard-of-hearing people are drawn into the social services system.

Finally, although anecdotal evidence points to large numbers of people from minority ethnic groups attending eye clinics, very few post-registration referrals reach social services – so this group is probably not receiving the services it needs (Williams 1994).

How registration works

VISUAL IMPAIRMENT

The legal definition of blindness in the UK states that someone can be certified blind if they are 'so blind that they cannot do any work for which eyesight is essential'. There is no legal definition of partial sight, but someone may be certified as partially sighted if they are 'substantially and permanently handicapped by defective vision, caused by congenital defect or illness or injury'.

In terms of a standard test, this means that someone who can see only the top letter of the eye test chart or less (even while wearing glasses), at a distance of 3 metres, could be eligible to be registered as blind by an ophthalmologist. If they can see it at a distance of 6 metres, they could be eligible to be registered as partially sighted.

The assessment for registration measures how well someone can read a sight chart with their correct glasses on. It does not measure near vision. There are clear guidelines for registration and little room nowadays for an ophthalmologist to register someone who does not strictly fit the criteria.

From November 2003, a new system for registering as blind or partially sighted began in England. Under the old system, a hospital eye specialist would decide whether someone should be registered. The specialist would issue a form BD8 for the visually impaired person to sign, and would then send it to the local authority, which would add the person to its register. This was a trigger for social services to assess the visually impaired person, but the system was slow and support was not always available as soon as they needed it unless they referred themselves.

Under the new system it should be easier for people to seek help from social services – even before they register or if they decide not to register. As before, local authorities – or voluntary organisations on their behalf – hold registers of people who are blind or partially sighted. Also as before, the hospital eye specialists decide who should be entered on the register. However, the new system makes it simpler for people to tell social services much earlier that they need help or advice.

In the new system, the term 'blind' has become 'severely sight impaired/blind'; 'partially sighted' has become 'sight impaired/partially sighted'.

The old form BD8 will not be phased out immediately, and will still be accepted by social services.

HOW THE NEW SYSTEM WORKS

- High street optometrists and hospital eye clinics can now issue a new standard referral letter, the Letter of Vision Impairment (LVI 2003). This letter is sent to social services.
- The visually impaired person fills in the LVI themselves. They can give information about their circumstances, difficulties or anxieties, and can ask for information about the services that are available to them. They will be given a leaflet helping them to fill in the form, and telling them where to seek advice locally and nationally.
- When a high street optometrist gives someone an LVI, they will probably also arrange for them to see a consultant ophthalmologist at the local hospital eye clinic.
- If the individual does not receive an LVI, or does not send it off, they can still ask for social services' help when they visit the hospital eye service. Eye clinic staff can fill in a form, Referral of Vision Impaired Patient (RVI 2003). This form tells social services about the individual's situation, asks for an assessment of their need for support, and states how urgently staff think the individual needs that support.
- If an individual's sight has deteriorated to a certain level, they may be eligible – as before – to be registered blind or partially sighted with

social services: the eye specialist must complete a Certificate of Vision Impairment (CVI 2003).

- The CVI is easier to complete than the old BD8, so the registration process should now be quicker.
- Registration should trigger a social services assessment of the individual's needs. However, anyone is entitled to ask for social services' help without going through the new system. They simply contact their social services department direct.

At time of writing, no decision had been taken about reforming the registration system in Scotland, Wales and Northern Ireland. For up-to-date information, contact the RNIB office in each country.

NATIONAL REGISTRATION CARD

In March 2004 a new National Registration Card was introduced, which is standard across all local authorities (previously each local authority issued its own style of card to people on its register). There are four templates: people who are registered as severely sight impaired/blind can have either a photocard or a basic card without a photo; people who are registered as sight impaired/partially sighted can also have a photocard or a basic card without a photo.

HEARING IMPAIRMENT

Relatively few people register with social services as deaf or hard of hearing: only about 194,000 people were registered in 2001 in England – out of over 9 million deaf and hard-of-hearing people. This is probably because registration is voluntary, and people are eligible for services whether or not they are registered.

Registration is carried out by social services themselves, or by a voluntary organisation to which they have contracted out hearing-impairment services.

The experience of registration

Registration can be very traumatic for a visually impaired person. Although their vision may have been deteriorating gradually for years, and they may have been coping well, being registered can make their blindness seem very real and depressing. This may be one reason why the RNIB found that only about a quarter of those with visual impairment are registered (Grindley 1997).

> 'It has been suggested that registration as visually impaired may symbolise the permanence of loss of vision for the patient and, as such, constitute a turning point in their ability to internalise and begin to respond to this loss.' *(Conyers 1986)*

Maria Conyers interviewed people about their experience of registering as visually impaired in the 1980s. Although it is to be hoped that more people now have a positive experience of the process than she found, their feelings of 'shock, disbelief and numbness' and of being 'unprepared for the possibility' almost certainly remain unchanged. Anecdotal evidence still suggests that people do not always have a good experience of registering, even today.

Conyers found that 'confusion and unrealistic expectations about the function of being registered abounded. ... Many reported feeling labelled and stigmatised.' One interviewee said:

> 'Stunned, did not expect it, disgusted that it had not been mentioned before.'

Another said:

> 'Shock; I felt it was just procedure for them, and what would follow? The consultant said he was unsure what was available.'

Perhaps surprisingly, many people (38 per cent) in Conyers' sample were unable to accept their loss of sight even after registration.

Benefits

There is a wide range of benefits available to people with a sensory loss in the UK. However, a great many of them are only for people under 65. This chapter focuses on those for people over 65, touching briefly on those for younger people.

Possibly the most important fact about benefits is that so few eligible people claim them. This is made doubly shocking by the poverty in which so many older people live. Nine out of ten older people with visual impairment are on an income of less than half the national average (Vale and Smyth 2003).

When you discuss benefits with older people, it is important to be sensitive, as many are unwilling to claim anything that is labelled as a benefit. Rehabilitation workers find that using the term 'entitlements' is generally more acceptable. Claiming a benefit can be a depressing task, as benefits forms emphasise what the person cannot do, rather than what they can, so tread carefully if you are helping someone.

Filling in a claim form can be a challenge at the best of times and, to someone with a visual impairment, it can seem impossible. Local authorities should provide benefits advice and help with form filling at the time of the financial assessment. If the person needs more help, try the Benefits Enquiry Line, the local Citizens Advice Bureau or a local sensory impairment organisation.

> 'Attendance Allowance forms are very lengthy. Most visually impaired people and elderly people need help with completing them.'
> *Chandra Beasley, KAB*

Attendance Allowance

The key benefit for older people with a sensory loss is Attendance Allowance (AA). It helps people aged 65 and over with the extra costs of their disability. For example, someone who is deaf could claim if they need help to communicate. AA is also granted when someone needs care or supervision.

AA is not means-tested, and there is no need to have paid National Insurance to receive it. It is not taxed. To claim it, the person needs to complete a form, available from the Benefits Enquiry Line (ask for Claim Pack DS2). Claiming AA does not mean losing Income Support, and may even lead to the Minimum Income Guarantee (Income Support) being increased.

To qualify for AA, a person must:

- be 65 or over;
- have been living in England, Scotland or Wales for 26 of the 52 weeks before the claim (and not away on holiday);
- have no limits on their right to live in the UK;
- need help with their care.

There are two levels of Attendance Allowance. The lower (Day) rate is for people who need care in the day or in the night. The higher (Night) rate is for people who need care both day and night, or who are terminally ill.

'Day condition' is defined as needing frequent help throughout the day with bodily functions, or continual supervision to prevent the person from coming to harm or harming others.

'Night condition' is defined as needing someone else to provide prolonged or repeated attention, help at night with bodily functions, or needing someone else to be awake for periods of 20 minutes or longer, or two or three times a night, in order to avoid substantial danger to the person or others.

There is much useful information about filling in the AA claim form, on the RNID website. It suggests that the claimant should keep a diary for a couple of weeks before filling in the form, noting when they usually need help with communicating, or other bodily functions such as cutting up food, or washing or dressing (note that 'bodily functions' includes hearing, speech and sight). It is important that the claimant be able to show that they need help often, throughout the day. It also notes that the claimant will probably not find the whole form relevant to their life, but should fill in the parts that relate to their need.

Someone with a sensory impairment may be able to claim AA because:

- they fall or stumble;
- they have dizzy spells or balance problems (eg if they have Menière's disease);
- they have other disabilities too (eg arthritis) that make certain tasks painful to carry out;
- they need help taking medication;
- it takes them a long time to carry out certain tasks;

- they need someone to wake them in the morning;
- they need help from someone else with communicating – whether in conversation or when listening to the radio or watching television;
- they need help when visiting the doctor or dentist, when using public transport, when shopping, or when taking part in hobbies and social activities.

It does not matter whether or not the claimant actually receives this help – they can still claim for the help that they 'reasonably require'.

AA is sometimes refused at the first claim, and the claimant will receive a letter from the Department for Work and Pensions to explain why. The claimant has one month to dispute the decision. It is quite common for appeals to be successful, but it is wise to enlist the help of an expert – perhaps from the person's social worker, the Citizens Advice Bureau, the welfare rights unit, law centre or local advice centre.

Some people do not claim AA because they do not want their difficulties made known. They may fear that they will be forced to go into residential care. You can reassure them that the claim for AA is separate from the social services assessment of care needs.

The rules about benefits while in residential care are complicated, and it is well worth seeking expert advice: if someone spends more than four weeks in hospital, or in residential care where the fees are wholly or partly publicly funded, they lose their AA. If they fund themselves in residential care, they should still be able to receive AA. They can also get AA even while the local authority is funding them pending, for example, the sale of their property and they will be paying it back at a later date.

> 'The irony of the DLA/AA system is that it is easier for people with quite active lives – due to work or study – to satisfy the "frequent attention test". A deaf older person who doesn't go out much or enjoy much of a social life will find it much harder because the instances when they will need help with communication are much less frequent. The need for communication support from another person is much harder to demonstrate if the only interactions you have are fairly basic – communicating with friends/family, neighbours, post office, local shops, etc.' *Duleep Allirajah, RNID*

Severe Disability Premium

Not a benefit as such, this is paid to people who receive AA, who live alone and who have no one looking after them who receives Carer's Allowance. Even if the person does not live alone, they might still receive the Premium.

Carer's Allowance

This benefit is paid to someone who cares (unpaid) for someone who receives AA or DLA (higher rate) for at least 35 hours a week. People 65 and over may find that their state retirement pension pays more than Carer's Allowance (CA), but if they receive a lower rate of state pension, CA will top them up to the level of a full pension. Note, however, that the AA claimant may lose their Severe Disability Premium if CA is awarded. It is therefore worth seeking advice before making a claim.

Benefits for people under 65

DISABILITY LIVING ALLOWANCE

This is a benefit for disabled children or adults under 65. It is very like Attendance Allowance (which is for people 65 and over), but it also includes a mobility component. If someone claims DLA before they are 65, they continue to receive it even after they are 65.

INCAPACITY BENEFIT

This benefit is for people who cannot work because of a disability. Someone with a sensory loss who has worked recently and paid National Insurance may be able to claim it. Severe Disablement Allowance has been abolished, although people who were already claiming it continue to receive it.

WORKING TAX CREDIT

This is for a disabled person working 16 hours a week or more.

ACCESS TO WORK

The Government's Access to Work scheme helps people with disabilities to work. It can help with the cost of special equipment, communications services and changes to the working environment. For information about this scheme, talk to the Disability Employment Adviser at the local JobCentre Plus.

Means-tested benefits

Means-tested benefits depend on the person's income and savings. The key benefits are the Pension Credit, which covers general living costs, Housing Benefit and Council Tax Benefit. Pension Credit tops up the claimant's income to a level defined each year by the Government.

Claiming AA does not automatically trigger a claim for the means-tested benefits, so a claimant needs to find out if they are eligible and make a claim as soon as possible. Someone successfully claiming AA is more likely to be eligible for a means-tested benefit.

A new system that provides financial support for older people is the 'Supporting People' Scheme. With this Scheme, local authorities receive a grant for funding support services, including those provided by wardens in sheltered housing.

Premiums

A premium is an increase on an existing benefit – not a separate benefit in its own right. Someone who is disabled or who is a carer may receive an additional premium if they receive, for example, Income-based Jobseeker's Allowance, Housing Benefit or Council Tax Benefit.

Industrial Injuries Benefit and War Pensions

To claim these, the person must be able to show a link between their current condition and their previous work, or their armed service or their experiences in wartime. The best sources of advice are often trade unions for Industrial Injury benefit; and the Royal British Legion (contact details on page 291) or SSAFA Forces Help (contact details on page 292) for War Pensions – which are payable to civilians injured in war as well as to combatants.

Direct Payments

Direct Payments are not benefits as such, just a way of enabling someone to arrange their own services rather than having social services commission it for them. See page 236 for more information on this.

16 Working with sensory specialists and other services

There is an enormous number of specialists who work with sensory-impaired people in the health and social services sectors. This chapter describes who they are, what they do and where to find them.

In health care:

- Who's who in health care for deaf or hard-of-hearing people
- The route to health care for deaf or hard-of-hearing people
- Who's who in health care for visually impaired people
- The route to health care for visually impaired people
- Emergency care
- Denial of care
- Access to health services for people in residential care

In social services:

- Who's who in social services
- The function of social services
- The assessment process
- Access to social services for people in residential care

When someone develops a visual or hearing impairment, they need help from specialists. Initially they seek a diagnosis, which will be delivered through the health care system. After diagnosis, they may need a range of support services, from emotional to practical. These might include counselling, information about their impairment, equipment to help them to cope with the impairment, communication support and training, rehabilitation, and general care. This support may be delivered through any of a number of agencies, including social services and specialist voluntary organisations.

The level and quality of care and support provided varies enormously, depending on where someone lives and how old they are. An additional factor is that many people in residential care find it difficult to access services.

WHERE ARE THE SPECIALISTS?

Health services: primary care groups; trusts; audiology departments; ophthalmology departments; district nurses; GPs; learning disability services

Social services: deaf teams; visual impairment teams; rehabilitation officers; older people's teams; learning disability services; disability services; sensory teams; home care; residential services; meals-on-wheels services; day centres

Housing services: social housing; housing associations; private sector housing

Voluntary sector: councils for voluntary services; local and national voluntary organisations connected in any way with sensory impairment; clubs and support groups for deaf, hard-of-hearing, visually impaired, older and/or disabled people; organisations serving ethnic minority communities and organisations; services for people with learning disabilities

There are so many people involved in providing health and social care, each with a distinct role to play, that each section below begins by listing the key people with whom you may work, and briefly describes their role.

Health care

This section is divided into those giving health care to people who are deaf or hard of hearing and those giving care to visually impaired people.

Who's who in health care for deaf or hard-of-hearing people

AUDIOLOGIST

An audiologist tests hearing and fits hearing aids. Audiologists are not medical doctors.

AUDIOLOGICAL PHYSICIAN

An audiological physician is a medical doctor who diagnoses conditions and sees difficult cases. They usually have a specialism.

EAR, NOSE AND THROAT (ENT) CONSULTANT

The consultant may be an audiological physician. Consultants see referrals from GPs and carry out surgery.

AUDIOLOGICAL SCIENTIST

An audiological scientist carries out research and more specialised tests of hearing and balance.

HEARING THERAPIST

A hearing therapist provides rehabilitation.

The route to health care for deaf or hard-of-hearing people

For diagnosis of a hearing problem and fitting of hearing aids, most people visit their hospital audiology department. They are usually referred to this department by their GP.

If the person with a hearing problem is over 60 and the GP sees no medical factor in their hearing problem, he or she will probably refer them straight to the audiology department for testing. If they are younger, or there might be a medical problem, they will be referred to a consultant in the ENT department. If the ENT consultant judges that the person needs a hearing aid, he or she will refer them to audiology. (See also Chapter 14 for a description of the testing procedure in audiology.)

Some people prefer to visit a private hearing-aid dispenser rather than using the NHS system.

Who's who in health care for visually impaired people

OPTOMETRIST

Optometrists are sometimes – inaccurately – known as opticians. They are trained to test vision and to prescribe lenses. They also detect eye disease and refer on to hospital eye clinics, via the GP, for diagnosis and treatment. Some are based in hospitals, but most work in private practice in the high street. Most hospital low-vision services are delivered by optometrists.

DISPENSING OPTICIAN

A dispensing optician is qualified to supply and fit lenses from a prescription completed by an ophthalmologist or optometrist.

OPHTHALMOLOGIST

An ophthalmologist is a medical doctor specialising in treating eye disease. Most are based in local hospital eye departments or in specialist eye hospitals. Some do not carry out surgery, and not all are consultants.

CONSULTANT OPHTHALMIC SURGEON

The consultant ophthalmic surgeon specialises in the medical and surgical management of eye disease.

OPHTHALMIC NURSE

An ophthalmic nurse is a nurse with an extra qualification in ophthalmology, who works in a hospital eye department. They may carry out low-vision work.

OPHTHALMIC MEDICAL PRACTITIONER

An ophthalmic medical practitioner is a medical doctor who is also licensed to test for and prescribe lenses.

ORTHOPTIST

An orthoptist is trained to assess binocular vision – the way that a person's eyes work together. Most work in hospitals and deal with squints. They sometimes provide low-vision services in hospitals.

EYE CLINIC LIAISON OFFICER

An eye clinic liaison officer's role is to coordinate post-diagnosis support services. They may provide some immediate information and support to newly diagnosed patients.

The route to health care for visually impaired people

If you feel that someone you work with has a sight problem, their first port of call is their optometrist. If the optometrist suspects that they have an eye condition, they will refer them to the ophthalmology department at hospital. The optometrist will make this referral via the person's GP in most cases. (See also Chapter 14 for further information on the testing process.)

Emergency care

It is rarely appropriate to seek help for a vision or hearing problem through a hospital's Accident and Emergency (A & E) department. However, if you suspect that someone you work with needs emergency care – for example, if they have an injury, or if they have severe pain in their eye or ear – and their GP is not available, you should take them straight to A & E.

Denial of care

Although most GPs are keen to help patients with their sensory loss, there may still be some who do not take the health care needs of older people seriously. An individual has the right to demand that their GP refer them to a specialist if they are unhappy about their sight or hearing, but many feel intimidated by medical staff and so do not press their case.

This is an area where a professional working with an older person can really help, by giving support and acting as an advocate. An example of the difference this can make is George:

George arrived at his local day-care centre with very poor vision. The staff were told that he was partially sighted as a result of a recurring detached retina, and that nothing could be done. He needed a great deal of support, as his mobility was limited by his poor vision, and staff had to hold his hand to write a cheque. His GP refused to refer him to the specialist.

The day-care centre staff persisted with the GP on his behalf, and eventually persuaded him to refer George to his local hospital, where the consultant prescribed him glasses. With these new glasses, George has regained much of his mobility, and not only can he now write cheques unaided but he can also read.

Another client at the same day-care centre is Rose:

Rose went to her optometrist when she first realised she could not see well, even though she had only recently bought new glasses. He gave her a letter to her GP asking him to refer her to the hospital. Rose says 'He was very offended and said "why didn't you come to me first?", and wouldn't refer me to the hospital'. It took Rose a year to get her hospital referral, where she was eventually diagnosed with glaucoma. Since then she has changed her GP, and sees her eye specialist regularly.

Access to health services for people in residential care

The above descriptions of how sensory-impaired people gain access to specialist services do not, unfortunately, strictly apply to people living in a care home, because it can be so hard for them to visit clinics.

Nadra Ahmed has found that audiologists are unwilling to visit the residents in her care home, who have to be taken to the hospital instead. If she were to ask a private dispenser to visit, residents would have to pay for their aids. This contrasts with the private domiciliary optometrist practice, which visits them free of charge because it is NHS subsidised.

Social services

This section describes in general terms the roles of social services staff and how sensory-impaired people can access the services they provide.

Who's who in social services

CARE MANAGER

A care manager's role is to work in partnership with an individual to assess that person's needs and decide what support they will receive. Many are generalists but some are specialists working only with sensory-impaired people.

SOCIAL WORKER FOR BLIND/DEAF PEOPLE

Some social workers also have specialist knowledge of a sensory impairment (rarely of dual impairment) and work in specialist sensory teams. They usually work either with visually impaired people or with deaf people but not both. They do not, though, carry out skills training.

REHABILITATION (REHAB) WORKER

Rehabilitation workers assess and teach independent living, communication and mobility skills; they provide information and advice, and give initial counselling. They may work alongside a low vision unit. (See also Chapter 8.)

TECHNICAL OFFICER FOR DEAF PEOPLE

Technical officers provide information and advice; they assess for equipment and adaptations, and train people in the use of the equipment.

MOBILITY OFFICER

Mobility officers provide information and advice, and assessment and teaching of orientation and mobility skills. They do not teach other practical skills.

SUPPORT WORKER

Support workers are members of staff who support individuals by enabling them to gain access to services.

INTERPRETER AND GUIDE COMMUNICATOR

Interpreters are fully trained and qualified to support people with particular communication needs; for example, interpreting into BSL.

Guide communicators support dual-sensory-impaired people in communication and mobility, enabling them to access services. Their role is described more fully on page 16.

People in any of these roles may be employed directly by social services, or may work for a voluntary organisation to which social services has contracted out this area of work.

COMMUNICATION SUPPORT WORKER

Communication support workers support deaf people, generally in an educational setting – helping in communication with the tutor and other students.

The function of social services

Social services are obliged by law to provide an assessment of anyone with a substantial and permanent disability. This means that they have to provide an assessment of the person's needs but they do not have to provide a response to those needs if they lack the resources. So although, officially, social care in this country is designed to be needs-led, it is in fact resource-led.

The assessment process

In 2003 a new mechanism for assessing all adults approaching social services was put in place. Called Fair Access to Care Services (FACS), it is designed to ensure that everyone has equal access to services. It means that local authorities may not prioritise one group of service users over another. For example, older people must be given the same access to services as younger adults. Instead, local authorities prioritise service delivery according to level of need.

Under FACS, anyone meeting the basic criteria should receive an assessment of need. These criteria may be as simple as 'appearing to have need of community care services' or 'having a disability'. The assessment of need will be carried out by the local social services. It may involve several sub-assessments by different professionals.

The information gathered in the assessment of need will be used to write a statement of needs. Each need in the statement is then evaluated against the FACS framework. FACS has four categories – Critical, Substantial, Moderate or Low – which are set nationally. But each local authority defines its own thresholds for provision of services. Many local authorities provide services only to the higher categories of need: some fund services only for needs within the Critical and Substantial categories; some cover Moderate needs, too. They must, however, provide information and advice on alternative sources of help to anyone whose needs are assessed as 'ineligible' – falling outside the local threshold.

Social services assessors are required to address four 'domains' of life in their assessments: health and safety; autonomy (the ability to control one's own life); personal and daily living activities; and maintenance of social or family involvement. Your local authority will be able to tell you in more detail about their assessment criteria.

> 'This begs the question: Does sight loss pose critical or substantial needs, or is its effect merely moderate or low? The answer appears to depend on whom you talk to!' *(Cox 2004)*

In principle, sensory impairment – depending on its severity or functional impact – could present needs at every level. For example, the need to access the TV guide might be moderate, on grounds of maintaining social involvement – it could be met by the provision of a specialist reading lamp. The need to prepare food more safely would probably be assessed as a substantial need in both health and safety and daily living – it might be met through rehabilitation, provision of equipment, additional lighting or meals provided in the home.

FACS is complicated and, as thresholds vary from local authority to local authority, it is best to seek advice from your local social services. Your local authority should have information about FACS on its website. However, it is worth remembering that, if an individual is experiencing any kind of difficulties in their day-to-day life because of a disability or chronic condition, they have a right to an assessment.

WHO CARRIES OUT THE ASSESSMENT?

Assessments are carried out by the social services care management team. This team consists of care managers, who are usually social workers but may have an occupational therapy or a nursing background. Their role includes assessment for, provision of, and coordination of care services.

The care management team will also work with specialist teams such as those for people with sensory impairments, and perhaps also with local voluntary organisations to whom they have contracted out services.

A specialist assessment may be carried out by a rehabilitation worker. Two such assessments are described below. In most areas they are carried out by members of a social services specialist team; unusually, they may be contracted out to local voluntary agencies.

Although a number of different health and social care professionals may assess an individual's needs, the end result should be a single assessment rather than several unconnected statements.

WHAT TRIGGERS AN ASSESSMENT?

An assessment may be triggered by any of a wide variety of events:

- Individuals may self-refer to social services.
- Their family or friends may refer them.
- The individual's GP or district nurse may refer them.
- A visually impaired person who is registered blind or partially sighted will be assessed automatically.
- Eye clinic staff can refer a visually impaired person for assessment.
- A visually impaired person's optometrist can issue them with a Letter of Vision Impairment, to send to social services.
- A hearing therapist or local audiology department may refer a deaf or hard-of-hearing person to social services.

SPECIALIST ASSESSMENTS: KAB'S VISUAL IMPAIRMENT ASSESSMENT

Kent Social Services has contracted out its registration assessments to the Kent Association for the Blind (KAB), a local voluntary organisation:

> 'The first thing I say on a visit is "I'm here to help you stay independent". The first time it's often about the eye condition: often the hospital just doesn't have time to explain their condition.' *Chandra Beasley, KAB*

The assessment lasts about an hour, after which there will be follow-up visits. The assessor discusses:

- the eye condition – what is wrong, what can be done;
- general health – for example, have they had a stroke? They may have an undiagnosed eye condition;
- the client's concerns – reading, television, going out, recognising people;
- the effects on the individual – their ability to cope;
- low-vision aids (magnifiers), which are issued following a low-vision assessment;
- mobility and guiding;
- daily living skills, which KAB feels are best assessed in the home;
- communication – reading, talking books/newspapers, television, telephone;
- finance and state benefits.

> 'It is far better to offer support at an early stage of sight loss rather than later when people have been struggling and may have become depressed.' *Ann Lewis, KAB*

SPECIALIST ASSESSMENTS: HI KENT'S HEARING IMPAIRMENT ASSESSMENT

Kent Social Services has also contracted out equipment assessments for people over 65 who have hearing impairment.

> 'If someone doesn't want help and feels they are coping, you have to respect their wishes. I tell them how to get in touch. They may do so later when their need is greater. The only time I would strongly encourage someone to accept help would be if they were potentially in danger, for example if they couldn't hear the doorbell to let the nurse in for medical help.' *Jacqui Jackson, Assessment Officer, Hi Kent*

Jacqui's assessment takes the following shape:

- She explains why she is there, and then asks to see the person's hearing aid. This gives her an idea about their hearing loss.
- She asks how the person is getting on with the aid. She may clean and retune it.
- If the person is still struggling to hear with the aid in, she will refer them back to audiology for an upgraded hearing assessment.
- If the aid is in good working order, they discuss what areas might be a problem – for example, the television or doorbell. She finds out what the person's priorities are.
- She and the person discuss equipment and she demonstrates it, where necessary.
- She may register the person as deaf.
- She may help the person with state benefits.
- If the person has a dual loss, she refers them to KAB.

Arranging services, and Direct Payments

A person who has been assessed by social services as needing support can:

- receive services direct from social services;
- receive services from an agency – such as a voluntary organisation – appointed by social services;
- arrange the services themselves and receive money from social services with which to pay for these services – a Direct Payment

The individual may use a Direct Payment only to meet the needs they were assessed as having. However, they decide how they would like to meet these needs; for example, for personal care, equipment or personal assistance. They can also decide that some aspects of their care will be provided direct by social services and receive Direct Payments for other aspects.

For more information about Direct Payments, see Age Concern's factsheet 24, *Direct Payments from social services*.

Access to social services for people in residential care

Most people in care homes never come into contact with social services, especially if they are living in a private home and are privately funded. They will only be reviewed by social services if they request help in paying the fees of the home.

17 Obstacles to receiving specialist sensory services

Most people with a sensory impairment are over 65. Yet older people with a sensory impairment often fail to obtain the services and support that they need. This chapter explores why. It looks at:

- Under-resourcing
- The status of sensory work
- The structure of care services
- Lack of understanding
- Ageism
- Ethnic groups

Many of the professionals described in Chapter 16 possess excellent skills and knowledge, and an incredible commitment to supporting people with sensory impairment. Why, then, do so many older people with sensory impairments find it hard to access the services they provide?

The health and social care systems are vast and complex, so it is perhaps not surprising that people do not always receive the care they need. There will always be some individuals who fall through the net. However, anyone who works with sensory-impaired older people will know that the system is not just over-stretched – in many ways it is quite simply not designed to recognise or supply the needs of this group.

The primary problems are under-resourcing, lack of understanding, the low status of sensory impairment as a specialty, and ageism.

Under-resourcing

The most obvious instance of under-resourcing is in audiology. Waiting lists for audiology can be extremely long – they can range from a few weeks to a few months, with considerable variation between districts. In its 2001 report, *Audiology in Crisis*, the RNID found that, in some areas, people were waiting over a year to have their hearing tested, and two years before they received a hearing aid.

The same report found that, in one in eight audiology departments, new patients did not receive hearing aids because money ran out in that year. And the funding crisis in audiology was expected to get worse.

Audiology in Crisis quotes Tina Pitcher, Audiology Service Manager at Chase Farm Hospital:

> 'The audiology centre was moved to this abandoned, decaying ward without proper test facilities or any provision for patient comfort. It was supposed to be a "temporary" emergency measure when the roof fell in on its previous place. That was five years ago! Other hospital departments are always first in the queue for resources.'

She did add, however, that 'Whatever we lack in equipment and space, we make up for in standard of care.' And work was about to start on new accommodation.

Since 2001, substantial new resources have been provided to modernise hearing aid services but the national shortage of trained audiologists remains, which means that waiting times are still unacceptably long.

Lack of funding is equally visible in social services sensory work. The lack of a National Service Framework for sensory impairment means that there is no impetus for social services departments to put money into sensory work. This has affected hearing-impairment services worse than those for visual impairment: in many areas, the hearing impairment service consists solely of an overworked British Sign Language (BSL) worker and a part-time technical officer.

The status of sensory work

There is a great lack of social workers specialising in sensory loss, largely because it has long been marginalised within the social work community. Because working with older people also tends to be a less popular choice for social workers, it is extremely hard to recruit people to work with older people with sight and/or hearing impairment.

> 'The problem is that there aren't enough people, not that the people who are there aren't committed.' *Chris Cogdell, Social Services District Manager*

> 'Sensory impairment is bottom of the heap – it's not trendy.' *Beryl Palmer, Sensory Disabilities Services*

The structure of care services

Many sensory professionals are frustrated by the disconnection between health care and social services, and also by the structure of those same social services.

Social services departments are generally split into teams, each of which focuses on one specific group of people – children, people with learning disabilities, older people, people with sensory impairments.

A sensory impairment team works with children and adults up to the age of 65: its members therefore generally have little experience of the way that sensory impairment affects older people. This is because, for the purposes of social services, people over 65 join a separate category of 'older people', and it is the service for older people that will be responsible for their care. Few social workers for older people have any specialist knowledge of sensory impairment. Lack of cooperation and planning between the sensory and older people's teams often means that they do not draw on each other's expertise.

Sensory specialists work in sensory impairment teams. Within a team, expertise is further split into people working with hearing impairment and those working with visual impairment. Few people in these teams have any expertise in dual impairment, and there is often little communication or planning between the two specialties. (See also Chapter 18 for information on Section 7 Guidance.)

Lack of understanding

> 'There seems to be an almost inverse ratio in the specialist literature … with the least numerous (children) being written about the most, and the most numerous (older people) being written about the least, leading me to question the commitment to the latter group, even within the specialist world itself.' *(Crossland, 2003)*

The low status of sensory work in both health and social care helps to explain the lack of awareness among non-specialists about sensory impairment.

When a non-specialist plans support for an older person, they are unlikely to give vision and hearing problems a high priority. This is largely a function of the way that care assessments are carried out by general teams: they focus on personal care and daily living tasks, and on mobility as defined by the need to use a wheelchair. Such assessments do not recognise the importance of communication in a person's life, nor the fact that someone may lose mobility because they cannot see where they are going, or are too afraid to leave the house because they cannot see or hear well enough to stay safe.

Where non-specialists – and indeed many specialists – do show an interest in sensory impairment, they may not have an understanding of the way that it affects the individual concerned. This can lead, for example, to futile efforts to teach BSL or Braille to someone in their 80s, because that is what they would teach a young adult who has recently become sensory impaired. But those who work with older people will know that most people who have lost hearing and vision in later life prefer to use speech, lipreading and printed text for as long as possible.

This lack of knowledge among non-specialists of sensory impairment, especially of dual loss, can have serious consequences. Beryl Palmer has found people who were wrongly put into residential care by an inexperienced assessor because they had such low preconceptions about a deafblind person's ability to live independently.

Ageism

> 'Ageism, however covert and subtle, is embedded in the funding and delivery of health and social care, and ... specialist sight and hearing services are among the worst examples.' *Graham Willetts, RNIB*

Although it is becoming rarer for people to be refused medical treatment because of their age, waiting times for referrals to hospital are often longer for older people. Social services departments have, since the early 1990s, put into place policies advocating an equal access to services regardless of a person's age – but these policies may not be implemented, or may be interpreted in an ageist way. (See also Chapter 18 for information about recent guidelines.)

Ageism is present in the segregation of older people into a separate service, so that they have little or no access to specialist sensory services. It is also present in the way that support for older people is funded: once someone is 65, their needs are assessed according to a much reduced set of criteria, and they are therefore eligible for less support and less equipment. This is despite the fact that many older people will be dealing with the combined effects of multiple impairments.

This reduced level of support manifests itself in many ways – from the denial of a vibrating alarm clock to a 66-year-old, to the forced removal of a 65-year-old resident from a specialist residential sensory unit, where he has lived for many years, into non-specialist, cheaper, residential care.

Ethnic groups

Relatively little research seems to have been done into the particular needs of members of ethnic groups with sensory impairment. Asian and African-Caribbean communities are known to be particularly prone to glaucoma and diabetic retinopathy. But we know little about the experience of members of these communities.

Language difficulties seem to prevent many people from knowing about their impairment and then obtaining services. In addition, the perception that older members of minority ethnic groups are cared for by large supportive extended families is often not entirely accurate. In reality, they may be lonely and isolated.

Looking on the bright side

In spite of these problems, there are also positive developments for older people with sensory impairment. There is exciting work going on across the UK, with specialist groups drawing together those with a particular interest in sensory loss in older people. They have been encouraged in this partly by the Government's Standards – which include a new set of social services guidelines for sensory impairment – and partly by voluntary sector organisations. The RNIB and Sense both have specialists in the field of late life sensory loss. The RNID has been active in campaigning for better audiology services; as a result, from 2005, all NHS patients will be given digital hearing aids.

As individuals, some specialists have also made a virtue out of a necessity, developing new ways of providing care that may have originated out of a desperate response to under-resourcing but have become something far more significant.

A good example is hearing therapist Alex Willoughby, one of only three in the whole of Kent, who cannot hope to provide support for the entire population of the county. Her waiting lists were growing faster than she could possibly deal with them, so she decided to change the way that she delivered her service.

Alex began running group 'Introduction to tinnitus' sessions, where people find out about the condition, have their audiograms explained, and look at hearing aids. They are given a pack to read, and a slip to return if they want to see someone again. She has set up a similar group for people needing help with communication, where they learn lipreading and tactics.

Both of these groups provide much-needed contact and advice for people with hearing problems who might otherwise have to wait two years for an individual appointment. They enable a tiny staff to see many more people than they would usually be able to. The group setting gets round the problem of people not turning up to appointments and provides mutual support to its members.

So, while many people do still struggle to obtain services to support their sensory impairment, there is hope that the situation will gradually improve and sensory impairment will be given the priority it deserves.

18 Legislation, standards and guidance

This chapter outlines the main legislation that underpins the provision of services to people with a sensory impairment. It then briefly describes the standards and guidance issued by the Government and major sensory organisations, some of which are legally binding on care providers. The following areas are discussed:

- Legislation
- Government Standards
- Voluntary Standards

Over the years, governments and interested parties such as campaigning bodies have tried to organise and improve services to impaired people by passing legislation and by setting standards.

Little of this framework focuses exclusively on sensory impairment – most legislation and standards are drawn up to cover large areas such as discrimination against disabled people, or provision of care to older people. The needs of sensory-impaired older people take their place alongside the needs of many others in this arena.

This chapter therefore briefly sums up the key legislation, standards and guidance that affect, directly or indirectly, the provision of care to older people with a sensory impairment. Only legislation has real teeth, as failure to comply can lead to legal action being taken against a service provider. Standards may be enforceable to some extent, but guidelines are just that – produced only as a guide to best practice.

Legislation

Legislation 1948–1990

John Crossland works as a sensory-loss specialist in social services. He identifies the lack of specific guidance relating to sensory loss in older people as one of the biggest problems for people working in his field: 'There's a kind of hotchpotch of bits and pieces.'

The key legislation is still the ***1948 National Assistance Act***, which gave local authorities responsibility for providing accommodation and services to disabled people, including those with a sensory impairment.

The ***Chronically Sick and Disabled Persons Act of 1970*** established social services departments' responsibility for assessing a disabled person's need for a range of services. The services covered are:

- practical assistance in the home;
- help to obtain radio and/or television, library or similar recreational services;
- help in obtaining education;
- help in travelling to activities listed above;
- adaptations or special equipment to provide greater safety, comfort or convenience at home for the disabled person;
- holidays;
- meals, at home or at a local centre;
- a telephone, and any special equipment needed to use it.

If social services finds that the person needs any of these services, it must provide them or help the person to obtain them.

The ***National Health Service and Community Care Act 1990*** provides the framework for supplying that care, ideally in the community, with individuals determining how to live their own lives. It should mean that care is driven by needs-led assessments. But this is not consistent in sensory loss: visual impairment provision is driven by the registration process but hearing impairment is not.

The Disability Discrimination Act 1995

The Disability Discrimination Act (DDA) of 1995 gives disabled people rights in the areas of:

- employment;
- access to goods, facilltles and services;
- buying or renting land or property.

Employers and service providers must treat everyone, whether disabled or not, equally. This means that they cannot refuse to provide a service on the grounds that a person is disabled. They should also make their goods, facilities and services accessible to everyone by making what the Act calls 'reasonable adjustments'.

Under the DDA, sensory impairment counts as disability if it has a 'substantial' effect on an individual's life.

The main principle behind the Act is whether an individual is treated differently because of their disability. So, for example, if a day centre is taking its clients on an outing but decides that two blind people cannot go because they do not have two members of staff to accompany them and guide them, those two individuals would have a case under the DDA.

The Disability Rights Commission has taken up a number of cases where blind and deaf people have claimed discrimination under the DDA after being refused service in pubs and restaurants because they use an assistance dog. In most cases the deaf and blind claimants have been successful.

Under the DDA, a sensory-impaired person can ask a service provider to enable them to access a service by supporting their communication needs. This support might take the form of an interpreter, or note-taker, provision of information in large print or audio format, or a loop system. However, the Act does not say that service providers must make their services equally accessible, only that they must make 'reasonable adjustments'. So if a service provider can prove that the adjustment requested would be unreasonable, the Act would not apply.

There is relatively little case law at present to show how the Act works in practice, and how 'reasonable adjustment' is defined. Until more cases have been heard, you should seek advice if you think that you might be contravening the DDA, or if you think someone you work with may have a case under the DDA.

The Disability Rights Commission, RNID and Age Concern all provide information on the DDA.

The Human Rights Act 1998

The Human Rights Act (HRA) enables UK citizens to challenge breaches of the European Convention on Human Rights (ECHR) in the UK courts. The ECHR includes the rights to life, to freedom of expression and to privacy.

The HRA applies only to 'public authorities'. These include government departments, local authorities, courts, schools, hospitals, GP surgeries, prisons and public libraries. However, it also covers activities that private organisations carry out for a public authority, such as looking after people in a private care home under a contract with the local authority.

The Act does not cover the activities of private companies that do not carry out any public function. If an organisation carries out both public and private functions, the HRA applies only to its public functions.

The HRA is a wide-ranging Act, and it is impossible to describe here all the areas it covers. As an example, however, of how it might be applied, Article 2 says that a public authority must do what it can to protect a person's right to life if the authority is responsible for that person. This means that, if someone were refused life-saving treatment by health-care services because they were deaf, this might be a breach of Article 2. If a local authority decided to close a care home, which put the life of an older resident at risk, this might also be a breach of Article 2.

For information about the Articles and Protocols of the HRA, ask the RNID for its Factsheet *The Human Rights Act 1998 – information for deaf and hard-of-hearing people*. For more information about the Act generally, contact RNID's Casework Service, the Citizens Advice Bureau, the

Disability Law Service, law centres or Liberty (details in the 'Useful addresses' section).

The HRA is a new piece of legislation and is as yet relatively untried. It is therefore hard to say how it might affect the rights of sensory-impaired people and those responsible for their care. If you want to bring a case under the HRA, or if a case is brought against you, you need to seek legal advice.

Government Standards

The National Service Framework (NSF) for Older People

The NSFs are the Government's plans for what should be achieved in health and social service provision in the future. They cover a ten-year period. There is a Framework for Older People, issued in 2001, but no specific Framework for sensory impairment.

The main voluntary organisations in the sensory impairment field were consulted when the Framework for Older People was put together but, despite this, there are relatively few specific mentions of sensory impairment.

The Framework for Older People should have the effect of coordinating different services and specialisms in order to improve the quality of social and health care for older people. It contains eight Standards, discussed below.

Although there is no Standard explicitly related to sensory impairment, local authorities and the NHS must address sensory impairment in older people in order to fulfil the requirements of the Standards. Taken Standard by Standard, this might have the following implications.

STANDARD 1: ROOTING OUT AGE DISCRIMINATION
STANDARD 2: PERSON-CENTRED CARE

These two Standards aim to ensure that older people with sensory impairment have the same access to services as other groups. This would include providing information in an appropriate format for the individual; for example, using large print in a hospital letter.

STANDARD 3: INTERMEDIATE CARE

When someone is discharged from hospital, they need to be assessed for sensory impairment and to have this taken into account when deciding intermediate care. This means that all health and social care staff should know about the full range of specialist services available – often they do not.

STANDARD 4: GENERAL HOSPITAL CARE

If hospital staff are unaware of someone's sensory impairment, they will be unable to provide a high-quality service, and may additionally cause significant distress. Ophthalmologists and eye clinic teams should refer people for social care assessment as soon as possible.

STANDARD 5: STROKE

Stroke can lead to sight problems, and pre-existing sight problems that have gone undetected can make rehabilitation more difficult.

STANDARD 6: FALLS

Sensory impairment – especially visual – is a significant factor in causing older people to fall: someone with a visual impairment is 1.5 to 2 times as likely to fall and fracture a hip. Dual sensory impairment affects balance, which also increases the likelihood of a fall. Many older people with a sensory impairment become housebound, and lose their fitness, which makes them more likely to fall.

STANDARD 7: MENTAL HEALTH

People with a sensory impairment in old age may be more prone to depression. In addition, the effects of sensory impairment need to be well understood when working with someone with dementia, where the symptoms are often confused.

STANDARD 8: PROMOTING ACTIVE HEALTHY LIFE IN OLDER AGE

In order to maintain independence and mobility, people need to exercise. But many older people with sensory impairment find it hard to exercise because of their social isolation, mobility problems, lack of awareness of their needs at leisure facilities, and their own and others' low expectations.

National Minimum Standards

These Standards cover residential care, and were issued by the Department of Health and the National Care Standards Commission (NCSC). In April 2004, the role of the NCSC was taken over by the new Commission for Social Care Inspection (CSCI). As part of its work the CSCI will:

- carry out local inspections of all social care organisations – public, private and voluntary – against national standards, and publish reports;
- register services that meet national minimum standards;
- carry out inspections of local social services authorities.

Many providers of residential care found it hard to meet all of the requirements under the National Minimum Standards when they were first put in place, and the Government responded by revising some standards, and dropping others altogether. These Standards are less prescriptive than the Best Practice Standards (see below), which give inspectors more freedom when registering homes. Once the CSCI has been up and running for a time, there may be further changes to the Standards.

There is no specific Standard for sensory loss. However, in order to meet the Standards, homes will have to ensure that the needs of residents with a sensory impairment are fully met. Areas that are most relevant in relation to these Standards are communication, information, environment, aids and adaptations, and training.

To date, the inspectors have not been universally rigorous in applying these Standards to the care of people with a visual and/or hearing impairment. However, as they are better trained, they are expected to become more experienced in judging what care is appropriate, and in offering advice.

You can find more information about the National Minimum Standards on the Care Standards' website (see page 278).

Section 7 Guidance

'Section 7 Guidance' is more properly known as 'Social Care for Deafblind Children and Adults'. It was issued by the Department of Health in March 2001 as guidance on Section 7 of the Local Authority Social Services Act 1970.

Deafblind UK and Sense campaigned hard for this government Guidance, which lays down the duty of social services to provide services for deafblind people. It has six main points:

- To identify, make contact with and keep a record of deafblind people in their catchment area (including those who have multiple disabilities that include dual sensory impairment).
- To ensure that an assessment is carried out by a specifically trained person or team equipped to assess the needs of a deafblind person – in particular to assess the need for one-to-one human support, assistive technology and rehabilitation.
- To ensure that appropriate services are provided to deafblind people, who are not necessarily able to benefit from mainstream services or those services aimed primarily at blind people or deaf people.
- To ensure that an accessible, specifically trained, one-to-one support worker is available for those assessed as requiring one.
- To provide information about services in formats and through methods that are accessible to deafblind people.
- To ensure that one member of senior management includes, within their responsibilities, overall responsibility for deafblind services.

As yet, Section 7 Guidance effectively means that each local authority must have a manager responsible for dual impairment, without checking that the manager is carrying out these responsibilities. So, in effect, it is down to individual, over-worked managers to decide how to respond to dual impairment. However, initial signs are positive, as Sense has been approached by a number of local authorities for advice on implementing Section 7 Guidance.

Voluntary Standards

Best Practice Standards

The Best Practice Standards for Social Services are voluntary standards. They have been put together by voluntary sector organisations and endorsed by the Government. They are not mandatory, and should be treated as best practice guidelines.

A set of Standards has been issued for those working with each of the following three groups:

- Deaf and hard-of-hearing people.
- Deafblind people.
- Visually impaired people.

Generally speaking, most social services departments have welcomed the Best Practice Standards. They are quite detailed, and can be useful for non-specialist managers looking for ways to improve the quality of their service and for specialists to use as benchmarks when arguing for extra resources.

RNIB accreditation

The RNIB receives many requests for recommendations of homes for people who have a visual impairment. In response it has started an accreditation scheme in order to be able to recommend homes that provide good care. The scheme focuses on three areas:

- Staff training.
- Communication and information.
- Environment (interior and exterior).

What are the advantages of accreditation for a home?

- Being accredited can increase the home's bed occupancy as a result of recommendations.
- Trained staff can help residents to live more independently. This will create more staff time for other activities.
- An accredited home is more likely to meet the demands laid down by the Care Standards Act and the DDA.
- In some areas, homes receive extra funding if they fulfil quality criteria.

Primarily, however, the RNIB's concern is to help ensure that people with a visual disability receive a good standard of care.

> **'It's about how much a home cares about its service.'** *Sandra Cronin, RNIB*

The RNID has an accreditation scheme, 'Louder than Words', for organisations that offer a high-quality deaf-aware service. Contact the RNID's Information Line (see page 289).

19 Training

Training is a vitally important part of developing your staff and helping them to provide good-quality support for sensory-impaired people. This chapter explores why you need to take training seriously, and how to plan it. In particular, the following areas are covered:

- The scope of sensory training
- What can training achieve?
- How does training benefit you and your staff?
- What training may cover
- Awareness training
- Tailor your training
- Choosing your training
- NVQ, level 2
- Is sensory impairment training a low priority?
- Government Standards and implications for training
- Where to get your training
- Funding support for training

Most people have preconceptions about visual and hearing impairment, even if they are in regular contact with people who have vision or hearing difficulties, and many of these preconceptions are wrong. This can severely affect the quality of care they provide.

This is what makes learning about sensory impairment worthwhile – it enables staff to make a huge difference to the quality of care they provide, and it also makes staff's own lives easier.

In Chapter 11 we saw an example of how training can improve someone's quality of life: a resident is having problems dressing because she cannot find her clothes, so her care worker – untrained in sensory impairment – chooses the resident's clothes and helps her to dress. The resident hates this – she is losing her dignity, self-esteem and independence because she cannot see well – and it takes up the care worker's valuable time.

Had the care worker been trained in visual impairment, she would have talked to the resident to find out why dressing is a problem. She would discover that the resident cannot find her clothes because they are never put back in the same place twice. So she would explain to the staff member responsible for delivering laundry the importance of putting it away in the correct drawer every time. The resident would regain her independence in dressing, and the care worker would no longer have to dress her.

The staff member responsible for laundry should also then be given training in sensory impairment.

> 'It is often the case that training is directed at managers and 'care/nursing' staff. But ancillary staff are likely to be in just as much contact with service users and therefore will also benefit from training.' *Graham Smith, RNIB*

The scope of sensory training

The laundry worker's training in this case would not just be in how to sort the washing but would also encompass the nature of visual impairment and what a particular eye condition means to the individual concerned. The more all staff understand about sensory impairment, the better they will be at supporting people with that impairment and at thinking of their own solutions to the problems created by it.

Training in this field should encourage people to look for individual solutions to individual problems. So, while this book proposes many solutions to problems caused by sensory impairment, they are of course general in nature. Training enables you to adapt other people's ideas and to try new ways until you arrive at something that works for you and the individuals you work with.

What can training achieve?

Good training looks beyond the purely practical, for example guiding skills or lipreading. It addresses the way that you and your staff think about sensory impairment and how you use that knowledge in your work.

Training can help you to:

- identify failing sight or hearing in someone you work with;
- learn how to communicate effectively;
- find out what facilities someone may need in order to help them with their impairment – from providing a speaking clock to help a vision-impaired person to adapting the environment for a dual-sensory-impaired person;
- provide the help that a sensory-impaired person needs in terms of care, service and information;
- make sure that people with a sensory impairment share all the opportunities available to those without one – you may be excluding people by not providing them with information about events, activities or services in a form they can use;
- know what help is available – you cannot help if you do not know what resources there are;
- understand what is helpful and what is not (you may have wasted much time looking for an appropriate magnifier when in fact a brighter light would have helped the person to read in comfort);
- learn about your responsibility to ensure that people have access to services;
- learn about the rights of disabled/older people.

Sensory impairment training will improve the quality of service you provide to all the people you work with, whether they are sensory impaired or not.

> 'To establish the practice of not passing a resident who is blind without a greeting, will also be beneficial to sighted residents.' *Graham Smith, RNIB*

How does training benefit you and your staff?

If you and your staff are properly trained, not only you will be able to improve the quality of life of those you work with but also:

- your staff will gain in confidence;
- they may be able to gain NVQs;
- you are more likely to comply with registration standards;
- you will provide a better service;
- you will therefore attract more people to your service.

> 'I took time out to qualify as a Communication Support Worker with Deaf People. I definitely feel that this was worth while.' *Jacqui Jackson, Assessment Officer, Hi Kent*

What training may cover

Areas that basic sensory training commonly covers are:

- the signs and symptoms of failing sight and hearing;
- common eye and ear conditions;
- the emotional impact of sight and hearing loss;
- mobility, guiding and orientation;
- communication;
- daily living skills;
- environmental factors (light, acoustics, and so on);
- multiple impairments;
- counselling skills.

Once staff have been trained at a basic level, some may wish to learn more advanced skills. For example, they may wish to learn more about working with people with severe dual-sensory impairment.

Awareness training

The most common training in sensory impairment is awareness training, which is designed to create a greater understanding of sensory impairment at a basic level. Most awareness training includes: information about the nature of sensory loss, the dispelling of myths, discussion about the needs of people with sensory loss, and simulation activities – where course members use simulation spectacles or ear muffs to imitate the effect of sensory loss.

This last aspect of awareness training is controversial in some quarters – some people with a sensory impairment argue that such simulation exercises cannot recreate the experience of a sensory impairment – being temporary and not taking into account the skills of a sensory-impaired person. There is also a fear that simulation will create pity rather than empathy and understanding, and help to compound an image of sensory-impaired people as victims – one that fundraisers in this field tend to play on to evoke sympathy. These images tie in very neatly with society's preconceptions about disability in general and sensory impairment in particular.

None the less, simulation activities remain a common and popular element in awareness training, and can give participants the beginnings of an idea about what sensory impairment might mean. Done well, and within a positive framework that does not victimise the impaired person, it can be an extremely powerful tool for enabling people to reassess their views of sensory impairment.

Awareness training tends to be more effective in promoting an understanding of the practical challenges brought about by sensory impairment than the psychological effects. If the staff of a day-care centre spend half a day doing a simulation exercise and come to realise that no visually impaired person would be able to find their toilets, or that a hard-of-hearing person cannot hear the bingo because of the radio behind them, they have learned something of real practical use – and should think more carefully in the future about the needs of the people they work with who have a sensory impairment.

The key to all awareness training is to learn not to inflict your own view of what people's needs are in a given situation but, rather, to find out and respond to what these needs are.

Tailor your training

It is important to think carefully about why you are providing a certain type of training. For example, one care home gave all its staff training in deaf-blindness, which included learning deafblind manual. However, no residents – even those with a dual loss – used deafblind manual: like most people who have age-related sensory loss, they preferred to continue to use speech. Precious training time was spent learning a skill that staff were unlikely to use or to see the point of, and this might consequently deter them from taking on other training. To avoid this pitfall, carry out an audit of your staff's existing skills and knowledge, look at the work that they do and establish what they need to know, before you plan their training.

Staff who meet the public regularly, such as reception staff, need basic awareness training. This will teach them to recognise and respect different sensory loss groups and give them basic communication skills. They may also need to learn telephone skills. Staff working in day care, residential care and domiciliary care, and any non-specialist staff working with sensory-impaired people on a regular basis need similar basic training. They also need specific training relating to the environment and the people they work with, together with more developed communication skills.

Specialist workers with sensory-impaired people such as specialist social workers, care managers and technical officers need a high level of skill; for example, if they work with deaf people, they will learn communication methods such as British Sign Language (BSL). They need a broad and in-depth level of knowledge, as they may be asked to act as advisers to others.

Training needs to reflect your local situation. If you use a non-local training provider, they may not provide information about local services and organisations, which can be a crucial part of your staff's knowledge base. You will need to ensure that staff acquire that local knowledge some other way.

Choosing your training

The Department of Health has set out some useful basic guidelines for choosing the right training for staff in its listing of courses available. They suggest assessing the training under the following headings.

Quality of the training

- The experience and qualification of the trainers.
- All practical activities, especially those involving high risks, such as outdoor travel, and food preparation and cooking, require supervised practice.
- Is the course accredited; if so, by whom?

Suitability of a course for local needs

- What kind of training do you need?
- If staff are upgrading their skills, they may need a top-up course.
- Awareness training and skill development may be most appropriate for staff in reception/day/residential settings.
- Do you need in-house or external training, or a mixture of both?
- Do some of your staff need additional or refresher courses? This may be negotiable.

Training methods

- Is the course mainly practical or academic?
- What is the size of the group being taught?
- Are there practice placements?

Selection methods

Most courses are suitable for all applicants. However, students for rehabilitation courses may be selected according to their:

- academic achievements;
- experience of sensory impairment;
- previous employment experience;
- personal qualities.

Practical details

- Duration of the course – it may be flexible or modular.
- Location of the course – this may be negotiable.
- Cost.

NVQ in Care, Level 2

A National Vocational Qualification (NVQ) or Scottish Vocational Qualification (SVQ) in Scotland is the main vocational qualification taken by care staff, and Level 2 was laid down by the Government as the minimum standard all staff should achieve. In practice, this target has proved impossible to meet, largely because of funding shortages, recruitment and retention problems in residential care, and the fact that it can take two years to achieve Level 2. The Government has therefore revised the target down to having 50 per cent of staff qualified to Level 2. Even this is regarded by some home owners as a tough target. However, an NVQ at Level 2 is a useful and valuable qualification for care staff and includes an important sensory impairment component. NVQs have two parts: underpinning knowledge and practice.

> 'The most useful part of the NVQ is the bit on communication. To understand their [people's] deafness, you've got to understand why they're deaf. And that helps you understand why they behave in a particular way.' *Gill, Senior Carer in a care home*

For more information on NVQs, get in touch with the Training Organisation in Personal and Social Services (TOPSS; contact details on page 294).

Note that although the courses accredited by the Council for the Advancement of Communication with Deaf People (CACDP) cover much of the required NVQ material, they do not qualify candidates for NVQ because of the need for additional evidence.

Is sensory-impairment training a low priority?

Some care staff receive training, such as a day course run by a local voluntary organisation. Some local authorities also run induction programmes for staff in their own care homes and centres, which include some awareness of sensory loss. But most staff in these environments receive no training at all, and those in related professions such as nursing and dentistry, and even audiology and ophthalmology, almost never receive training. The Kent Association for the Blind finds that nurses often do not take up training even when it is offered.

> 'We offer awareness training to the residential care sector, but there's very little take up because of fast staff turnover, and lack of money and time.' *Ann Lewis, Rehabilitation Services Manager, KAB*

> 'I don't see sensory loss necessarily as a separate issue. It should be an integral part of staff training. Training is expensive, and specialised training costs are often prohibitive. It is therefore essential that it is part of induction rather than separate.

> 'Often, staff are reluctant to attend sessions, as they may lose time and/or money. For providers, a day's training can cost up to £700, taking into account the trainer cost and staff pay, including replacement costs. Add to this the current retention issues and the picture becomes more difficult.' *Nadra Ahmed, National Care Homes Association and care home owner*

But Nadra's own care manager found that her staff were keen to learn from her:

> 'We're forever going on to the net – say, the BUPA website to find out about strokes – the staff are all very keen to learn. It helps the staff and the residents. They've all got their specialities – for example, one does wound care. We put information about an issue affecting a resident on the board, and staff read it and sign. So we've just put up stuff about the types of stroke there are, and ways of making the resident more comfortable.' *Pauline, Senior Carer*

Graham Willetts, at RNIB, puts the lack of training in sensory loss down to five main reasons:

- Poor pay in the sector, with unqualified and undervalued staff.
- Pressure groups seeking better care have tended to ignore sensory impairment.
- Sensory impairment is perceived to be less disabling than other conditions affecting older people, and its incidence is hugely underestimated.

- Social services have not committed resources to sensory loss in older people.
- Too many myths and stereotypes make people feel that 'there is nothing to be done', and that sensory loss is just something older people have to accept; service providers and users both have low expectations and feel that older people 'do not have the capacity to learn skills and benefit from either habilitation or rehabilitation', finds Willetts.

He adds that 'the qualifications framework has been woefully underdeveloped', so work in sensory disability is not seen as fashionable or rewarding as a career. In addition, such training as there is 'has not taught or emphasised the skills necessary for working with older people'.

Government Standards and implications for training

This lack of emphasis on training may change, however, because recent Government Standards give proper training a high priority. For example, Standard 20 of the National Minimum Standards requires all staff to receive foundation training within six months of appointment, which equips them to meet the assessed needs of the service users. As so many older people have a sensory impairment, staff will need to be trained to look after them.

Section 7 Guidance establishes that social services departments must ensure that they have a suitably trained specialist and non-specialist workforce in relation to dual impairment.

There are also signs that there has been a general growth of interest in sensory impairment by the social care sector: in the last few years, Best Practice Standards have been issued, giving guidance for service providers working with people with sight loss, hearing loss and dual loss. These have all been endorsed by the Department of Health and/or the Association of Directors of Social Services. In order to achieve the improvements set out in these documents, training will have to be taken seriously.

The new National Service Framework for Older People raises the profile of the needs of older people, which can only be provided by staff who are fully trained in all areas, including sensory impairment.

(See also Chapter 18 for more information on these Standards and guidelines.)

Where to get your training

All the main campaigning organisations offer training, as do many other smaller organisations. The Department of Health put together lists of training courses in visual impairment, hearing impairment and dual impairment. They have stopped updating these lists but in late 2003 free copies were still available from the Department of Health (address on page 280).

It is also well worth contacting your local voluntary organisations for people with vision or hearing difficulties, and your local social services and rehabilitation workers. They may be able to recommend locally run courses tailored to local conditions.

The Council for the Advancement of Communication with Deaf People (CACDP) is an excellent source of information about courses relating to hearing and dual impairment; it is the accrediting body for such courses.

Distance learning

Distance learning can provide an effective alternative to face-to-face training, or a valuable supplement to it.

Useful materials include packages such as the RNIB's *Older people and sight loss – the basics* (RNIB 2002), which is good for all staff, and *New Independence* (Beliveau-Tobey 1994), which is for people working in residential care. The Department of Health's lists of training courses includes a number of distance learning packages; it is also useful to contact major sensory-impairment organisations to find out what they can offer.

Major course providers

Major course providers for hearing impairment and dual impairment include:

- Royal Association for Deaf People – offers courses in BSL, and deaf, deafblind and disability awareness.
- RNID – training courses cover general awareness, the Disability Discrimination Act (DDA) and its implications, equipment, BSL, deaf-blind awareness, age-related sensory loss and its emotional impact.
- The Centre for Deaf People, at the City Lit, London, runs courses for community-based support workers for people who are deaf or hard of hearing.
- Sense courses include deafblindness awareness, communication strategies, aromatherapy and relaxation, communication and guiding, and technology. Sense operates from regional offices – contact its headquarters to find the one nearest you (see page 293).
- Manchester Metropolitan University offers a postgraduate Diploma and MA in Social Work with Deaf People for experienced practitioners.

Major course providers for visual impairment and dual sensory loss include:

- RNIB
- Guide Dogs for the Blind Association
- Henshaws Society for Blind People
- Queen Alexandra College
- Royal London School for the Blind
- Royal National College for the Blind

The future of the School of Vision and Rehabilitation studies, which over-sees the training of guide dogs, is under discussion.

New courses

The University of Central England has established a whole framework of courses, from foundation to degree, for training in rehabilitation, including a basic course for those working in the area who do not want to become rehabilitation workers.

CACDP has accredited three new NVQ courses in working with deafblind people – they cover awareness, support work and communication/guiding. These are especially suitable for staff working with older people with acquired dual sensory loss.

Funding support for training

Local authorities and voluntary organisations with a service contract can apply for help with funding for sensory-impairment training from the Department of Health (for social services departments) or the local authority (for organisations with a local authority contract). There are details on the DoH website.

GLOSSARY

Terms given in *italics* are also defined in this glossary.

audiologist audiologists test hearing and fit hearing aids; they are not necessarily medical doctors

audiology the testing of hearing and treating of hearing problems; the audiology department is where hearing tests are carried out and hearing aids fitted

binocular vision vision using both eyes

block a means of communicating with someone with very poor vision and hearing by using your finger to 'write' letters on the person's hand

Braille a means of writing using raised dots on paper that a blind person can feel and 'read'

British Sign Language (BSL) the main sign language used by the Deaf community in the UK

cataract a clouding of the lens in the eye, causing poor vision

cochlear deafness *see* sensorineural deafness

conductive hearing loss the deafness resulting when sounds cannot get through the outer or middle ear

deafblind impairment of both vision and hearing

deafblind manual using the hands to spell out letters: each letter of the alphabet is represented by a different shape on the fingers (see Figure 10.2)

decibel (dB) a measurement of the intensity (loudness) of a sound

detached retina the retina becomes partly or completely detached from the back of the eye: the symptoms are a black patch across the *field of vision* and possibly bright flashes and many 'floaters' (black spots floating in the eye's fluid); if someone experiences these, they should go straight to hospital

diabetic retinopathy changes in the retina, causing poor vision; they are caused by diabetes

dual sensory impairment also called 'deafblindness', this is when some-one has significant loss of both sight and hearing

field of vision the total area of what we can see (*see also* peripheral vision)

fingerspelling a means of spelling out letters on the hands (*see Figure 10.1. and see also* deafblind manual)

glaucoma a range of eye conditions resulting from high pressure inside the eye

glue ear the Eustachian (pharyngotympanic) tube gets blocked and air can-not reach the middle ear, reducing hearing

guide communicator someone who works beside a dual-sensory-impaired person to help them to remain independent and to relieve isolation

inductive listener a device used by a hard-of-hearing person to listen to sound relayed by an inductive loop

lipreader someone who watches the shapes made on another's lips as they speak, in order to read what they are saying

lux a measurement of light intensity

macular degeneration a disease of the retina, causing poor vision; it affects the centre of the *field of vision*

magnifier a lens used to enlarge close objects or type; it may be hand-held or in a frame

Makaton a communication system for people with speech and learning difficulties

Menière's disease the main effect is dizziness; it can also cause nausea, *tinnitus* and hearing loss

monocular using only one eye

neck loop a small induction loop worn round a hearing-aid user's neck to enable them to listen to selected sound sources

ophthalmologist a medical doctor specialising in eye disease

optometrist a practitioner who tests vision and prescribes corrective lenses

otosclerosis the chain of tiny bones inside the ear become rigid, causing *tinnitus* and hearing loss

peripheral vision what you can see around the sides of your *field of vision*

presbyacusis age-related deafness

registered blind someone whose sight is extremely poor; to obtain support from social services, a visually impaired person must be registered as blind

retinitis pigmentosa an eye condition causing loss of *peripheral vision*

Section 7 guidance more properly known as 'Social Care for Deafblind Children and Adults', this was issued by the Department of Health in March 2001 as guidance on Section 7 of the Local Authority Social Services Act 1970; it places the onus on social services departments to provide specifically for dual-impaired people

sensorineural deafness hearing impairment caused by damage to the inner ear

sensory impairment hearing or sight (or both) is impaired

Sign Supported English (SSE) a form of English with key signs added

stetoclip a small receiver through which a deaf person who does not wear a hearing aid may receive signals from a listening device

symbol cane a short white cane, used by someone to indicate to others that he or she is visually impaired

tinnitus noises in the ears or head

tunnel vision being able to see only a narrow area

typoscope a small sheet of black card or plastic with a wide slot through which a visually impaired person can look at a single line of text

Usher syndrome a condition that causes deafness, followed by visual impairment

vertigo a symptom of some conditions, vertigo is a kind of dizziness where the world seems to spin

visual field *see* field of vision

REFERENCES AND FURTHER READING

Ainlay SC (1989) *Day brought back my night: aging and new vision loss*. London: Routledge

Anand JK and Court I (1989) 'Hearing loss leading to impaired ability to communicate in residents homes for the elderly', *British Medical Journal*, vol 298 (issue 6685), pages 1429–1430

Ashley J (1991) 'The silent house', in Taylor G and Bishop J (eds) *Being deaf: the experience of deafness*. London: Pinter Publishers in association with the Open University

Bagley M (1998) 'Communication and people who have lost vision and hearing in late life'. Proceedings from Expert Meeting on Older People with Vision and Hearing Loss, 18–24 March, Copenhagen, Denmark. Published on website: www.deafblindinternational.org

Baker M (1998) *Lost vision: older visually impaired people in the UK*; Campaign Report 6. London: RNIB

Barker P, Barrick J and Wilson R (1995) *Building sight: a handbook of building and interior design solutions to include the needs of visually impaired people*. London: HMSO for RNIB

Beliveau-Tobey M (1994) *New independence*. London: RNIB/Aware

Bernardini L (1985) 'Effective communication as an intervention for sensory deprivation in the elderly client', *Topics in Nursing*, vol 61 (issue 4), pages 72–81

Browne M (2002) *Patient support services in eye clinics – a nationwide survey*. London: RNIB

Bruce I and Walker E (1991) 'Challenges and opportunities: blind and partially sighted adults in Britain: the RNIB needs survey', *New Beacon*, vol 75 (issue 8892), pages 413–420

Caissie R and Rockwell E (1994) 'Communication difficulties experienced by nursing home residents with a hearing loss during conversation with staff members', *Journal of Speech–Language Pathology and Audiology*, vol 18 (issue 2), pages 127–134

Conyers MC (1986) 'Emotional and practical adjustment to loss of sight', paper presented at XXV International Congress of Ophthalmology, May, Rome [Available from the RNIB library]

Costie J (2001) 'We speak through our hands; we need yours too', *Baptist Times* (London), 25 January

Counsel and Care (1993) *Sound barriers: a study of the needs of older people with hearing loss living in residential care and nursing homes*. London: Counsel and Care

Cox R (2004) 'On the critical list?', *New Beacon*, vol 88 (issue 1029), pages 28–30

Crossland J (2003) 'Re-visioning services for "the Blind": how have specialist rehabilitation services for visually impaired people responded to the effects of the demographic transition on the profile of the service user group over recent decades?' MA Thesis

Cullinan T (1986) *Visual disability in the elderly*. London: Croom Helm

Deafblind Services Liaison Group (1988) *Breaking through: developing services for deaf-blind people*. London: The Group

Department of Health (1995) *Think dual sensory*. London: DoH

Department of Health (2001a) *Courses by trainers in hearing impairment and dual sensory loss*, 1st edition. London: DoH

Department of Health (2001b) *Courses by trainers in visual impairment and dual sensory loss*, 7th edition. London: DoH

Erber NP (1993) *Communication and adult hearing loss*. Clifton Hill, Victoria, Australia: Clavis Publishing

Erber NP, Lamb NL and Lind C (1996) 'Factors that affect the use of hearing aids by older people: a new perspective', *American Journal of Audiology*, vol 5 (issue 2), pages 11–18

Evans JR, Fletcher AE, Wormald RP, *et al* (2002) 'Prevalence of visual impairment in people aged 75 years and older in Britain: results from the MRC Trial of the Assessment and Management of Older People in the Community', *British Journal of Ophthalmology*, vol 86 (issue 7), pages 795–800

French S, Gillman M and Swain J (1997) *Working with visually disabled people: bridging theory and practice*. Birmingham: Venture Press

Gerson LW, Jarjoura D and McCord G (1989) 'Risk of imbalance in elderly people with impaired hearing or vision', *Age and Ageing*, vol 18 (issue 1), pages 31–34

Gilhome Herbst K (1982) 'Social attitudes to hearing loss in the elderly', in Glendenning F (ed) *Acquired hearing loss and elderly people*. Stoke-on-Trent: Beth Johnson Foundation in association with the University of Keele

Gilhome Herbst K (1986) 'Hearing aids for the elderly: expediency versus felt need', *British Journal of Audiology*, vol 20 (issue 2), pages 91–93

Gilkes M (1979) 'Eyes run on light', *British Medical Journal*, vol 1 (issue 6179), pages 1681–1683

Goffman E (1963) *Stigma*. Englewood Cliffs, New Jersey: Prentice-Hall

Grindley S (1997) *Losing sight of blindness*; Campaign Report 2. London: RNIB

Hi Kent (1993) *Communicating with hearing impaired*. Information sheet 4.2 (1) 4/93. Maidstone, Kent: Hi Kent

Hull RH (1992) 'The impact of hearing impairment on aging persons: a dialogue', in Hull RH (ed) *Aural rehabilitation*, 2nd edition. London: Chapman and Hall

Huvenaars A and Wijnhoven R (1998) 'Kalorama', in Proceedings from Expert Meeting on Older People with Vision and Hearing Loss, 18–24 March, 1998, Copenhagen, Denmark. Published on website: www.deafblindinternational.org

James P and Thomas M (1996) 'Deconstructing a disabling environment in social work education', *Social Work Education*, vol 15 (issue 1), pages 34–45

Kaplan HF (1992) 'The impact of hearing impairment and the need to facilitate adjustment', in Hull RH (ed) *Aural rehabilitation*, 2nd edition. London: Chapman and Hall

Lewycka M (2001) *Caring for someone with a hearing loss*. London: Age Concern

Lewycka M (2002) *Caring for someone with a sight problem*. London: Age Concern

McBride S (2001) *Patients talking 2*. London: RNIB

McCall R (1982) 'Communication and acquired hearing loss', in Glendenning F (ed) *Acquired hearing loss and elderly people*. Stoke-on-Trent: Beth Johnson Foundation in association with the University of Keele

Oliver M (1983) *Social work with disabled people*. London: Macmillan

Palmer B (unpublished) *Enforced isolation. a study of the needs of dual sensory disabled people living in Leicestershire*. Leicester: Royal Leicestershire Rutland and Wycliffe Society for the Blind

Perry C (2002) *Improving environments for people with dementia and sight problems*. London: RNIB

Ringgold N (1991) *Out of the corner of my eye: living with vision loss in late life*. New York: American Foundation for the Blind

RNIB (2002). *Older people and sight loss – the basics*. London: RNIB

RNIB/Health Promotion England (2001) *Older people, visual impairment and accidents*, RNIB Factsheet 3. London

RNID (2000). *General statistics on hearing*. London: RNID

RNID (2001a) *Audiology in crisis: still waiting to hear*. London: RNID

RNID (2001b) *Your home is your castle … make it theirs*. London: RNID

RNID (2002) *A good audiology service: what you can expect*. London: RNID

RNID (2003a) *The Disability Discrimination Act 1995 (DDA) – a guide for providers of goods, facilities and services* (factsheet). London:RNID

RNID (2003b) *The Human Rights Act 1998 – information for deaf and hard of hearing people* (factsheet). London: RNID

Scott R (1969) *The making of blind men*. New York: Russell Sage Foundation

Smeeth L, Fletcher AE, Ng ES, *et al* (2002) 'Reduced hearing, ownership, and use of hearing aids in elderly people in the UK – the MRC Trial of the Assessment and Management of Older People in the Community: a cross-sectional survey', *The Lancet*, vol 359 (issue 9316), pages 1466–1470

Stephens SDG (1982) 'What is acquired hearing loss in the elderly?' in Glendenning, F (ed) *Acquired hearing loss and elderly people*. Stoke-on-Trent: Beth Johnson Foundation in association with the University of Keele

Taylor G and Bishop J (eds) (1991) *Being deaf: the experience of deafness*. London: Pinter Publishers in association with the Open University

Taylor G and Gregory S (1991) *Being deaf: perspectives on deafness: an introduction*. London: Open University

Tester S (1989) *Caring by day: a study of day care services for older people*. London: Centre for Policy on Ageing

Vale D and Smyth C (2003) *Changing the way we think about blindness*. London: RNIB

Weddell L (2003) 'Examining the elderly population: strategies for the optometrist', *Optometry Today*, 7 February, pages 31–34

Willetts G (2002) 'Loss of hearing – a contributory factor to frailty in older blind and partially sighted people, and some possibilities for developing service responses', presented to the 2002 RNIB conference on visual impairment and older people

Williams PC (1993) 'Care management and assessment with blind and partially sighted people', in Stevens A (ed) *Back from the wellhouse: discussion paper on sensory impairment and training in community care services*. London: Central Council for Education and Training in Social Work

Williams PC (1994) In Waterson, J and Willetts G (eds) *Reaching the needs of people with visual disabilities* (training package). London: RNIB/HMSO

Woodcock K (2001) 'All roads lead to ALDA'. On the Association of Late-Deafened Adults' website: www.deafened.org

Age Concern, RNIB and RNID publish a wide range of extremely useful, regularly updated factsheets, many of which can be downloaded from their websites. They have been invaluable in the preparation of this book.

USEFUL ADDRESSES

Action for Blind People
14–16 Verney Road
London SE16 3DZ
Tel: 020 7635 4800
National Information Hotline: 0900 915 4666
Fax: 020 7635 4900
Email: info@afbp.org
Website: www.afbp.org
A charity that promotes equality for blind and partially sighted people. Offers advice and support, with particular expertise in housing, welfare, employment and leisure.

Age Concern England
see page 301

ALDA (Association of Late-Deafened Adults, USA)
Website: www.deafened.org
A support and information website for people who became deaf in late childhood or adulthood.

Association of Lipspeakers (ALS)
ALS Information Office
5 Furlong Close
Upper Tean
Stoke-on-Trent ST10 4LB
Tel: 01538 722482
Fax/textphone: 01538 722442
Email: information@lipspeaking.co.uk
Website: www.lipspeaking.co.uk
The professional association for lipspeakers, it can advise on choosing and booking a lipspeaker; runs a list of qualified lipspeakers.

Association of Optometrists
61 Southwark Street
London SE1 0HL
Tel: 020 7261 9661
Fax: 020 7261 0228
Website: www.assoc-optometrists.org
The professional association for optometrists.

Association of Teachers of Lipreading to Adults (ATLA)
PO Box 506
Hanley
Stoke-on-Trent ST2 9RE
Fax: 0870 706 2916
Email: ATLA@lipreading.org.uk
Website: www.lipreading.org.uk
The professional association for teachers of lipreading to adults; will send information about lipreading classes.

Benefits Enquiry Line for people with disabilities
Tel: 0800 882 200
Textphone: 0800 243 355 (Mon–Fri 8.30am–6.30pm. Sat 9am–1pm)
Run by the Department for Work and Pensions, it gives information about elgibility for state benefits.

NORTHERN IRELAND
Tel: 0800 220 674
Textphone: 0800 243 787 (Mon–Fri 9am–5pm)

Better Hearing
2B Lynwood Close
Harrow
Middlesex HA2 9PR
Advice line: 07830 179084
Fax: 020 8248 1179
Email: advice@betterhearing.co.uk
Website: www.betterhearing.co.uk
Information about hearing aids provided by private audiologists.

British Cochlear Implant Group
Website: www.bcig.org
Provides information about cochlear implants for health professionals and people with cochlear implants.

British Deaf Association (BDA)
1–3 Worship Street
London EC2A 2AB
Tel: 0870 770 3300
Textphone: 0800 652 2965
Videophone: 020 7496 9539
Fax: 020 7588 3527

Email: helpline@bda.org.uk
Website: www.britishdeafassociation.org.uk
Represents the Deaf community – British deaf people who use British Sign Language.

British Retinitis Pigmentosa Society
PO Box 350
Buckingham MK18 1GZ
Tel: 01280 821 334
Helpline: 0845 123 2354 (Mon–Fri 9.30am–1pm, Mon–Thu 1.30pm–5pm)
Fax: 01280 815900
Email: lynda@brps.org.uk
Website: www.brps.org.uk
Provides information on all matters of interest to people with retinitis pigmentosa and their families.

British Society of Audiology
80 Brighton Road
Reading RG8 1PS
Tel: 0118 966 0622
Fax: 0118 935 1915
Email: bsa@b-s-a.demon.co.uk
Website: www.thebsa.demon.co.uk
One of the organisations for audiology professionals.

British Society of Hearing Therapists
12 Southend Avenue
Darlington DL3 7HL
Tel: 01325 358185
Fax: 01325 469433
Email: dthearing@gofree.co.uk
Website: www.hearingtherapy.org
Professional body for hearing therapists.

British Telecom (BT)
Tel: 0800 919591
Textphone: 18001 0800 919591
Fax: 020 8326 9339
Email: disability@bt.com
Website: www.btplc.com/age_disability/
Information about telephone products and services useful for sensory-impaired people.

British Tinnitus Association
Ground Floor, Unit 5
Acorn Business Park
Woodseats Close
Sheffield S8 0TB
Tel: 0800 018 0527 (free in UK)
0845 4500 321 (local rate in UK)
0114 250 9922 (national rate)
Fax: 0114 258 2279
Email: info@tinnitus.org.uk
Website: www.tinnitus.org.uk
Advice and support for people with tinnitus. Details of local support groups.

Care Council for Wales
6th Floor
South Gate House
Wood Street
Cardiff CF10 1EW
Tel: 029 2022 6257
Fax: 029 2038 4764
Email: info@ccwales.org.uk
Website: www.ccwales.org.uk
Regulates and registers social care workers in Wales. Provides information about training.

Care Standards
Website: www.carestandards.org.uk
For information about the National Minimum Standards.

Chest, Heart and Stroke Scotland
65 North Castle Street
Edinburgh EH2 3LT
Tel: 0131 225 6963
Fax: 0131 220 6316
Website: www.chss.org.uk
Provides advice, information and support, and funds research into stroke, chest and heart illness.

City Literary Institute (City Lit)
16 Stukely Street
London WC2B 5LJ
Tel: 020 7242 9872

Fax: 020 7405 3347
Email: infoline@citylit.ac.uk
Website: www.citylit.ac.uk
The Centre for Deaf People at the City Lit offers a wide range of BSL and lipreading classes for deaf people, and professional training for people working with deaf people.

Council for the Advancement of Communication with Deaf People (CACDP)
Block 4
University Science Park
Stockton Road
Durham DH1 3UZ
Tel: 0191 383 1155
Text: 0191 383 7915
Fax: 0191 383 7914
Email: durham@cacdp.org.uk
Website: www.cacdp.org.uk
Accredits courses in subjects relating to deafness and supplies information on training providers. It also maintains a database of BSL/English interpreters, level 3 lipspeakers, interpreters for deafblind people and speech-to-text reporters.

Deaf Club
Email: info@DeafClub.co.uk
Website: www.DeafClub.co.uk
A deaf search facility providing links to a wide range of organisations, services, campaigns and information relating to deafness.

Deafblind International
Website: www.deafblindinternational.org
Network of deafblind specialists, with a subgroup focusing on late acquired deafblindness.

Deafblind UK
John and Lucille van Geest Place
Cygnet Road
Hampton
Peterborough PE7 8FD
Tel/Textphone: 01733 358 100
Fax: 01733 358 356
Email: info@deafblind.org.uk

Website: www.deafblind.org.uk
The National Centre for Deafblindness welcomes visitors, runs a helpline, has a research centre, runs training and houses its campaign and support teams.

Defeating Deafness (The Hearing Research Trust)
330–332 Gray's Inn Road
London WC1X 8EE
Tel: 020 7833 1733
Information service: 0808 808 2222
Textphone: 020 7915 1412
Fax: 020 7278 0404
Email: ddeafness.info@ucl.ac.uk
Website: www.defeatingdeafness.org
Funds medical and scientific research into deafness and provides medical information about deafness.

Department of Health
Disability Policy Branch 2
Room 544
Wellington House
133–155 Waterloo Road
London SE1 8UG
Tel: 020 7972 4121
Training website: www.doh.gov.uk/scg/training.htm
Until 2003 this team produced a listing of major training providers. The list is still being distributed, free, but there are no plans to update it. The website provides links to information about social care training.

Diabetes UK
10 Parkway
London NW1 7AA
Tel: 020 7424 1000
Fax: 020 7424 1001
Email: info@diabetes.org.uk
Website: www.diabetes.org.uk
Provides help and support to people diagnosed with diabetes, their families and those who care for them.

Disability Alliance
Universal House
88–94 Wentworth Street
London E1 7SA

Tel/Textphone: 020 7247 8776 (Mon–Fri 10am–4pm)
Rights Advice Line (for benefits enquiries; tel/textphone): 020 7247 8763 (Mon and Wed 2–4pm)
Fax: 020 7247 8765
Email: via the website
Website: www.disabilityalliance.org
Leading authority on social security benefits for disabled people.

Disability Benefits
Helpline: 08457 123 456
Website: www.disabilitybenefits.co.uk
Information about state benefits and other services (businesses catering for disabled people, website and equipment suppliers, etc).

Disability Law Service (DLS)
Ground Floor
39–45 Cavell Street
London E1 2BP
Tel: 020 7791 9800 (Mon–Fri 10am–1pm, 2–5pm)
Textphone: 020 7791 9801
Fax: 020 7791 9802
Email: advice@dls.org.uk
Website: www.abilityonline.org.uk/charity_links/disability_law_service.htm
Provides free legal advice to disabled people, and representation where appropriate.

Disability Rights Commission
DRC Helpline
FREEPOST MIDO2164
Stratford upon Avon CV37 9BR
Tel/Helpline: 08457 622 633
Fax: 08457 778 878
Textphone: 08457 622 644
Email: via the website
Website: www.drc.gov.uk
Provides legal support and advice for disabled people, employers and service providers. Campaigns for better rights for disabled people.

Disabled Living Foundation
380–384 Harrow Road
London W9 2HU
Tel: 020 7289 6111

Helpline tel: 0845 130 9177
Helpline textphone: 020 7432 8009
Equipment centre: 020 7289 6111 ext 247
Website: www.dlf.org.uk
Provides advice and information on equipment and assistive technology for disabled and older people. Runs advice services and equipment demonstration centre, training programmes and an equipment database.

Guide Dogs for the Blind Association
Burghfield Common
Reading
Berkshire RG7 3YG
Tel: 0870 600 2323
Email: guidedogs@guidedogs.org.uk
Website: www.guidedogs.org.uk
Provides guide dogs, mobility and other rehabilitation services for blind and partially sighted people. Runs two Schools of Vision and Rehabilitation Studies, which see.

Hearing Aid Council
Witan Court
305 Upper Fourth Street
Milton Keynes MK9 1EH
Tel: 01908 235700
Fax: 01908 233770
Email: hac@thehearingaidcouncil.org.uk
Website: www.thehearingaidcouncil.org.uk
Regulates the sale of hearing aids.

Hearing Dogs for Deaf People
The Grange
Wycombe Road
Saunderton
Princes Risborough
Buckinghamshire HP27 9NS
Tel: 01844 348 100 (voice and minicom)
Fax: 01844 348 101
Email: info@hearing-dogs.co.uk
Website:www.hearing-dogs.co.uk
Provides hearing dogs for deaf people.

Hearing Exchange
Website: www.HearingExchange.com
A US-based site on which deaf people and those working with them exchange information and ideas.

Help the Aged
207–221 Pentonville Road
London N1 9UZ
Tel: 020 7278 1114
Benefits advice line (tel): 0808 800 6565; Northern Ireland 0808 808 7575
Benefits advice line (textphone): 0800 269 626
Fax: 020 7278 1116
Email: info@helptheaged.org.uk
Website: www.helptheaged.org.uk
A voluntary organisation working with older people in the UK, giving advice and information.

Henshaws Society for Blind People
John Derby House
88–92 Talbot Road
Old Trafford
Manchester M16 0GS
Tel: 0161 872 1234
Fax: 0161 848 9889
Email: info@hsbp.co.uk
Website: www.hsbp.co.uk
Offers courses in rehabilitation, care for people with a visual impairment, mobility, awareness training, working with older people.

International Glaucoma Association
108C Warner Road
Camberwell
London SE5 9HQ
Tel: 020 7737 3265
Fax: 020 7346 5929
Email: info@iga.org.uk
Website: www.iga.org.uk
Organisation creating public awareness about glaucoma. Offers reassurance and support through its information service.

Law Centres Federation
Duchess House
18–19 Warren Street
London W1T 5LR
Tel: 020 7387 8570
Fax: 020 7387 8368
Email: info@lawcentres.org.uk
Website: www.lawcentres.org.uk
Law centres provide free legal advice and representation.

Liberty
21 Tabard Street
London SE1 4LA
Tel: 020 7378 8659
Email: info@liberty-human-rights.org.uk
Website: www.liberty-human-rights.org.uk
Gives free advice on the Human Rights Act.

LINK Centre for Deafened People
19 Hartfield Road
Eastbourne
East Sussex BN21 2AR
Tel/Textphone: 01323 638230
Fax: 01323 642968
E-mail: linkcntr@dircon.co.uk
Website: www.royaldeaf.org.uk
Provides intensive residential rehabilitation courses for people who have become profoundly deaf in adulthood.

Macular Disease Society
Darwin House
13A Bridge Street
Andover
Hampshire SP10 1BE
Helpline: 0845 241 2041
Email: info@maculardisease.org
Website: www.maculardisease.org
Advice and information on macular disease and how it can be treated.

Menière's Society
98 Maybury Road
Woking GU21 5HX

Tel: 01483 740597
Textphone: 01483 771207
Fax: 01483 755441
Email: info@menieres.org.uk
Website: www.menieres.org.uk
A membership organisation giving information and support to people with Menière's disease and their families and carers.

Manchester Metropolitan University
Faculty of Community Studies
799 Wilmslow Road
Didsbury
Manchester M20 2RR
Tel: 0161 247 2020
Fax: 0161 247 6392
Email: commstud.fac@mmu.ac.uk
Website: www.did.stu.mmu.ac.uk
Offers a postgraduate diploma and MA in Social Work with Deaf People for experienced practitioners.

National Association for Deafened People (NADP)
PO Box 50
Amersham
Buckinghamshire HP6 6XB
Tel: 01227 379538
Textphone: 01227 762879
Fax: 01227 379538
Email: enquiries@nadp.org.uk
Website: www.nadp.org.uk
Run by deafened people for deafened people, providing information and support.

National Federation of the Blind
Sir John Wilson House
215 Kirkgate
Wakefield
West Yorkshire WF1 1JG
Tel: 01924 291313
Fax: 01924 200244
Email: nfbuk@nfbuk.org
Website: www.nfbuk.org
Campaigns, holds local meetings and publishes a magazine for blind and partially sighted people.

National Library for the Blind
Far Cromwell Road
Bredbury
Stockport
Cheshire SK6 2SG
Tel: 0161 355 2000
Text: 0161 355 2043
Fax: 0161 355 2098
Email: enquiries@nlbuk.org
Website: www.nlb-online.org
Provides library and information services for visually impaired people. Has largest collection of Braille and Moon books in Europe.

Northern Ireland Social Care Council (NISCC)
7th Floor
Millennium House
19–25 Great Victoria Street
Belfast BT2 7AQ
Tel: 028 9041 7600
Textphone: 028 9023 9340
Fax: 02890 417601
Email: info@niscc.n-i.nhs.uk
Regulates and registers social care workers in Northern Ireland. Provides information about training.

Partially Sighted Society
PO Box 322
Doncaster DN1 2XA
Tel: 01302 323132
Fax: 01302 368998
Website: www.jim.leeder.users.btopenworld.com/LHON/UK-pss.htm
Offers information and advice, low-vision aids, transcription service (large print, including large-print music), local support through branch network.

Queen Alexandra College
Court Oak Road
Harborne
Birmingham B17 9TG
Tel: 0121 428 5050
Fax: 0121 428 5048
Email: enquiries@qac.ac.uk
Website: www.qac.ac.uk

Offers training in rehabilitation, awareness training, residential care, counselling, and mobility for people with visual impairments.

RADAR (Royal Association for Disability and Rehabilitation)
12 City Forum, 250 City Road
London EC1V 8AF
Tel: 020 7250 3222
Textphone: 020 7250 4419
Fax: 020 7250 0212
Email: radar@radar.org.uk
Website: www.radar.org.uk
Campaigning organisation run by and for disabled people; runs the National Key Scheme for disabled people to have access to locked public toilets.

Ricability
30 Angel Gate
City Road
London EC1V 2PT
Tel: 020 7427 2460
Textphone: 020 7427 2469
Fax: 020 7427 2468
Email: mail@ricability.org.uk
Website: www.ricability.org.uk
Produces consumer reports on products and services for older people and people with disabilities.

RNIB (Royal National Institute of the Blind)
105 Judd Street
London WC1H 9NE
Tel: 020 7388 1266
Helpline: 0845 766 9999
Fax: 020 7388 2034
Email: helpline@rnib.org.uk
Website: www.rnib.org.uk
See page 299 for information about the RNIB.

RNIB Scotland
Dunedin House
25 Ravelston Terrace
Edinburgh EH4 3TP
Tel: 0131 311 8500
Email: rnibscotland@rnib.org.uk

RNIB Northern Ireland
40 Linenhall Street
Belfast BT2 8BA
Tel: 028 9032 9373/028 9027 8119
Email: rnibni@rnib.org.uk

RNIB Cymru
Trident Court
East Moors Road
Cardiff CF24 5TD
Tel: 029 2045 0440
Fax: 029 2044 9550
Email: gwenda.fitzpatrick@rnib.org.uk

RNIB LIBRARY
105 Judd Street
London WC1H 9NE
Tel: 020 7391 2052
Fax: 020 7391 2210
Email: library@rnib.org.uk
A research library. Has an online catalogue, accessible via RNIB's website.

RNIB MAIL ORDER CATALOGUE
PO Box 173
Peterborough PE2 6WS
Tel: 0845 7023 153
Textphone: 0845 7585 691
Fax: 01733 375001
Email: cservices@rnib.org.uk
Website: www.rnib.org.uk
Equipment and catalogue of spoken-described videos.

RNIB TALKING BOOK SERVICE
PO Box 173
Peterborough PE2 6WS
Tel: 0845 762 6843
Email: cservice@rnib.org.uk
A library of audio books, delivered to people's homes.

RNID
19–23 Featherstone Street
London EC1Y 8SL

Information line: 0808 808 0123
Textphone: 0808 808 9000
Fax: 020 7296 8199
Email: informationline@rnid.org.uk
Website: www.rnid.org.uk
For a wide range of information on many aspects of deafness and hearing loss. *See also page 300.*

RNID CASEWORK SERVICE
19–23 Featherstone Street
London EC1Y 8SL
Tel: 0808 808 0123
Textphone: 0808 808 9000
Fax: 020 7296 8199
Email: caseworkteam@rnid.org.uk
Provides information and advice to the public and professionals on the Disability Discrimination Act 1995 in relation to employment, education and the provision of goods, services and facilities. In some situations the Casework Service may be able to help bring your case to court and provide representation in court.

RNID LIBRARY
330–332 Gray's Inn Road
London WC1X 8EE
Tel/Textphone: 020 7915 1553
Fax: 020 7915 1443
Email: rnidlib@ucl.ac.uk
Website: www.ucl.ac.uk/Library/RNID
Has specialist publications ranging from books for children to academic journals.

RNID SOUND ADVANTAGE
1 Haddonbrook Business Centre
Orton Southgate
Peterborough PE2 6YX
Tel/Textphone: 0870 789 8855
Fax: 0870 789 8822
Email: solutions@rnid.org.uk
Website: www.rnidshop.org
Sells a range of equipment for deaf and hard of hearing people. Visit the website or send for a copy of the RNID Sound Advantage 'Solutions' catalogue.

RNID TINNITUS HELPLINE
19–23 Featherstone Street
London EC1Y 8SL
Tel: 0808 808 6666
Textphone: 0808 808 0007
Fax: 020 7296 8199
Email: tinnitushelpline@rnid.org.uk
Website: www.rnid.org.uk
Offers information and advice to people with tinnitus, their families and friends, and the professionals who work with them.

RNID TRAINING SERVICES
19–23 Featherstone Street
London EC1Y 8SL
Tel/Textphone: 020 7296 8060
Fax: 020 7296 8128
Website: www.rnid.org.uk
Provides training for employers and individuals.

RNID TYPETALK
PO Box 284
Liverpool L69 3UZ
and

RNID TYPETALK CUSTOMER SUPPORT
(Mon–Fri 8am–8pm; Sat, Sun 9am–5pm)
Tel: 0800 7311 888
Textphone: 0800 500 888
Fax: 0151 709 8119
Email: helpline@rnid-typetalk.org.uk
Website: www.typetalk.org.
Telephone relay service connecting textphone and voice phone users.

Royal Association for Deaf People
Walsingham Road
Colchester
Essex CO2 7BP
Tel: 01206 509509
Textphone: 01206 577090
Fax: 01206 769755
Email: info@royaldeaf.org.uk
Website: www.royaldeaf.org.uk

Support and information for deaf people and those working with them; also provides awareness and BSL training.

Royal British Legion
48 Pall Mall
London SW1Y 5JY
Helpline: 0845 772 5725
Tel: 020 7973 7200
Fax: 020 7973 7399
Website: www.britishlegion.org.uk
Information about possible help for serving and former members of the armed forces and their dependants.

Royal College of Ophthalmologists
17 Cornwall Terrace
London NW1 4QW
Tel: 020 7935 0702
Fax: 020 7935 9838
Website: www.rcophth.ac.uk
The professional body for ophthalmologists. Provides information about eye conditions to the general public.

Royal London Society for the Blind
Dorton House
Wildernesse Avenue
Seal
Sevenoaks
Kent TN15 0ED
Tel: 01732 592500
Fax: 01732 592506
Email: enquiries@rlsb.org.uk
Website: www.rlsb.org.uk
Offers distance learning courses in visual impairment studies at various levels.

Royal National College for the Blind
College Road
Hereford HR1 1EB
Tel: 01432 265725
Fax: 01432 376628
Email: info@rncb.ac.uk
Website: www.rncb.ac.uk
Offers courses for visually impaired people.

Samaritans
Tel: 08457 90 90 90 (Ireland 1850 60 90 90)
Textphone: 08457 90 91 92
Email helpline: jo@samaritans.org
Postal helpline: Chris, PO Box 9090, Stirling FK8 2SA
Website: www.samaritans.org
A 24-hour helpline every day for people needing to talk.

SSAFA Forces Help
(formerly Soldiers, Sailors and Air Force Association)
Special Needs Adviser
19 Queen Elizabeth Street
London SE1 2LP
Tel: 020 7403 8783
Fax: 020 7403 8815
Website: www.ssafa.org.uk
National charity offering information, advice and financial aid to serving and ex-service men and women and their families who are in need.

School of Vision and Rehabilitation Studies
Rehabilitation training to degree level for professionals working, or planning to work, with visually impaired people. Part of the Guide Dogs for the Blind Association *(see page 282).*

ENGLAND
Highcombe Edge
Churt Road
Hindhead
Surrey GU26 6SJ
Tel: 01428 606022
Fax: 01428 602727
Email: Rehabhindhead@guidedogs.org.uk
Website: www.visionschool.org.uk

SCOTLAND
28 Park Circus
Glasgow G3 6AP
Tel: 0141 331 0391
Fax: 0141 331 0390
Email: Rehabglasgow@guidedogs.org.uk
Website: www.visionschool.org.uk

Scottish Social Services Council (SSSC)
Compass House
11 Riverside Drive
Dundee DD1 4NY
Tel: 0845 60 30891/01382 207101
Fax: 01382 207215
Email: enquiries@sssc.uk.com
Website: www.sssc.uk.com
Regulates and registers social care workers in Scotland. Provides information about training.

Sense
11–13 Clifton Terrace
London N4 3SR
Tel: 020 7272 7774
Textphone: 020 7272 9648
Fax: 020 7272 6012
Email: enquiries@sense.org.uk
Website: www.sense.org.uk
A national organisation for deafblind people, offering advice, information, self-help groups and a wide range of support services such as communicator guides and training. *For the transcription service, see page 297.*

Sense Scotland
5th Floor
45 Finnieston Street
Glasgow G3 8JU
Tel: 0141 564 2444
Textphone: 0141 564 2442
Fax: 0141 564 2443
Email: info@sensescotland.org.uk
Website: www.sensescotland.org.uk
A national organisation for deafblind people, offering advice, information, self-help groups and a wide range of support services such as communication guides and training.

Stroke Association
Stroke House
240 City Road
London EC1V 2PR
Tel: 020 7566 0300

Helpline: 0845 3033 100
Fax: 020 7490 2686
Website: www.stroke.org.uk
Information and advice about stroke, and support for stroke patients and their carers.

Subtitles at Your Local Cinema
Website: www.subtitles@yourlocalcinema.com
An online campaign for better access to cinema for people who are disabled by blindness or deafness. Shows cinema listings.

Training Organisation in Personal and Social Services (TOPSS) England
Albion Court
5 Albion Place
Leeds LS1 6JP
Tel: 0113 245 1716
Fax: 0113 243 6417
Email: info@topssengland.org.uk
Website: www.topss.org.uk
Develops social care training standards and provides information about training, in particular about NVQs.
Sister organisations are Care Council for Wales, Northern Ireland Social Care Council and Scottish Social Services Council, which are also listed in this appendix.

Traveline
Tel: 0870 608 2608 (7am–8pm daily)
Website: www.traveline.org.uk
Information about all public transport in the UK (bus, train, coach, ferry, etc), including timetables.

Information for Northern Ireland is available only through the website.

UK Council on Deafness
Westwood Park, London Road
Little Horkesley
Colchester CO6 4BS
Tel: 01206 274075
Textphone: 01206 274076
Fax: 01206 274077
Email: info@deafcouncil.org.uk
Website: www.deafcouncil.org.uk
An umbrella body for organisations representing the needs of deaf people.

Usher UK
Email: enquiries@usheruk.org.uk
Website: www.usheruk.org.uk
Voluntary organisation for people with Usher syndrome and their families, providing support, information, training and events.

Videospec Ltd
30A High Street
Old Woking
Surrey GU22 9ER
Tel: 01483 722273
Fax: 01483 728343
Website: www.videospec.co.uk
Makers of Eezee Readers.

Visual Impairment North East (VINE)
Fred Hodson
c/o Pearey House
Preston Park
North Shields NE29 9JR
Tel: 0191 257 4388
Website: www.vine-simspecs.org.uk
Suppliers of Simspecs.

Audiovisual aids for people who have hearing or vision loss

Asian language talking newspapers and magazines:

Gujarati and Punjabi (Vista)	0116 249 0909
Urdu (Asian Awaz)	01772 744 148
Punjabi (GhalBaat), Urdu (Bhol Chal)	01274 848 150
Bengali, Gujarati and Punjabi (several publications)	0121 428 5046

Big Print News
PO Box 308
Warrington WA1 1JE
Tel: 0800 124 007
Website: www.big-print.co.uk
A weekly large-print newspaper, which includes TV and radio listings.

Calibre
New Road
Weston Turville
Aylesbury
Buckinghamshire HP22 5XQ
Tel: 01296 432339
Fax: 01296 392599
Email: enquiries@calibre.org.uk
Website: www.calibre.org.uk
Publishers of audio books.

Chivers Large Print
FREEPOST SW10541
Bath BA1 3ZZ
Tel: 01225 335 336
Freephone (orders): 08081 727 475
Customer services: 01225 336552
Fax: 01225 448005
Email: info@largeprintdirect.co.uk
Website: www.largeprintdirect.co.uk
Suppliers of large print books.

Forest Books
Unit 2, New Building
Ellwood Road
Milkwall
Coleford GL16 7LE
Tel: 01594 833858
Textphone: 01594 833507
Videophone: 01594 810637
Fax: 01594 833446
Email: forest@forestbooks.com
Website: www.forestbooks.com
Books and resources for deaf people, their families and those who work with them.

ISIS
7 Centremead
Osney Mead
Oxford OX2 0ES
Tel: 01865 250 333/0800 731 5637
Fax: 01865 790358

Email: sales@isis-publishing.co.uk
Website: www.isis-publishing.co.uk
Publishers of large print and audio books.

Listening Books
12 Lant Street
London SE1 1QH
Tel: 020 7407 9417
Fax: 020 7403 1377
Email: info@listening-books.org.uk
Website: www.listening-books.org.uk
A charity providing audio books by post to people who cannot read print.

St Cecilia's Guild for the Blind
St Joseph's
Watford Way
London NW4 4TY
Tel: 020 8202 5749
Talking book library of Christian materials (mostly Catholic).

Sense Transcription Service
Coventry Society for the Blind
33–35 Earlsdon Avenue
South Earlsdon
Coventry CV5 6DR
Tel/Textphone: 024 76 717522
Fax: 024 76 717067
Email: csb@sensewest.org.uk
Website: www.sense.org.uk
For transcription into a range of formats, including audio cassettes and large print.

Talking Newspaper Association of the United Kingdom
Browning Road
Heathfield
East Sussex TN21 8DB
Tel: 01435 866102
Fax: 01435 865422
Email: info@tnauk.org.uk
Website: www.tnauk.org.uk
Provides national and local newspapers and magazines in a range of formats: audio tape, computer disk, email, internet download, CD-ROM.

Torch Trust
Torch House
Hallaton
Market Harborough
Leicestershire LE16 8UJ
Tel: 0870 7700 272
Email: info@torchtrust.org
Website: www.torchtrust.org
Produces a wide range of Christian literature and study books in large print, cassette and Braille.

Ulverscoft and Magna
The Green
Bradgate Road
Anstey
Leicestershire LE7 7FU
Tel: 0116 236 4325
Fax: 0116 234 0205
Website: www.ulverscroft.co.uk
Large print and audiobook publishers, with an extensive and regularly updated catalogue.

ABOUT THE RNIB

There are about 2 million people in the UK with sight problems. RNIB's pioneering work helps anyone with a sight problem – not just with Braille, Talking Books and computer training but also with imaginative and practical solutions to everyday challenges.

We help people with sight problems to live full and independent lives. We campaign to change society's attitudes, actions and assumptions so that people with sight problems can enjoy the same rights, freedoms and responsibilities as fully sighted people. We fund pioneering research into preventing and treating eye disease and we promote eye health by running public health-awareness campaigns.

As a charity we need your support to fund our vital work. With your generosity we can help people with sight problems now and in the future. If you or someone you know has a sight problem, RNIB can help.

For contact details for the RNIB and its services, see the entries on pages 287–288.

ABOUT RNID

RNID is the largest charity representing the 9 million deaf and hard of hearing people in the UK. As a membership charity, we aim to achieve a radically better quality of life for deaf and hard of hearing people. We do this in the following ways:

- Campaigning and lobbying to change laws and government policies.
- Providing information and raising awareness of deafness, hearing loss and tinnitus.
- Training courses and consultancy on deafness and disability.
- Communication services, including sign language interpreters.
- Training of interpreters, lipspeakers and speech-to-text operators.
- Seeking lasting change in education for deaf children and young people.
- Employment programmes to help deaf people into work.
- Care services for deaf and hard of hearing people with additional needs.
- RNID Typetalk, the national telephone relay service for deaf and hard of hearing people.
- Equipment and products for deaf and hard of hearing people.
- Social, medical and technical research.

For contact details about the various services offered by RNID, including Typetalk, see the entries on pages 288–290.

ABOUT AGE CONCERN

Hearing and Sight Loss is one of a wide range of publications produced by Age Concern England. Age Concern is the UK's largest organisation working for and with older people to enable them to make more of life. We are a federation of over 400 independent charities that share the same name, values and standards.

We believe that ageing is a normal part of life, and that later life should be fulfilling, enjoyable and productive. We enable older people by providing services and grants, researching their needs and opinions, influencing government and media, and through other innovative and dynamic projects.

Every day we provide vital services, information and support to thousands of older people of all ages and backgrounds.

Age Concern also works with many older people from disadvantaged or marginalised groups, such as those living in rural areas or black and minority ethnic elders.

Age Concern is dependent on donations, covenants and legacies.

Age Concern England
1268 London Road
London SW16 4ER
Tel: 020 8765 7200
Fax: 020 8765 7211
Website:
www.ageconcern.org.uk

Age Concern Cymru
4th Floor
1 Cathedral Road
Cardiff CF11 9SD
Tel: 029 2037 1566
Fax: 029 2039 9562
Website:www.accymru.org.uk

Age Concern Scotland
113 Rose Street
Edinburgh EH2 3DT
Tel: 0131 220 3345
Fax: 0131 220 2779
Website:
www.ageconcernscotland.org.uk

Age Concern Northern Ireland
3 Lower Crescent
Belfast BT7 1NR
Tel: 028 9024 5729
Fax: 028 9023 5497
Website: www.ageconcernni.org

PUBLICATIONS FROM AGE CONCERN BOOKS

Dementia Care ***A handbook for residential and day care***

2nd edition

Alan Chapman, Donna Gilmour and Iain McIntosh

This revised edition of a successful book stresses a more holistic approach to the support of people with dementia: in essence, dementia, as an illness, does not rob the person of the influence of their past life. Topics include:

- the individual and their previous lifestyle;
- staff teamwork;
- approaches to the person;
- issues for day care;
- what is dementia and what is not?
- health matters;
- behaviour as a response to the living environment;
- behaviour as a response to the daily routine and staff actions;
- dilemmas and challenges;
- feelings of loss, pain and palliative care.

A comprehensive, practical guide to the delivery of care to people with dementia, this book has been designed for use by those working in both residential and day-care settings, providing sound advice on good practice and offering reassurance and support.

£14.99 0-86242-313-9

An Introductory Guide to Community Care

Alan Goodenough

This book is a useful starting point for new or inexperienced carers, particularly paid carers, who are unsure of what services are available or who they can turn to for support or advice. It guides them through the basics of care plans, relevant legislation and regulations, useful contacts, and the roles of other professionals they will encounter. The book encourages the carer to feel part of a team, offers self-assessment opportunities, and encourages them to seek further training opportunities.

£6.99 0-86242-340-6

If you would like to order either of these titles, please write to the address below, enclosing a cheque or money order for the appropriate amount (plus £1.99 p&p for one book; for additional books, please add 75p per book up to a maximum of £7.50) made payable to Age Concern England. Credit card orders may be made on 0870 44 22 120. Books can also be ordered online at www.ageconcern.org.uk/shop

Age Concern Books
Units 5 & 6
Industrial Estate
Brecon
Powys
LD3 8LA

Bulk order discounts

Age Concern Books is pleased to offer a discount on orders totalling 50 or more copies of the same title. For details, please contact Age Concern Books on 0870 44 22 120.

Customised editions

Age Concern Books is pleased to offer a free 'customisation' service for anyone wishing to purchase 500 or more copies of the title. This gives you the option to have a unique front cover design featuring your organisation's logo and corporate colours, or adding your logo to the current cover design. You can also insert an additional four pages of text for a small additional fee. Existing clients include many of the biggest names in British industry, retailing and finance, the trades unions, educational establishments, the statutory and voluntary sectors, and welfare associations. **For full details, please contact Sue Henning, Age Concern Books, Astral House, 1268 London Road, London SW16 4ER. Fax: 020 8765 7211. Email: hennins@ace.org.uk**
Visit our Website at www.ageconcern.org.uk/shop

Age Concern Information Line/ Factsheets subscription

Age Concern produces more than 45 comprehensive factsheets designed to answer many of the questions older people (or those advising them) may have. Topics covered include money and benefits, health, community care, leisure and education, and housing. For up to five free factsheets, telephone 0800 00 99 66 (7am–7pm, seven days a week, every week of the year). Alternatively, you may prefer to write to Age Concern, FREEPOST (SWB 30375), ASHBURTON, Devon TQ13 7ZZ.

For professionals working with older people, the factsheets are available on an annual subscription service, which includes updates throughout the year. For further details and costs of the subscription, please write to Age Concern England at the above Freepost address.

We hope that this publication has been useful to you. If so, we would very much like to hear from you. Alternatively, if you feel that we could add or change anything, please write and tell us, using the following Freepost address: Age Concern, FREEPOST CN1794, London SW16 4BR.

INDEX

Numbers in *italic* refer to pages with illustrations.